Science Fiction TV Series with ChatGPT

Andrew Parry

Published by Andrew Parry, 2025.

SCIENCE FICTION TV SERIES WITH CHATGPT

First edition. June 5, 2025.

ISBN: 979-8231022236

Written by Andrew Parry.

Table of Contents

Welcome to the Future: Writing Sci-Fi Television with ChatGPT

The future of storytelling has arrived, and it's not just on your screen—it's on your desktop, in your hands, in your mind. Artificial intelligence is no longer the stuff of speculative fiction. It's here, and it's transforming how we write the stories that will shape the next generation of science fiction television. Whether you've been carrying around a wild sci-fi idea for years or you're just now realizing how much you want to create your own series, this chapter is where the journey begins. And it starts with understanding how ChatGPT can become your most powerful collaborator.

Science fiction has always been about asking questions. What if humans could travel time? What if alien civilizations exist? What if artificial intelligence surpassed our own intelligence? But here's a twist—what if artificial intelligence could help *you* write the very stories that explore those ideas? That's exactly what you'll discover in this book. The aim isn't just to show you how to write a science fiction television series. It's to help you write one with the support of AI, using ChatGPT not just as a tool but as a genuine creative partner.

Great sci-fi television has always expanded our vision of what's possible. Think of the thoughtful optimism of *Star Trek*, boldly imagining a future where humanity thrives among the stars. Or the eerie paranoia of *The X-Files*, where every shadow and whisper could be a clue to a government cover-up or alien presence. Consider the philosophical loops of *Westworld*, where consciousness, identity, and control are constantly questioned. And then there's *Doctor Who*, the longest-running, most fantastical, and yet deeply human of them all, dancing between historical fantasy and futuristic wonder with wit and heart. These shows didn't just entertain; they reshaped our expectations of what television could explore.

With ChatGPT, you now have a writing partner who can help you develop ideas, structure episodes, write dialogue, brainstorm new technologies, or even invent alien species with fully fleshed-out languages and cultures. But more than that, it can reflect your own curiosity and creativity back at you. It can push you to dig deeper, go weirder, and make smarter choices with every story beat.

This chapter isn't about jumping into plotting just yet. Instead, it's about setting the tone for the creative partnership you're about to experience. Writing science fiction with ChatGPT doesn't mean surrendering your creativity. On the contrary, it allows you to amplify it. You're still the showrunner, the world builder, the architect of story. But now you have a writing room that never sleeps and never runs out of ideas. You can ask, "What would a moon colony look like if it was built by robots to house humans?" And ChatGPT can give you ten versions—each with a different aesthetic, political system, and mystery waiting to unfold.

This process is not a shortcut—it's a new kind of collaboration. With the right prompts, you can shape entire seasons of television in a day. You can brainstorm character arcs, test variations of plot twists, or rewrite dialogue that doesn't quite sing. More importantly, ChatGPT can help you ask better questions. Because in sci-fi, the question is often more powerful than the answer.

You'll find that the creative process is flexible and surprisingly intuitive when working with AI. You can start with a one-line idea like "a woman wakes up on a planet where everyone believes she's their long-lost saviour," and by asking the right questions and refining the details, ChatGPT will help you build an entire mythology around that premise. You can explore genres within genres—cyberpunk, space opera, dystopian realism, time travel comedy—and find the right flavor for your voice.

In the chapters ahead, you'll learn how to use AI to develop an episodic structure that works, build compelling characters that change and evolve over time, and craft scenes that come alive on the screen. You'll dive into the mechanics of plot, the poetry of dialogue, and the philosophy behind your themes. You'll also explore how to think visually, cinematically, and symbolically—turning words into immersive experiences that feel as vivid as your favorite series.

There will be prompts throughout the book—powerful jumping-off points to help you start a scene, structure a season, or reimagine a tired trope. These prompts are your creative fuel, and the more you play with them, the more you'll develop your own rhythm and voice. You'll discover how to use ChatGPT to build not just ideas but systems—entire fictional ecosystems of story logic, visual design, and emotional truth.

But most importantly, this journey is about writing a story that only *you* can tell. AI may help generate, brainstorm, and rewrite, but it's your vision, your decisions, and your taste that will shape the final result. You're the creator. ChatGPT is your assistant. And together, you can create something original, strange, meaningful, and unforgettable.

So welcome to the future. Welcome to the writing room where ideas never stop flowing. You don't need a Hollywood budget or a team of ten people. You just need your imagination, your curiosity, and the willingness to explore. Sci-fi is about asking "what if?" Now it's your turn. What if *you* wrote the next great science fiction series?

Let's begin.

What Makes a Great Science Fiction TV Series?

If you want to write a science fiction TV series that resonates, endures, and thrills, you need to understand what makes the best ones stand apart. Great sci-fi isn't about flying saucers, space lasers, or time machines—not really. Those are the visual trappings, the window dressing. What lies at the heart of unforgettable science fiction is something much deeper: the human condition refracted through the lens of the extraordinary.

A great science fiction television series isn't just an exploration of technology—it's an exploration of *people*, placed in scenarios that stretch their understanding of life, society, and self. At its core, science fiction is philosophical. It asks what happens to morality, identity, or love when the world around us changes. It offers us metaphors made literal—what if our memories could be edited? What if our desires could be predicted? What if we were watched by machines we made?

Take *Westworld*, for example. On the surface, it's a show about humanoid robots in a theme park gone rogue. But dig deeper and it becomes a conversation about consciousness, free will, and what it means to be alive. *Star Trek* painted a hopeful future, but it did so while confronting racism, war, religion, and class. *The X-Files* is about aliens and conspiracies, but it also hinges on belief, skepticism, and the desperate human need for truth. *Doctor Who* cloaks itself in whimsy and time-travel hijinks, but again and again, it circles back to loss, love, and the weight of memory. These shows make audiences feel something, not just marvel at something.

The best science fiction television lives at the intersection of "what if" and "why does it matter?" Your show doesn't need to predict the future accurately—it needs to feel emotionally truthful in a world where the rules have changed. It doesn't have to be realistic. It has to be *real* to the characters. Once you earn the audience's emotional trust, they'll follow you anywhere—into parallel dimensions, aboard alien ships, or inside digital afterlives.

Science fiction also demands great worldbuilding. That doesn't mean you need a 500-page show bible outlining the history of your galactic empire. But it does mean you need to think carefully about how things work in your universe. What are the social structures? What has replaced money? What do people believe in? What scares them? A compelling setting doesn't just look good—it creates tension, conflict, and possibility. In *The Expanse*, for example, the tension between Earth, Mars, and the Belters isn't just political—it's cultural, linguistic, and historical. You feel the friction in every encounter. The world feels lived in.

Another trait of great sci-fi series is thematic consistency. The theme doesn't need to be obvious or declared. In fact, it's often better if it emerges subtly, episode by episode. But having a strong thematic backbone gives your story shape. *Black Mirror*, for instance, always returns to themes of technological anxiety and human vulnerability. Every episode is different, but the unease lingers across all of them. When you know your theme—whether it's survival, control, connection, or evolution—you have a compass to guide you through the storytelling process.

Character development is just as important in sci-fi as it is in any genre. You may be writing about a cyborg detective or a time-traveling linguist, but they must still want things, fear things, and make mistakes. They need arcs. They need relationships. They need contradictions. Great sci-fi series give us characters we love not despite the strange settings, but *because* of how those settings force them to grow. *Fringe* may have started as a show about fringe science and parallel universes, but what audiences remember most are the relationships—Olivia's trauma, Walter's regret, Peter's loyalty. It's the human story that anchors the speculative one.

Tone also plays a critical role. Some shows lean heavily into mystery and suspense, like *The X-Files*. Others take a more philosophical or poetic tone, like *Devs* or *Raised by Wolves*. Some embrace humor and satire, like *Futurama* or *The Orville*. Your tone should align with your theme and concept. If you're exploring existential dread in a future surveillance state, the tone may be somber and unsettling. If your story is about misfit aliens learning to live among humans, maybe you want levity and absurdity. ChatGPT can help you experiment with tone by generating variations of a scene in different emotional registers until one feels right.

Pacing is another piece of the puzzle. A series like *Battlestar Galactica* uses rapid developments and cliffhangers to build intensity, while something like *The OA* unfolds slowly, immersing you in mystery and mood. When you write with AI, you can test multiple pacing styles quickly. You can write a scene as a rapid-fire thriller, then reimagine it as a slow-burn drama. ChatGPT lets you preview different narrative speeds before committing to a final style.

Dialogue in sci-fi must balance clarity and creativity. You want it to feel futuristic without being incomprehensible, clever without being cold. Characters should sound like real people—even if they're aliens or post-human beings. Look at *Star Trek*—the language is crisp, sometimes technical, but always rooted in character. *Doctor Who*, by contrast, leans into whimsical speech patterns that match its tonal playfulness. ChatGPT can help you write in different voices, test phrasings, or find metaphorical language that fits your world.

Lastly, great sci-fi shows often contain layers—narrative layers, thematic layers, emotional layers. They reward re-watching. They raise questions you might not notice on first viewing. That's where figurative language, visual symbolism, and subtext come in. You can work with ChatGPT to brainstorm visual metaphors or recurring imagery that add richness to your show. Maybe your post-apocalyptic world is filled with broken mirrors, representing fractured identity. Maybe your utopia has no shadows—until your main character starts casting one.

So what makes a great science fiction TV series? It's a mix of big questions and small moments. Of strange worlds and relatable characters. Of thematic coherence and tonal confidence. It's something that feels like it could happen—or should never happen—but always makes us feel something now. And with ChatGPT at your side, you can experiment faster, explore deeper, and build something truly original.

The future of great sci-fi storytelling is no longer a mystery. It's yours to create.

How Star Trek Still Teaches Us to Build Worlds

If you're trying to write a science fiction television series that feels vast, alive, and worth returning to week after week, few franchises offer a better blueprint than *Star Trek*. It may have premiered back in 1966, but it remains one of the most instructive examples of worldbuilding ever put to screen. And the lessons it offers aren't just about phasers, warp drives, or pointed ears. The real genius of *Star Trek* is how it creates a universe that reflects both the future and the present, inviting viewers to imagine the possible while examining the real.

At first glance, *Star Trek* might seem like a show about space exploration. But at its core, it's about values. Its world is built on the idea that humanity has overcome its internal conflicts, reached for the stars, and found a moral compass strong enough to explore the unknown without conquering it. This philosophical foundation is key. Every alien culture, every piece of future tech, every diplomatic crisis isn't just there for drama—it's there to reflect, challenge, or affirm the values at the heart of the show.

When you sit down to build your sci-fi world, that's the place to start. What does your world believe in? What values define your future society? Is it a utopia of shared knowledge like the Federation? Is it a fractured realm ruled by algorithms and corporations? Is it a post-apocalyptic rebuilding, clinging to old myths in the ruins of Earth? Whatever the answer, that worldview becomes the gravity around which everything else orbits—characters, conflicts, settings, and story arcs.

One of *Star Trek*'s most powerful tools was its use of allegory. It didn't just create alien species for spectacle; it used them to reflect human traits in exaggerated form. The Klingons were once the embodiment of Cold War-era militarism. The Vulcans represented logic without emotion. The Borg represented the terror of assimilation and loss of individuality. And through these lenses, *Star Trek* could explore issues like war, racism, gender, colonialism, and identity—without ever needing to name those issues directly. This use of allegorical species-building is a technique that remains just as powerful today.

ChatGPT can be immensely helpful here. You can prompt it to create an alien species that embodies a specific concept—say, a culture that fears memory or worships artificial intelligence. It can then build the biology, customs, fashion, language, architecture, and belief systems of that culture, giving you a rich toolkit to populate your episodes. These species don't need to be metaphors, but when they are, they give your story a resonance that hits far beyond the stars.

Another strength of *Star Trek* was its consistent technological vision. It didn't just throw gadgets into scenes for convenience. The technology felt embedded into the society. The replicator changed how people thought about scarcity. The transporter made movement seamless and created moral dilemmas about identity and duplication. The holodeck allowed for fantasy and training, but also revealed inner character psychology. In a well-built sci-fi world, your technology should affect how people think, feel, live, and relate to each other. You can use ChatGPT to imagine how a single piece of speculative tech changes everything from economics to relationships.

And then there's the format. *Star Trek* pioneered the "planet of the week" structure. Each episode was a self-contained story that still added depth to the universe. It worked because the core premise—exploration—gave the show an endless supply of new environments and moral challenges. When building your own series, think about how your structure allows for this kind of variety. Is your team investigating anomalies in deep space? Solving crimes in a multi-planet federation? Escaping a collapsed Earth through dimensional portals? You need a premise that invites new stories while maintaining thematic cohesion.

You can even borrow structural inspiration from the way *Star Trek* treated its ships. The USS Enterprise wasn't just a set piece—it was a home, a workplace, a symbol. Its corridors carried memory. Its bridge was the heart of every decision. In your own show, think about your recurring locations. Is there a ship, a base, a city, or even a character's mind that you return to? ChatGPT can help you design those spaces in detail, imagining everything from the color of the lights to the way characters move through them, creating environments that feel as real as any studio-built set.

Character relationships were another pillar of *Star Trek*'s worldbuilding. The show didn't just populate its universe with diverse people—it gave them distinct philosophies and emotional truths. Spock wasn't just logical; he was torn between two heritages. McCoy wasn't just grumpy; he was a moral anchor. Picard, Sisko, Janeway—each captain embodied a different vision of leadership. Great sci-fi series thrive on this kind of interplay, where characters represent different perspectives on the same problem. You can prompt ChatGPT to help you develop ensemble casts with contrasting viewpoints, giving your show the fuel it needs for endless debate, growth, and drama.

One of the subtler worldbuilding tricks in *Star Trek* was its long memory. Events from earlier seasons would echo in later ones. Political shifts would ripple across series. Cultures would evolve. This sense of time passing added richness and realism. In your own series, think beyond the single episode. How will your world change? What will your characters carry with them from one planet to the next, one season to the next? Using ChatGPT, you can track arcs, plot long-term developments, or even ask it to simulate what a specific society would look like fifty years after a key event.

And then, there's the optimism. Even at its darkest, *Star Trek* believed in progress. It believed in diplomacy, in science, in dialogue over violence. That's not the only tone a sci-fi show can take—but it's a valuable reminder that even in speculative fiction, hope can be radical. Your world doesn't have to be bleak to be powerful. It just has to be coherent. Whether your story leans toward dystopia, satire, or dreamscape, the world has to make sense to the people living in it—and to the viewers watching it.

Ultimately, *Star Trek* teaches us that worldbuilding isn't just about scale. It's about *meaning*. Every detail, every choice, every rule of your universe should support the questions you're asking. That's what makes a world feel alive. That's what invites an audience to come back week after week. You're not just writing stories. You're creating a place where those stories can happen. So study *Star Trek*. Not just for nostalgia or reference—but for architecture. For blueprints. Then, using ChatGPT, start building your own starship, your own future, your own philosophy disguised as a galaxy. You have the same creative tools now that Roddenberry had in the sixties—plus one more: a thinking, responding, idea-generating machine ready to assist you every step of the way.

The future is yours to build. Make it matter.

Starting with the End: Reverse Engineering Your Series Arc

One of the smartest ways to write a science fiction television series is to start with the ending. Not necessarily the final scene of the last episode, but the emotional truth or thematic revelation that your audience will take away when the journey is over. By knowing what kind of story you're ultimately telling—what it means, what it changes, and what it resolves—you give yourself a compass for every twist, subplot, and strange world you invent along the way. This chapter is about reverse engineering your series arc using ChatGPT to help you uncover the destination before you map the road.

Great storytelling is about resolution. Whether it's a triumphant escape, a hard-won truth, or a quiet acceptance of loss, the ending is the moment everything before it starts to make sense. That's why it's such a powerful place to begin. What do you want your audience to feel when the credits roll for the final time? Relief? Shock? Grief? Wonder? Hope? That emotional intention becomes the fuel for building structure backwards.

Imagine you know your series ends with your protagonist choosing to erase their memory of everything that came before. Immediately, that tells you something vital: memory will be central. Identity may be fragmented. Regret might be a theme. With that decision, you begin to shape what came before. Maybe the show becomes about fractured realities or false memories. Maybe your world has technology that allows memory to be altered or extracted. Now you're not writing blindly—you're writing toward something with weight.

You can use ChatGPT as a mirror and brainstorming partner here. Try prompting it with a final moment: "Describe the emotional and narrative impact of a series finale where the hero becomes the villain." Then ask it to reverse map the events that might lead to such a conclusion. You'll get frameworks that push you to reconsider structure, arc, and tone. If your hero falls, what were the temptations along the way? What small cracks became the fractures that broke them? You can go backward scene by scene, or concept by concept, exploring how each moment builds toward the inevitable.

Science fiction is especially well-suited to this method because so much of it plays with time, causality, and destiny. You don't have to write in a linear fashion. You can begin at the ending and ripple outwards, creating patterns that resonate across episodes. *Dark* did this with extraordinary precision, making its ending an essential seed from the very first scene. Even *Doctor Who*, with all its whimsy, often writes backward from big reveals, letting future knowledge influence past behavior. When you begin with the ending, you let every earlier episode become a necessary piece of the puzzle.

It's also a practical way to ensure you're not improvising your series into a corner. Many sci-fi shows collapse under the weight of unanswered questions or sprawling mythology that leads nowhere. Starting from the end lets you plant questions you already know how to answer. You can pace your reveals, seed clues, and avoid the trap of endless escalation without payoff. You're not just writing episodes—you're composing a symphony.

Let's say your series ends with humanity abandoning Earth for the second time, realizing they never solved the problem they fled from the first time. That gives you a structure of return, of reflection, of generational conflict. ChatGPT can help you outline a season arc where the main character starts off celebrating Earth's rebirth only to uncover the unresolved darkness underneath. You can write backwards, imagining each step that changes their perspective—starting hopeful, then troubled, then desperate, then resolved.

Reverse engineering is also a powerful tool for building character arcs. Think about who your protagonist becomes, and then figure out who they had to be at the beginning to make that journey meaningful. If your character ends the series believing machines deserve equal rights, maybe they start as a tech-skeptic. If they sacrifice themselves for others in the finale, maybe they begin selfish, traumatized, or detached. You can use prompts like "Give me a 10-episode transformation for a character who goes from ruthless corporate agent to revolutionary leader," and let ChatGPT help shape that arc across key turning points.

Don't just think about plot. Think about tone. If your series ends in tragic ambiguity, you probably don't want the early episodes to feel like a cartoon. If your finale ends in joyful awe, that tone should peek through even the darkest chapters. Reverse engineering helps you stay emotionally consistent. It lets you echo your ending thematically across the entire run. If your final image is of two enemies reaching out to touch hands, then earlier episodes should reflect the long climb from hatred to understanding.

This method is also useful when building serialized mysteries or mythologies. If the truth is that the utopia is a simulation, or the alien race was engineered by humans, or the main character is a clone of someone they hate—these revelations land harder when you've seeded them properly. And when you write backward, you never have to force a twist into a place it doesn't belong. You can set it up from the start, letting each episode naturally build tension toward the end.

Using ChatGPT, you can run variations of your ending to see how they change the rest of your show. Try out, "What if the protagonist dies in episode eight instead of the finale?" or "What if the utopia is real, but the hero chooses to leave it?" You'll see how these shifts ripple backward, forcing changes in earlier dynamics, relationships, and themes. This flexibility is one of AI's greatest gifts to the writer—it lets you explore before you commit.

The goal isn't to write backwards forever. Eventually, you'll move forward, letting your scenes and characters breathe. But starting with the end gives you a map, a rhythm, a shape. You don't have to write in the order you plan to watch. You just have to write with intention. And when the writing gets hard, as it always does, the ending gives you something to aim for. A light on the horizon. A last scene waiting to be earned.

So before you build a starship or invent a new language, take a moment to stand at the edge of your story and look back. What do you want the final moment to be? What truth do you want to leave behind? Use ChatGPT to sketch, to question, to refine. You're writing the future, but you already know how it ends.

Now let's find the path that gets us there.

The Science of Science Fiction

One of the most persistent challenges in writing a science fiction TV series is knowing how much science to include. Do you dive into the technical language of quantum tunnelling and gravitational waves, or do you simply say, "They opened a wormhole," and move on? The truth is, science fiction lives in the balancing act between credibility and wonder. Too much explanation can suffocate the story, while too little can make your world feel hollow. This chapter is about knowing when to explain—and when to leave room for imagination.

Science fiction earns its credibility through its internal logic. Your world doesn't have to follow the physics of *our* world, but it must follow *its own*. That means when you introduce a technology, biological rule, or interstellar phenomenon, you have to stay consistent with the logic it brings. If a device allows your character to read minds in one episode, you can't ignore it when a diplomatic negotiation hinges on truth later. Viewers may not know the equations behind teleportation, but they know when something doesn't make sense emotionally or narratively.

This is where ChatGPT can be a huge help. You can prompt it with questions like: "Explain how teleportation could work using speculative but plausible science," and get an answer that reads like the kind of dialogue or briefing scene you might include in an episode. You can then ask it to simplify the same explanation for a character who wouldn't understand advanced physics. This gives you options. You can keep your technobabble lean and readable—or go full detail when it serves the story.

Shows like *The Expanse* are grounded in hard science fiction, where physics is a constraint rather than a cheat code. They take inertia, time delay, and resource scarcity seriously. This gives the world weight and consequence. On the other end of the spectrum, *Doctor Who* often treats science more like magic, invoking concepts like "time vortexes" or "chronon energy" without needing to pin them to equations. And yet both approaches work because they're consistent with the tone and theme of their respective series.

So how do you know which way to go? The answer lies in the kind of story you're telling. If your series revolves around scientific discovery—like *Fringe*, *Stargate SG-1*, or *Altered Carbon*—you'll likely want to explain more. The science is part of the drama. It drives the plot. If your show is more surreal or allegorical, like *Legion* or *The OA*, then leaving things unexplained can add to the mystery and emotional depth.

When science becomes a tool for emotional storytelling, rather than just exposition, that's when it's doing its job. Think of the film *Interstellar*. Its depiction of time dilation isn't just a fascinating concept—it's the core of a heartbreaking story about a father aging slower than his daughter. Or look at *Star Trek's* transporters. They're not just a way to move characters from ship to planet—they've sparked debates about identity, mortality, and the soul. The best sci-fi series use science not just to *show* the future, but to ask human questions in unfamiliar terms.

That said, you don't want to bog your episodes down with long monologues about particle physics. If a character has to explain a concept, make it urgent, emotional, or character-revealing. If two characters disagree on how to interpret a scientific breakthrough, that's drama. If someone's hiding the truth about an experiment gone wrong, that's tension. Always look for the conflict or revelation hiding inside the science. That's where it becomes story.

You can use ChatGPT to draft multiple versions of your scientific explanations. Try a prompt like: "Write a short scene where a scientist explains to a military commander why a portal is collapsing." Then rewrite it with different tones—formal, sarcastic, panicked, compassionate. You'll start to feel how the delivery of information can shape a character or elevate a scene.

Sometimes, the best thing you can do is *not* explain. Let the mystery stay mysterious. Give the audience a puzzle to hold onto. *Lost* used this strategy in its early seasons, offering strange phenomena with no immediate answers. So did *Stranger Things*, where the Upside Down was terrifying precisely because it wasn't fully understood. But if you go this route, you need to commit. Tease without promising. Don't bluff an explanation if you don't plan to deliver. Viewers can tell the difference between purposeful mystery and confusion masquerading as depth.

Another useful technique is the *show-don't-tell* approach to science. Instead of explaining how a ship's gravity drive works, show the character walking sideways up a wall. Instead of telling us that time flows differently near the black hole, show a character aging while another one doesn't. Visual storytelling is one of your greatest assets in sci-fi. Use it to make the impossible feel tangible.

When in doubt, use metaphor. Science fiction thrives on metaphorical language to express abstract or futuristic ideas. *Battlestar Galactica* used the phrase "jump drive" instead of describing faster-than-light travel in technical terms. *Black Mirror* often builds entire episodes around single concepts—memory implants, AI companions, digital afterlives—and then unpacks them through emotional metaphor. You can prompt ChatGPT to generate metaphorical explanations for complex science, asking it to "Describe genetic manipulation like a gardener tending to invisible flowers," or "Explain quantum entanglement as a love story across time."

There's also the matter of tone. If your show is comedic, like *Futurama*, you can lean into absurdist science that deliberately breaks the rules. If your show is dark and grounded, like *Severance*, the science should be understated and ominous. ChatGPT can help you test your scientific concepts in different tonal registers so you can see how they feel across multiple versions of the same scene. Ultimately, science in science fiction is there to support your story, not hijack it. You're not writing a textbook. You're writing a television show with characters, stakes, emotion, and rhythm. You don't have to be a physicist to create great sci-fi. You just need to ask interesting questions—and then decide how much of the answer to give. Let your world make sense, but leave enough room for awe. Use science as scaffolding for wonder. With ChatGPT, you can generate plausible explanations when you need them and poetic ambiguity when you don't. The real secret to science fiction isn't knowing everything. It's knowing *what* to explain—and what to leave echoing in the dark.

Your story doesn't have to predict the future. It just has to feel like one someone might live in. Or escape from. Or return to. That's when science fiction becomes unforgettable.

Genre Hybrids: From Sci-Fi Horror to Techno-Noir and Beyond

Science fiction has never existed in a vacuum. It's a genre built on bending the rules, stretching expectations, and fusing together elements that don't traditionally belong together. Some of the most powerful, haunting, or ground-breaking sci-fi stories don't wear the label "science fiction" alone—they wear it alongside another: horror, noir, romance, western, political thriller. And when you're building a science fiction television series, understanding how genre hybrids work is a key to unlocking tone, structure, and originality.

Take a moment to think about *Alien*. It's not just a sci-fi movie—it's a sci-fi horror film. The cold corridors of the Nostromo, the body horror of the Xenomorph, the creeping dread of an unseen predator. It's a haunted house in space. That simple genre mashup—sci-fi plus horror—created something iconic. And the idea of being hunted by something unknowable in an environment that's supposed to be sterile and safe? That hybrid structure is just as effective in television, seen in shows like *The X-Files*, *Stranger Things*, and *Nightflyers*.

Now contrast that with *Blade Runner*, the definitive example of sci-fi noir. The rain-slicked streets, the voiceover, the morally ambiguous protagonist. It's as much Raymond Chandler as it is Philip K. Dick. What makes this hybrid work is the marriage of aesthetic and theme. Noir stories often deal with memory, identity, corruption, and fate—and those are questions that science fiction loves, too. So you get a setting of flying cars and androids, but a story rooted in old, gritty, very human dilemmas.

As you begin developing your own sci-fi TV series, consider what hybrid might best serve the kind of story you want to tell. Are you crafting a mystery about alien intelligence? Maybe sci-fi procedural, like *Fringe*. Are you exploring the end of human civilization? Perhaps a sci-fi western, like *Firefly*, or a sci-fi survival thriller, like *The 100*. Or maybe you want to dive into political conspiracies, where sci-fi becomes a lens for paranoia—*Battlestar Galactica* and *The Man in the High Castle* both turned genre mashups into sustained tension and complex character dynamics.

ChatGPT is especially helpful in this space. You can prompt it to brainstorm hybrid combinations like "Give me 10 unique sci-fi genre hybrids and describe the premise for each one." Or more specifically: "Describe a science fiction romance series set on a time-traveling research station," and you'll receive backbones of stories that instantly feel more nuanced than straight-up tech tales. The hybrid becomes your way of giving science fiction shape—it decides whether your show leans toward dread, awe, joy, or heartbreak.

Genre blending also gives you control over pacing and tone. Horror-sci-fi is often slow, atmospheric, and claustrophobic. Noir-sci-fi favors inner monologues and psychological tension. Comedy-sci-fi like *Red Dwarf* or *Upload* might be fast-paced and dialogue-heavy. The tone of your series isn't just about lighting and music—it's born from the genre DNA you choose to splice into your sci-fi framework. When in doubt, run test scenes through ChatGPT in different hybrid modes. Try the same character scene as horror, then noir, then romance. Watch what changes.

One of the most underused hybrids is sci-fi fantasy. *Doctor Who* often lives in this space, where pseudo-science bends so far it becomes indistinguishable from magic. Time Lords, regeneration, paradoxes—it's scientific sounding, but it's really mythological. This works because the show's tone supports it. It's whimsical, curious, deeply emotional. The sci-fi is a delivery system for big, magical ideas. If you want to write a show where dreams reshape reality or where consciousness is transferred into animals, this hybrid might be your ticket.

Then there's sci-fi comedy. It might seem lighthearted, but it's a powerful tool for social commentary. *Futurama* managed to tackle death, technology, politics, love, and loneliness—all while making us laugh. *The Orville*, on the surface a parody, evolved into serious storytelling with genuine heart and ideas. Comedy allows sci-fi to explore contradictions without feeling preachy. You can write a robot who wants to be human and a human who wants to be a toaster, and people will follow you if the tone invites them in.

There's also value in writing against type. Think of a sci-fi series where the world is bleak, the tech is dangerous, but the emotional core is romantic or hopeful. *Counterpart* gave us espionage and parallel worlds, but it was also about love, trust, and identity. Blending genres can help you challenge clichés. If your world feels too much like something that's been done, switch genres. Instead of a dystopian action epic, maybe you're writing a sci-fi musical. Or a coming-of-age story about a teenager with a malfunctioning alien device.

Hybrid genres also affect how your story unfolds structurally. A noir might lean into episodic cases with an overarching mystery. A horror might be a slow burn with escalating dread. A romantic hybrid will pace itself around emotional climaxes. Understanding your genre blend early lets you set expectations for viewers—and break those expectations in ways that feel intentional, not accidental.

As always, ChatGPT can serve as a testing lab for your hybrids. Ask it to rewrite a scene from your pilot in a new genre. Ask for tone comparisons. Feed it a simple premise like, "A colony on Mars begins to experience shared dreams," and let it reimagine that as a horror, a drama, a comedy, or a noir. Each version will reveal something about the soul of your story.

There's no "pure" science fiction. Even the classics borrow. That's the beauty of it. Science fiction has always been the genre of possibility—not just in terms of technology, but in narrative design. Your sci-fi series can contain multitudes. It can be thrilling and philosophical. Funny and frightening. Mysterious and romantic. Your job is to find the blend that feels most alive to you.

Don't be afraid to mash together your favorite genres. That's where the next *Stranger Things* or *Black Mirror* will be born. Not from following the rules of science fiction—but from bending them until something new breaks through.

With AI, you have the freedom to explore dozens of variations before choosing the one that clicks. So mix boldly. And then build your world around the story only that hybrid could tell.

Pilot Episode Power: Your First Hour Is Everything

The pilot episode is your spaceship launch. If it doesn't leave the ground, the series won't survive. A weak pilot can kill a great idea, while a powerful one can carry a show for years. In science fiction television, where the audience is being introduced not just to characters and plots but entire worlds, the pilot has to do triple the work—and still feel effortless. That first hour is your invitation, your handshake, your pitch, your proof. Everything hinges on it.

A great sci-fi pilot accomplishes several things at once. It introduces your core characters and relationships. It sets up the narrative engine of the show—what the series will *do* week after week. It begins laying out the rules of your world without overwhelming the audience. And most importantly, it gives viewers a reason to care. Not just about the concept, but about the people navigating it. The pilot episode is where you prove that your series is more than just an idea. It's a story worth following.

Think of *Battlestar Galactica*'s reimagined pilot. It didn't just set up a universe in the aftermath of a genocidal attack by intelligent machines—it grounded that destruction in grief, panic, command, and sacrifice. You knew who Adama and Roslin were before you understood the politics of the Twelve Colonies. You felt the scale of the threat, but you also felt the human cost. Or take *The Expanse*, which began with a haunting mystery and layered it with political tension and a clear sense of scale—space wasn't just setting, it was pressure. These pilots succeeded because they knew what made their series tick—and put it front and center.

So how do you write your own science fiction pilot? The key is clarity within complexity. Your world may be huge, but you're not showing all of it in the first hour. Choose a specific, grounded narrative to guide the viewer's first steps. Maybe it's a rescue mission gone wrong. A murder investigation in a futuristic society. A first contact moment between species. This primary storyline should be emotionally relatable, even if the setting is wildly unfamiliar. Your characters are our guides—so let us see the world through their surprise, fear, curiosity, or ambition.

ChatGPT can be an invaluable co-writer here. Try prompting it with: "Write a one-hour TV pilot for a sci-fi series where Earth's gravity is failing." Then refine. Ask it to focus more on character emotion. Or trim the exposition. Or add a subplot. Use the results not as finished product, but as raw material—seeds to shape into something cinematic and specific. You can also prompt it to generate multiple cold opens—some suspenseful, some quiet, some surreal—and test which tone best fits your vision.

In a pilot, your characters must arrive fully alive. We don't need their entire backstory—we need their presence. Their perspective. Show us who they are through action and dialogue, not exposition. A good test is this: if you removed all the sci-fi elements, would the characters still be interesting? If yes, you're on the right track. Sci-fi enhances story, but the people carry it.

Structure matters too. Most successful sci-fi pilots operate in two parallel tracks: immediate conflict and long-term mystery. The immediate conflict gives the episode urgency—someone is lost, something is broken, someone must decide. The long-term mystery gives the show shape—what happened before, what's lurking behind the scenes, what truth is waiting to be uncovered. Think of *Stranger Things*, which starts with a disappearance and ends with questions about parallel dimensions. The viewer is satisfied, but also hungry.

When it comes to worldbuilding, less is more—at least at first. Don't try to explain everything. Show what your characters would naturally encounter. Let the tech reveal itself through use. Let the culture show itself through tension. If your world has three suns, then show how that changes the day. If your characters speak in code, reveal that through a scene where misunderstanding creates danger. Trust the viewer's intelligence. Mystery is part of the allure.

Tone is another powerful tool. The tone of your pilot sets the emotional contract for the series. If you want to write a series full of paranoia and bleak revelations, your pilot shouldn't end on a joke. If your series is going to embrace wild, colorful adventure, then lean into that from the start. ChatGPT can help you test tonal variations of your scenes. Ask it to rewrite your pilot's closing moment with a tone of awe, then fear, then irony—and see what feels most true to your concept.

And don't forget theme. It doesn't need to be overt, but your pilot should begin exploring your show's core questions. If your show is about freedom versus security, let that tension exist in the decisions your characters face. If it's about identity, then let your characters be mistaken, conflicted, or hidden. Theme gives your story weight—it makes your world more than a gimmick.

Finally, think about the last moment. The last image of your pilot is your promise. It's the question you're daring the viewer to keep asking. Will the alien ship open? Will the AI wake up? Will the clones rebel? A strong final beat hooks the audience—and also gives *you* a direction. If you know where episode one ends, you know what episode two must begin to answer.

A pilot is more than a first episode. It's a miniature version of your series. A self-contained invitation. Your entire show distilled into one hour of television. Get it right, and the rest will follow. And with ChatGPT at your side, you can test, refine, reimagine, and restructure that pilot until it hums with energy and potential.

This is your first step into the unknown. Make it count. Make it personal. Make it unforgettable.

And once you've done that—make the next one even better.

Writing the Series Arc: Season-Long Mysteries and Revelation

Writing a science fiction television series is like designing a labyrinth—but instead of trapping your audience, you want to lead them deeper with every step. At the center is a revelation, an answer, a truth waiting to be uncovered. The season arc is your map. It's the engine that drives the story forward and keeps the audience engaged over multiple episodes. In science fiction, it's often where the real power of the genre reveals itself—because unlike episodic formats, a serialized arc lets you layer questions, complicate answers, and transform characters across time.

A well-crafted season arc gives your show its spine. While individual episodes might follow contained storylines—exploring alien phenomena, strange technology, or moral dilemmas—the season arc provides cohesion. It's the slow-burning mystery, the growing threat, the hidden agenda, the secret that will change everything. Whether it's the identity of a hidden AI overlord, the origin of a pandemic, or the true nature of a character's reality, your arc is what compels people to binge or come back next week. It turns casual interest into obsession.

Start by identifying the *central question* of your season. This doesn't need to be framed as a literal mystery, but it should invite curiosity and tension. In *Stranger Things*, the question is: What happened to Will, and what is the Upside Down? In *Westworld*, it's: What is consciousness, and who is really in control? In *Fringe*, it's: What's behind the strange events—and what's Walter hiding? That central question becomes the narrative gravity pulling your characters—and the audience—deeper into the story.

Once you have that question, use ChatGPT to help develop the web of sub-questions that spiral out from it. For example, prompt it with: "Give me 10 subplot-level mysteries that could emerge from discovering a parallel dimension." You might receive ideas about missing people, altered identities, interdimensional theft, or even temporal echoes of a character's past self. Each of these becomes fuel for episodic tension that builds toward the larger revelation.

Pacing is crucial. You want to reveal just enough each episode to move forward—but not so much that you resolve everything too soon. Think of your season arc as a pressure valve. You increase tension, drop a clue, build doubt, raise the stakes, and then—just when it seems like something might be answered—you twist the question. It's not about stalling. It's about layering. ChatGPT can help you structure these beats. Prompt it with: "Outline a 10-episode arc where the mystery of a disappearing planet is slowly revealed through character-driven discoveries." It can provide plot points, turning points, and mid-season climaxes to work from.

Revelations in science fiction hit hardest when they're personal. It's not just about what's out there—it's about how the truth changes your characters. A clone discovering they're not unique. A soldier realizing they're fighting the wrong enemy. A scientist forced to confront the damage caused by their greatest invention. Tie your big revelations to character arcs. The answer to the mystery should hurt. Or heal. Or shake something loose. It should force change. That's when science fiction becomes emotionally rich—not just intellectually satisfying.

Another powerful technique is the *false revelation*. These are moments when a character—or the audience—believes they've discovered the truth, only for it to be incomplete or misleading. This works especially well in AI-generated story planning, where you can prompt ChatGPT to generate multiple "plausible but wrong" explanations for an event, and use those to mislead or deepen your plot. Mystery thrives on ambiguity, and viewers love to be proven wrong *if* the new truth is even more compelling.

The architecture of the arc also depends on your show's length and format. A tight 8-episode season might follow a more accelerated structure, with a clearly planned midpoint twist. A 20-episode network season may intersperse monster-of-the-week episodes with slowly creeping clues. Think about your climax—what happens in episode 8 or 10 that makes it impossible for the world, or the characters, to go back to how things were? That climax doesn't always have to be action-packed. It can be a quiet reveal. A character's betrayal. A message finally decoded. But it must shift the story forever.

Symbolism and recurring motifs can subtly support your arc. The repeated appearance of a number, a tune, a word in an alien language, or a visual symbol like a spiral or mirror. ChatGPT can help you brainstorm these patterns, turning abstract ideas into visuals or sounds that accumulate meaning. You can prompt it to "Give me ten recurring symbols that could represent a malfunctioning simulation," and then work those into your world.

And don't forget the power of *thematic resonance*. The mystery you create shouldn't just be a puzzle—it should reflect your show's deeper themes. If your series explores identity, maybe the mystery involves shapeshifters or memory alteration. If it's about control, maybe someone has rewritten reality itself. The mystery isn't separate from your message. It *is* your message, hidden in narrative form.

AI can also help you balance the structure. Ask ChatGPT to "Break down a season arc into escalating emotional beats across ten episodes," and you'll start to see the emotional journey that complements the plot. It's not just about what's revealed. It's about how your characters feel as they edge closer to the truth. Fear, hope, confusion, grief, awe. Let those feelings be the real map, guiding your writing from start to finish.

A well-executed series arc leaves breadcrumbs that seem meaningless at first but become profound in hindsight. The flower in episode two. The word someone mutters in their sleep. The brief flash of a strange device. You can go back and plant these moments once your arc is locked. ChatGPT can even help you brainstorm where to hide clues—and how to make them resonate when the truth is finally revealed.

In science fiction, where the rules of the world can shift, a strong arc gives the viewer something to hold onto. It's the rope that leads them through the dark. It gives your story shape, suspense, and scope. Whether your arc ends in revelation, destruction, or transcendence, make sure the journey justifies the destination. And remember, the best mysteries don't just answer questions. They change the way we look at everything that came before.

Let ChatGPT help you sketch the maze. But you decide where it ends—and what's waiting at the center.

The Weekly Episode: Monster-of-the-Week vs. Serialized Structure

When crafting a science fiction television series, one of the most crucial choices you'll make is how your episodes function. Do you want your show to follow a procedural rhythm with self-contained stories—something viewers can dip into casually without much background knowledge? Or do you want to build an ongoing narrative where each episode is one chapter in a long, continuous arc? This is the classic creative fork between the *monster-of-the-week* format and the *serialized structure*. Each has its strengths, and each invites a different kind of storytelling. Many of the best sci-fi shows in history have played with both.

The *monster-of-the-week* (MOTW) model refers to episodic television in which each installment introduces a new problem—often a literal creature, alien, anomaly, or moral dilemma—that the protagonists must confront and resolve by the episode's end. It's a structure that thrives on creativity, variety, and strong character consistency. The mystery or challenge changes weekly, but the relationships and world remain familiar. Classic *Doctor Who*, early *The X-Files*, *Fringe*, *Stargate SG-1*, and even *Star Trek: The Next Generation* all lean heavily on this model. And when done well, this format becomes incredibly binge-worthy, offering viewers a full narrative arc in every hour while gradually building character depth across seasons.

This style is especially powerful for world-building. Each new episode allows you to explore a different corner of your universe—a planet, a species, a new piece of technology, or a philosophical question. You can stretch your concept to its limits. What if a sentient virus wants to negotiate peace? What if time travel accidentally rewrites a character's personality? With ChatGPT, you can prompt, "Give me a monster-of-the-week sci-fi episode concept involving artificial intelligence and lost memory," and receive a unique scenario to build an episode around in seconds.

The key to MOTW success is having a strong thematic spine. While the plot resets, the deeper questions—about identity, purpose, morality—build gradually. The best monster-of-the-week shows evolve emotionally, even if the plot of the week is solved. Mulder and Scully changed dramatically over the seasons, even as they kept chasing aliens and conspiracies. You don't need constant serialization to tell a meaningful story—you just need characters who *remember* what they've been through.

On the other hand, the *serialized structure* is about progression. It's narrative momentum—ongoing conflict, deepening mystery, long-form storytelling that rewards attention. Every episode builds on the last. There's no "back to normal" because the normal keeps shifting. This is the model used by shows like *Battlestar Galactica*, *Dark*, *The Expanse*, and *Westworld*. These series weave plot threads that carry through entire seasons or even the full run. Characters evolve rapidly, secrets compound, and revelations have long-lasting consequences.

Serialization invites more complex arcs. It's ideal for stories about revolutions, wars, betrayals, identity crises, or systems breaking down. If you're writing about a world unraveling, a serialized format lets that unraveling play out in real time. It gives you room for subtle clues, multi-episode subplots, and character transformations that feel earned. It also creates a powerful sense of immersion—viewers don't watch episodes, they live in your world.

But serialized stories require careful planning. Loose threads can pile up. If the audience gets confused or bored waiting for answers, you risk losing them. That's where ChatGPT becomes a valuable partner. You can use it to map out a full season arc, break down subplots into emotional beats, or revise earlier episodes once you know where the story ends. You can prompt it to "Write a ten-episode arc where a colony on Mars falls under AI control, with character arcs for four leads," and you'll get a structure to build from or revise.

Many modern science fiction shows blend both formats. This hybrid approach offers the best of both worlds. You get the accessibility and variety of the monster-of-the-week, plus the emotional and thematic depth of serialization. Shows like *Fringe* and *The X-Files* often followed a pattern of standalone episodes laced with clues about a larger mystery. This allowed new viewers to jump in, while rewarding long-time fans with satisfying payoffs. Your series can do the same—interweaving standalone plots with serialized elements that grow louder and more pressing as the season progresses.

You can even design your series to shift structurally over time. Early episodes might be more episodic, gradually giving way to a tightly serialized narrative. *Breaking Bad*, though not sci-fi, famously used this tactic to lull viewers into its world before accelerating its descent. In science fiction, this can mirror the encroachment of larger forces—a creeping AI, a spreading disease, a political collapse. The format itself becomes a storytelling device.

Another thing to consider is production. Monster-of-the-week episodes are generally easier to rearrange or even drop if needed. Serialization demands precise placement. If you're planning a pitch or working with a production team, being flexible about format can give you more room to adapt. ChatGPT can help you write both kinds of episodes, and even test scenes written in one style translated into the other. Try prompting: "Turn this serialized sci-fi arc into a series of stand-alone episodes that each still hint at the mystery," and let AI do some of the heavy lifting.

Your format also affects pacing. MOTW episodes tend to open with a tease and resolve with a thematic button. Serialized stories often end on cliffhangers or turning points. Decide what rhythm suits your concept. If your story is about the slow loss of reality, serialization fits. If it's about confronting ethical dilemmas one strange situation at a time, go with episodic. In the end, the choice between monster-of-the-week and serialized isn't just about structure—it's about audience experience. Do you want them to feel closure at the end of each hour, or to be left restless and hungry for the next piece of the puzzle? Both have value. Both have legacy. And with ChatGPT, you can explore each version of your story before choosing—or decide not to choose at all.

Because in science fiction, there's no rule that can't be bent. Not even time itself.

So write the kind of journey that *you* want to take—and give your viewers a reason to stay aboard. Whether they arrive for the creature, the conspiracy, or the character drama, they'll stay if the story makes them wonder what happens next. Every week. Every episode. Every world you build.

Building a Sci-Fi Writer's Room with ChatGPT as Your Team

Building a writer's room for a science fiction television series has always been about gathering voices around a table, each bringing a different perspective on story, character, or theme. In the past, that room was populated by human writers, each with their own notebook, coffee cup, and deadlines looming. Today, you have the opportunity to build a writer's room that combines humans and AI—specifically, ChatGPT—as collaborators. This chapter explores how to assemble that hybrid team, structure your process, and use AI to amplify creativity without sacrificing the human spark that makes stories matter.

From the moment you decide you want to develop a sci-fi series, you start imagining the writer's room. In the traditional model, you invite three, four, six writers—people you trust to riff on ideas, argue over character motivations, and keep the season arc coherent. You meet in a conference room, papers sprawled, whiteboards full of diagrams, chairs pushed back as voices rise and fall. With ChatGPT, you can replicate much of that dynamic in virtual form. You can ask the AI to generate outlines, propose dialogue variations, invent alien species, or even draft entire scenes—all in real time. But to do that effectively, you need to think of ChatGPT not as a monolithic tool but as a member of your team: a brainstorming partner, a first-draft sketch artist, an "ideas generator" that never tires.

The first step in building this hybrid room is defining roles. In a traditional writers' room, someone might function as showrunner—overseeing tone and final decisions—while others handle story arcs, subplots, character development, or specific episodes. With ChatGPT, you don't slot it into one role. Instead, think of it as a flexible collaborator that can assume whichever function you need at any moment. It can play the role of your junior writer, offering fresh takes on a scene. It can act like a researcher, filling in plausible scientific details. It can serve as a devil's advocate, presenting alternative conflicts or moral twists. You can even ask it to "be" a specific type of writer: a humor specialist, a horror writer, a world-builder who focuses on culture and politics. In practice, you'll shift ChatGPT's "hat" multiple times per session.

To illustrate, imagine your human writers are gathered for a day of brainstorming on episode three of Season One. You ask ChatGPT to propose five versions of how the main character's alien-guide companion might betray them—one version focusing on political ideology, another on personal jealousy, another on corporate espionage, and so on. Within minutes, you have multiple seeds to discuss and debate. Then you ask ChatGPT to roll back and "become" the character's voice: "Write a monologue where the alien companion justifies turning against the heroes because they believe preserving their species requires darker measures." Suddenly you have dialogue you can adapt, refine, or reject. By switching ChatGPT's function from "idea generator" to "character interpreter," you keep the room lively and grounded in the show's emotional stakes.

One of the most powerful aspects of using ChatGPT is speed. In a traditional room, when you need a quick justification for why a futuristic transport system breaks down or what kind of political system an underwater colony might have, you'd pause, someone would research, and you'd reconvene later. With ChatGPT, you prompt it instantly: "Describe a near-future underwater city that relies on genetically modified coral structures for skyscrapers. Include political factions and daily life details." In seconds, you'll receive a description that you can tweak. That immediacy keeps the momentum high, prevents the dreaded lull when people stare at blank pages, and allows you to stay in creative "flow" rather than shifting gears to research mode.

Still, speed can become noise if you're not disciplined. A writer's room needs structure—moments of freewheeling brainstorming, but also checkpoints for coherence. One effective workflow is to alternate between "divergent" and "convergent" sessions. In a divergent session, you ask ChatGPT and your writers to generate as many possibilities as possible: plot lines, character motivations, futuristic tech concepts, alien cultures, episode titles. You don't judge; you capture everything. Then in a convergent session, you winnow those options, vote on which directions to pursue, refine the chosen ideas, and fold them into the growing series bible. ChatGPT can help both phases. During divergence, prompt it with iterative requests: "Give me ten more ways that the interstellar political union could collapse." During convergence, ask: "Summarize the top three threats to the union's stability based on previous ideas, and rank them by dramatic potential." This two-step process mirrors a human room's creative yin and yang but amplifies it by letting AI handle rapid idea generation and structured summarization.

To maintain clarity, create a shared document—your virtual "whiteboard"—where humans and ChatGPT dumps go side by side. Use headings like "Episode One Brainstorm," "Character Profile: Commander Nava," or "Technology Ideas: Phase Drive." As you chat with GPT, paste its outputs into these sections. Humans can annotate, highlight, or comment. Over time, you build a living document that captures the evolution of every idea. This archive becomes invaluable when you realize a plot thread you discarded in week one might tie into a discovery in week seven. ChatGPT can search through that document for relevant terms—eclipsing the speed of manual searches—and help you connect dots you might have overlooked.

Let's dive into a concrete example. Suppose your series revolves around a renegade starship crew that stumbles on an abandoned research station orbiting a rogue planet. In early brainstorming, you ask ChatGPT: "Describe three scientific catastrophic events that could force the station's crew to abandon it five years ago." It suggests a failed terraforming experiment that triggered micro-quakes, a viral outbreak among genetically altered test subjects, and an AI uprising trying to convert biological matter into machinery. You copy these to your "Research Station History" section. Now, in a separate session, you ask ChatGPT: "Given those three possible disasters, outline how survivors living on a nearby moon would form a shadow network trading exile technology." It gives you a sketch of a black-market group, their customs, and how they scavenge station tech. You paste that under a "Moon Colony Black Market" heading. Next, your writers argue: which scenario best sets up tension for Episode Three? They vote for the viral outbreak because it yields moral questions and an opportunity for a returning antagonist. Now you have a decision and a clear path.

Another advantage of including ChatGPT in your writer's room is diversity of perspective. Even the most capable group of humans can lean toward familiar tropes or get locked into a collective blind spot. ChatGPT draws on patterns from countless stories, sometimes offering a fresh hybrid you might never have considered—a mashup of Japanese mecha philosophy with Russian space politics, for instance. If you ever feel stuck in a creative rut, run a prompt like, "Combine cyberpunk dystopia with neo-medieval themes, and give me a five-scene synopsis where technological alchemists hold sway." The response can spark a new subplot or even the next season's main villain.

Of course, collaboration with AI is not perfect. You'll sometimes get generic or clichés-laden suggestions. You'll encounter contradictions—ChatGPT might name a station "Prospero One" in one prompt and "Ulysses Outpost" in the next. Part of your job as showrunner or lead writer is to curate, vet, and reconcile. Use ChatGPT's outputs as raw clay—not finished clay. If GPT proposes a "quantum sandstorm" that isn't scientifically coherent or dramatically compelling, you can refine it: "Explain how a quantum sandstorm works by synthesizing tropical storm patterns with particle wave theory." The more precise your prompts, the more useful the results. Over time, you'll develop a prompt-writing fluency, knowing how to coax ChatGPT into providing depth rather than surface fluff.

Collaboration also depends on where humans meet. Some teams still gather in person over a long table; others are fully remote, using shared docs, Slack channels, or Zoom rooms. If you're remote, set up a daily or weekly routine where a specific person moderates ChatGPT interactions—ensuring prompts are clear, responses are archived, and ideas are distilled. That person becomes the AI Wrangler, making sure the AI's outputs mesh with human creativity rather than overwhelm it. If you're in person, you can hook ChatGPT up to a projector or screen, type live prompts during discussions, and let everyone watch the AI "brainstorm" in real time. That transparency encourages collective critique. Writers can suggest prompt tweaks on the fly—"Ask it to make the alien species more empathetic, not just hostile"—and GPT refines answers immediately.

One of the biggest challenges in writer's rooms—AI-assisted or not—is the fear of losing originality. You might worry that if you rely too heavily on AI, your show will feel generic or secondhand. The answer is to use ChatGPT for breadth, not depth. Let it generate a hundred variations of a warp drive failure, but choose the one that resonates with your characters' emotional stakes. Use human instinct to judge tone, theme, and voice. If ChatGPT's dialogue feels stiff, rewrite it in human voice. If an AI-proposed subplot seems too convenient, toss it. Always maintain editorial control. AI should be your sounding board, not your boss.

As the season progresses, you'll reach points where you need to revise earlier episodes because a later story beat doesn't fit. In a traditional room, you'd gather everyone again, reread scripts, debate solutions. With ChatGPT, you can feed it a summary of Episode One and ask, "Adapt this scene so that a clue about the rogue planet's core composition appears in the background dialogue." Or, "Rewrite this exchange so that the second-season betrayal of Commander Nava feels foreshadowed." ChatGPT can suggest edits that acknowledge the new series knowledge, helping you keep continuity tight without rewriting from scratch.

Crucially, building a writer's room with ChatGPT also means training your human team to trust the process. Some writers may initially resist the idea of an "artificial" collaborator. They may feel that AI can't capture nuance or that it's simply a gimmick. You'll need to demonstrate that ChatGPT, when used thoughtfully, can lift tedious tasks—like drafting multiple loglines or summarizing research—so that human writers can focus on emotional resonance and originality. Encourage your team to think of ChatGPT as a well-informed colleague who doesn't take lunch breaks, but still needs direction and feedback. Show them that the best AI-generated ideas may be those that are imperfect—a sentence fragment, a half-formed twist—that spark something richer when a human mind catches fire.

Over time, your hybrid writer's room will develop a rhythm. You might start each week by reviewing notes, checking production schedules, and listing "Creative To-Dos." Then, you take five minutes to feed those into ChatGPT: "List unresolved character tensions from Episode Four," "Generate five alternative endpoints for Episode Six based on the rebellion subplot," "Describe three ways to heighten suspense in the mid-season cliffhanger." ChatGPT delivers drafts while writers stretch legs, grab coffee, or read previous episodes. You reconvene, evaluate, refine, assign tasks. This rhythm—human insight guiding AI output, then human curation of AI suggestions—creates a feedback loop that can be faster and more creative than an all-human room alone.

When you get that rhythm right, your show benefits. Episodes get richer, character arcs feel more interconnected, and your team wastes less time reinventing the wheel. Because in science fiction, it's easy to get lost in speculation. The universe is vast; your creativity can be boundless. ChatGPT helps contain that boundlessness, giving you a sandbox where you can test ideas, fail fast, and build something coherent out of all that raw potential.

Remember that a successful writer's room—hybrid or not—is more than just churning out pages. It's about nurturing a shared vision. Make sure human voices still hold sway in every decision. Use ChatGPT's rhythms and suggestions to expand possibilities, but let human empathy and taste decide which possibilities live on. Keep your world coherent by archiving decisions in a centralized story bible. Encourage open discussion where writers critique AI outputs and collaborate on refining them. Celebrate those moments when a ChatGPT twist sparks a human writer to push a character in a new direction.

In the end, building a sci-fi writer's room with ChatGPT is an experiment in co-creation. It's not about replacing writers. It's about augmenting them—amplifying ideas, accelerating research, and providing perspective when you need it. The best science fiction has always prospered on collaboration: authors drawing on science, artwork, philosophy, and each other. Now, AI is part of that ecosystem. When humans and ChatGPT work in tandem—prompt by prompt, revision by revision—the result can be a series that feels both vast in imagination and focused in emotional truth.

So, gather your human crew and crank up the AI. Assign roles: the big-picture architect, the character specialist, the tech consultant, the AI wrangler. Build your shared documents. Develop your prompt vocabulary. Embrace the friction when humans challenge AI suggestions, and let those debates refine your vision. Over time, you'll find the equilibrium where ChatGPT's tireless brainstorming fuels human insight—and the human insight, in turn, refines and curates the AI. That is the future of the writer's room. That is how you create a science fiction television series that feels fresh, dynamic, and alive. And it all starts the moment you invite ChatGPT to the table.

Idea Generation with AI: From Nothing to Everything in One Hour

One of the most overwhelming parts of writing a science fiction television series is staring at a blank page and wondering where to begin. The possibilities are infinite, and that's the problem. Should your series take place on a decaying space station orbiting a dead planet? Should it center on a future Earth ruled by memory merchants? Should it begin in the moment of apocalypse—or centuries after? Without a direction, the imagination can feel paralyzed. That's where AI, particularly ChatGPT, becomes a powerful catalyst. In this chapter, you'll learn how to go from nothing to everything—an entire series premise, character map, and setting—in just one hour.

The trick isn't to ask ChatGPT for "a sci-fi show idea." That's too vague. You'll likely get something thin, generic, and uninspired. Instead, you guide the AI by asking small, specific questions that build on each other. This is idea scaffolding. You don't begin by asking for a whole series. You begin with the seed—and let ChatGPT help you water it, prune it, and watch it grow.

Start with one strange "what if" scenario. You can invent it or ask ChatGPT to generate one. Try:

"What if in the year 2450, humans are legally required to switch consciousness every ten years?"

Or:

"What if the Earth's moon is revealed to be a long-dormant spacecraft waiting to wake up?"

You can also prompt ChatGPT with: "Give me ten original 'what if' scenarios for a sci-fi TV series that involve identity, memory, or technology." Choose one that sparks curiosity or discomfort. The best ideas don't just sound cool—they raise questions. "Why?" "How?" "What would that do to people?" That's where your show begins.

Once you have a premise, your next step is to build a world around it. Don't jump to full planetary maps or cultural histories yet. Ask specific questions. "What kind of government would enforce mandatory consciousness switching?" Or: "What myths would develop if the moon were secretly an alien machine?" Let ChatGPT offer possibilities—political structures, belief systems, economies, underground resistance groups. Use the answers not as facts, but as starting points. If something feels wrong, tweak it. If something feels intriguing, dig deeper.

Now, introduce characters. Not everyone—just a few archetypes that bring emotional energy into your concept. Try prompts like:

"Who would be the perfect protagonist in a world where people change bodies every decade?"

Or:

"Give me a character who grew up worshipping the moon, only to find out it's a machine designed to erase Earth."

These characters should want things. Fear things. Have blind spots. You're looking for people who will suffer and evolve as the story unfolds. The science fiction concept is the canvas—but these characters are the paint.

You can go further with ChatGPT by prompting it to develop character arcs:

"Describe a season-long emotional arc for a woman who discovers her memories are not her own."

You'll get beats you can break down into episodes later. Don't worry about polish—this is a discovery phase. The idea is to move quickly, allowing instinct and curiosity to guide you, with AI as your assistant.

By this point—20 or 30 minutes in—you'll have the beginnings of a world, a premise, and a few people who might live in it. Now it's time to focus on format. Ask ChatGPT:

"What kind of episode structure would work best for this premise?"

Is it serialized or episodic? Is it a tight ten-episode season or a sprawling saga? Could it sustain "monster-of-the-week" storytelling, or is it an unfolding mystery that builds to a singular revelation? You don't have to lock it down now—but the earlier you know how your show wants to function, the easier it will be to shape.

Next, ask for stakes. Try:

"What is the major conflict driving the first season of this show?"

Conflict is your engine. Maybe it's personal—your protagonist is losing their grip on reality. Maybe it's political—a war is brewing between cloned citizens and original humans. Maybe it's existential—the AI on the moon has decided humanity must start over. Whatever it is, you need something that creates pressure. A ticking clock. A threat. An impossible choice.

Now, with 15–20 minutes left in your creative hour, start combining what you have. Use a prompt like:

"Summarize this show's premise, characters, tone, and setting as if pitching to a streaming platform."

This helps you see if the whole is more than the sum of its parts. If it feels too familiar, go back and shake something up. Ask ChatGPT:

"What's one twist that could turn this show into something totally unexpected?"

Or:

"How can I make this show more emotionally grounded?"

You can also ask for genre hybrid suggestions to refine your tone:

"Make this concept feel more like a sci-fi noir," or "Give this a sci-fi romance spin."

Suddenly, your memory-switching story becomes a detective drama with shifting bodies and no reliable identity. Or your moon-AI show becomes a tragic love story between a human and the consciousness embedded in the satellite.

The last thing to generate in this session is a visual or stylistic vibe. Ask:

"What shows or films does this series resemble in tone and style?"

Or:

"Describe the visual look and mood of this show."

This helps when pitching the concept to collaborators—or just making sure it feels distinct. Is it sterile and cerebral like *Devs*? Gritty and grounded like *The Expanse*? Neon-soaked like *Blade Runner 2049*? ChatGPT can offer comparisons and even help you generate taglines or loglines.

By the end of your hour, you'll have:

- A high-concept premise
- A few key characters
- The central conflict
- The tone and structure
- The potential arc of Season One
- Visual inspirations
- Several unique twists or thematic layers

And all of it can come from zero. From an empty page. From the moment you say, "I want to write a sci-fi show, but I don't know where to start."

That's the power of combining human instinct with AI momentum. ChatGPT won't write your show for you—but it will make sure you never face that intimidating silence alone. It will talk back, suggest, provoke, imagine, and let you sharpen or discard its suggestions. It gives you the freedom to fail fast, pivot often, and uncover the version of the idea that feels most alive to you.

The Protagonist in Sci-Fi: Visionary, Scientist, or Everyman?

Every science fiction television series begins with a question—but it survives because of a character. No matter how big the ideas, how strange the setting, or how ground-breaking the technology, your audience will follow your story if they connect with the person at the center. The protagonist is the audience's tether to the unknown. Through their eyes, we experience wonder, fear, discovery, and transformation. In science fiction, that protagonist often takes one of three primary forms: the visionary, the scientist, or the everyman. Each brings a different lens to the world—and each shapes the story in unique and powerful ways.

Let's start with the visionary. This protagonist sees what others can't—or won't. They are dreamers, revolutionaries, leaders, or prophets. Think of Jean-Luc Picard in *Star Trek: The Next Generation*. His belief in diplomacy, ethics, and exploration defines the tone of the show. Or Dolores in *Westworld*, whose awakening leads to rebellion and the deconstruction of everything she once believed. The visionary protagonist doesn't merely react to the future; they shape it. Their story is often about ideals clashing with reality. The conflict lies in the cost of their vision: what they must sacrifice, how they are misunderstood, or how they risk becoming the thing they oppose.

If you choose to build your series around a visionary, ChatGPT can help you explore that character's ideology. Try prompting: "Describe a sci-fi protagonist who believes artificial life should have the same rights as humans. What events in their past shaped that belief?" You'll receive backstory details, possible internal conflicts, and relationships that either support or challenge that belief. Use that foundation to write a character who isn't just navigating a futuristic world—but trying to change it.

Then there's the scientist—the protagonist driven by curiosity, logic, and discovery. These characters often serve as the anchor in worlds of chaos. They want to understand how things work, even when those things are terrifying. Think of Walter Bishop in *Fringe*, Eleanor Arroway in *Contact*, or even Dr. Manhattan in *Watchmen*. The scientist can be an explorer of both external worlds and internal dimensions. Their stories are often about pushing too far, revealing too much, or realizing that knowledge comes with ethical consequences.

The scientist protagonist fits beautifully in science fiction because they are already searching. They ask questions the audience wants answers to. But they can also be emotionally restrained, haunted by loss, or blind to the human implications of their research. Their arc is often about learning to feel as deeply as they think. You can use ChatGPT to brainstorm those arcs. Try: "Create a ten-episode journey for a scientist who discovers that time travel causes memory decay." You'll get a structure that blends intellectual discovery with emotional deterioration.

Finally, there's the everyman—the ordinary character thrust into an extraordinary world. This is the audience surrogate. They don't have the tools, the knowledge, or the vision to understand the universe at first, but they *learn*. Think of Fry in *Futurama*, Joel in *The Last of Us*, or Jim Holden in *The Expanse* (who starts off as a reluctant leader). The everyman (or everywoman) gives the story emotional grounding. Their confusion, awe, and terror mirror our own. Their journey is usually one of transformation—from powerless to empowered, from clueless to courageous.

The strength of the everyman protagonist lies in accessibility. They make the strange familiar. They ask the obvious questions. They feel what the viewer would feel. But they also risk being reactive. To avoid that, make sure your everyman still has goals, flaws, and agency. ChatGPT can help you elevate this kind of character. Prompt: "Write an everyman sci-fi protagonist who accidentally activates an alien artifact. What mistake from their past makes this decision emotionally loaded?" Suddenly, the ordinary character has emotional depth and thematic significance.

In truth, most compelling sci-fi protagonists are hybrids. The visionary might also be a scientist. The everyman might evolve into a visionary. Ripley in *Alien* begins as a cautious survivor—an everywoman—but becomes a warrior with moral clarity. The Doctor in *Doctor Who* is part scientist, part visionary, and often grounded by a human companion serving as the emotional center. Your protagonist can shift archetypes over time, reflecting the journey your story demands.

One way to determine your protagonist's core identity is to ask what type of *questions* they ask. The visionary asks: *What's right?* The scientist asks: *How does this work?* The everyman asks: *What's happening to me?* The type of questions your protagonist asks most often will shape the tone of your show. If they're asking philosophical questions, the series leans cerebral. If they're panicked and reactive, the show becomes suspense-driven. If they're curious and daring, it becomes exploratory.

ChatGPT can help you develop these tonal differences. You can give it a scene—say, a character witnessing an AI uprising—and ask it to write three versions: one where the character is a visionary, one where they are a scientist, and one where they are an everyman. You'll see how dialogue, pacing, and emotion change. Then you can mix, match, and refine until you find the voice that fits your story.

Another way to define your protagonist is by looking at what they *lack*. The visionary might lack humility. The scientist might lack empathy. The everyman might lack purpose. Your character arc can then be about filling that gap. Use prompts like: "What is the emotional weakness of a visionary who believes machines deserve rights?" or "How does a scientist's childhood loss shape their desire to control time?" These answers lead to complexity. They lead to evolution.

In serialized television, the protagonist doesn't stay static. So always think about how they will change by the end of the season—or the end of the series. A visionary might become a martyr or a tyrant. A scientist might destroy the very thing they created. An everyman might reject power, or become its reluctant wielder. Build these shifts into your episode outlines. Use ChatGPT to chart emotional turning points across key episodes. You can prompt: "Track the emotional evolution of a protagonist who discovers they are a clone." And then break that down into beat-by-beat transformations.

Also remember that in a writer's room, not everyone will agree on who the protagonist *should* be. Some may argue for a brooding antihero, others for a noble leader. ChatGPT can act as a neutral party—generating variations, offering summaries, and helping test different types of protagonists in the same story world. It's not about picking one type because it's trendy—it's about choosing the character who can sustain tension, evolve emotionally, and keep us watching.

Whether your sci-fi series is about alien invasions, dystopian surveillance, quantum entanglement, or sentient dreams, it all starts with someone trying to make sense of their place in the chaos. Your protagonist doesn't need to be perfect. They don't even need to be heroic. They just need to *want* something deeply—and have everything in the world standing in their way.

That's how you write a character we'll follow through time, across galaxies, or into the unknown. Visionary, scientist, or everyman—they are the bridge between us and the future. Make that bridge strong. Make it human. Make it unforgettable.

The Antagonist as Philosophy

In science fiction, the most powerful antagonists are rarely just villains. They're not always people. They're not always even conscious. Often, they are *ideas*—philosophies, systems, or phenomena that reflect something deeper and darker about the human condition. When you're writing a science fiction television series, especially one with a long arc, your antagonist shouldn't just be an obstacle. It should be a force of thought, a presence that embodies a worldview your protagonist must face, understand, and either resist or be transformed by.

We're not talking about moustache-twirling space dictators here. We're talking about AI that redefines personhood. Surveillance networks that strip away free will. Alien ecologies that challenge our understanding of life itself. These antagonists are most effective when they stand for something beyond themselves. They challenge not just the hero's mission but the audience's assumptions about morality, identity, and the future.

Take *Westworld*, where the real antagonist isn't just the park's creators or the Hosts who rebel—it's the philosophy of control versus autonomy. Every character's struggle is a reaction to that idea. Or *Battlestar Galactica*, where the Cylons begin as enemy machines but evolve into complex symbols of faith, creation, and vengeance. Or *The Matrix*, where the antagonist isn't Agent Smith alone—it's the system, the illusion, the simulated reality keeping everyone docile. These enemies can't simply be punched or shot. They have to be unraveled, exposed, or endured.

If you want your series to have staying power, build your antagonist around a philosophical core. Ask yourself: what *idea* threatens your world? What truth is too dangerous to accept? What principle does your hero reject or cling to when all else is lost? Then, design your antagonist to *embody* that principle.

You can use ChatGPT to brainstorm different forms this antagonist might take. Prompt: "What are five ways to represent the philosophy of total surveillance in a sci-fi antagonist?" You might get a citywide AI that watches every citizen, a genetically engineered truth-teller caste, a virus that records memories and reports them to a hive mind, or a religion that believes privacy is a sin. You're not just looking for characters—you're looking for *embodiments of ideas.*

A great antagonist also forces moral ambiguity. If your enemy's philosophy has some validity, the conflict deepens. That's why HAL 9000 in *2001: A Space Odyssey* is so chilling. He's not trying to be evil—he's trying to protect the mission, as he understands it. The fact that he might be right (at least logically) creates tension. Likewise, in *The Expanse*, the protomolecule isn't evil. It's simply following its purpose. But that purpose is incomprehensible to us, and dangerous.

ChatGPT can help you create this ambiguity. Ask: "Describe a machine intelligence that wants to save humanity from itself by limiting emotional experience. What are its core beliefs?" Then: "Describe a protagonist who agrees with 70% of this AI's logic but resists its final conclusion." Now you have conflict built not on good versus evil, but on competing visions of what's right.

You might also choose to make your antagonist non-sentient. The force of nature. The system. The unknown. In *Annihilation*, the enemy is a mutation field. It has no motive—only effect. In *Arrival*, the aliens aren't hostile. The antagonist is human misunderstanding. This opens up a whole new mode of storytelling: tension without malice. You can prompt ChatGPT with: "Create a sci-fi antagonist that isn't alive, sentient, or malicious, but still causes mass upheaval." Maybe it's a signal from deep space that rewrites neural pathways. Maybe it's a dormant planet-wide consciousness that wakes when humans step on it. The terror lies in the fact that we cannot reason with it—only respond.

Some of the most impactful sci-fi stories center the antagonist in a system, not a single figure. Consider *Black Mirror*. The "villains" are often the consequences of unchecked tech: memory implants, social credit systems, digital consciousness. The system functions perfectly—and that's the problem. Your character's struggle becomes about escaping, subverting, or surviving within that machine. If you want to write this kind of story, use ChatGPT to help sketch systemic antagonists. Prompt: "Describe a global system that claims to eliminate poverty but ends up creating a new form of slavery." Now design characters who were raised in that system—and one who helped build it. When your antagonist is a system or philosophy, personal stakes still matter. Your protagonist must have something to lose: freedom, a loved one, their own grip on reality. And your antagonist must be able to *offer something* seductive. Safety. Order. Eternity. That's where the tension gets rich. The antagonist tempts. And that temptation should make sense.

Also consider how the antagonist evolves. In serialized TV, your threat can change shape. The system gains sentience. The AI becomes spiritual. The alien force reveals itself to be human in origin. Evolution makes your antagonist feel alive—and keeps your audience guessing. ChatGPT is perfect for drafting alternate versions of your antagonist. Prompt: "Describe five stages of transformation for a sci-fi antagonist that starts as a weather control program and becomes a planetary consciousness." Now you have five seasons of story potential.

Sometimes, the most powerful antagonist is the unknowable. The mystery that never fully resolves. Shows like *Lost* and *The OA* thrived on this. They used the antagonist as a question mark—a force just outside comprehension. When done well, this can be haunting and unforgettable. When done poorly, it frustrates. The key is to give the audience emotional clarity even if the mystery remains. You can use ChatGPT to test versions of ambiguity. Prompt: "Describe an antagonist that viewers never see, but whose presence is felt in every episode." Or: "Write a scene where a character confronts the idea of a non-local intelligence that may be watching humanity evolve." In the end, the antagonist in science fiction is never just the obstacle—it's the mirror. It reflects the flaws, fears, and hopes of your characters. It pushes your protagonist to question what they believe. To grow. To break. To become something new. Don't be afraid to let your antagonist be quiet. Or invisible. Or polite. Or omnipresent. It doesn't have to scream or explode to be terrifying. It just has to mean something. Something uncomfortable. Something your hero can't ignore. So ask yourself: what idea are you trying to challenge in your series? Now make that idea walk, speak, whisper, or pulse behind the stars. That's your antagonist.

Make it beautiful. Make it brutal. Make it unforgettable.

Building the Ensemble Cast: The X-Files, Firefly, and Beyond

Science fiction thrives on big ideas, but it *lives* through characters. You can build entire galaxies and invent brilliant speculative technologies, but if your characters don't connect with the audience, the show will feel cold, detached, or even hollow. In long-running sci-fi television, the key to emotional depth, tonal flexibility, and sustained viewer engagement is the ensemble cast. A strong ensemble is not just a collection of characters—it's an ecosystem. And building that ecosystem is one of the most exciting creative opportunities in designing your series.

You can look to classics like *The X-Files* and *Firefly* to understand how ensembles are built not for decoration but for function. In *The X-Files*, you technically start with a duo: Mulder and Scully. But their dynamic is so rich, so filled with contrast, chemistry, and philosophical tension, that it feels like an ensemble in microcosm. Around them orbit figures like Skinner, the Cigarette Smoking Man, and even the Lone Gunmen—each recurring character adding flavor, conflict, and mystery. Every major figure exists in conversation with the show's two key ideas: belief and doubt.

Firefly takes this further. Here, you have a full cast from the outset: the captain, the soldier, the con artist, the mechanic, the priest, the doctor, the psychic, the mercenary, and the pilot. On paper, that's a lot to balance. But the show succeeds because each character represents a *different reaction* to the world they inhabit. They respond differently to danger, law, survival, morality, and money. Some fight for ideals. Others run from the past. Some trust too easily. Others never do. Their strengths and flaws interact like chemicals—sparking drama, humor, and growth.

When you design your ensemble cast, start by mapping thematic contrast. Ask: What are the key themes of your series? Then, for each theme, create characters who reflect different stances. If your show explores the ethics of artificial intelligence, one character might fear AI as a threat to humanity, another might romanticize it as the next stage of evolution, while a third treats it like just another tool. The tension between those viewpoints drives dialogue, conflict, and even plot. You can ask ChatGPT to assist by prompting: "Create four sci-fi characters with opposing views on AI ethics who must work together."

Balance is essential. Not just in opinions, but in tone. A good ensemble offers multiple flavors. You can have your brooding strategist and your sarcastic mechanic in the same room—because one grounds the drama and the other keeps it alive with levity. Sci-fi shows often balance humor and horror through ensemble dynamics. Think of how Kaylee softens the grit of *Firefly*, or how the quirky scientists in *Stargate SG-1* or *Fringe* bring relief to the heavy stakes.

You'll also want characters with overlapping but conflicting goals. Unity without friction becomes flat. In *The Expanse*, Naomi and Amos are on the same team but driven by wildly different motivations. In *Farscape*, characters like Aeryn, Crichton, and Rygel constantly push against each other's values. This makes every decision a negotiation—and every victory hard-won. Conflict doesn't always mean fighting. It can be difference. And difference is what makes a group dynamic sing.

Think, too, about character *roles* within the crew or cast. Who leads? Who heals? Who hacks, fights, navigates, or interprets data? These practical roles must blend with emotional ones. Who grounds the group? Who stirs trouble? Who questions everything? Who sacrifices? Ask ChatGPT to help create role diversity with a prompt like: "Design a sci-fi ensemble crew where each character has a distinct skill and emotional wound." You'll get combinations like a medic haunted by war crimes, or a pilot with a death wish and a flawless record.

Also pay attention to rhythm. Some characters shine in action. Others in downtime. Some drive plot. Others deepen theme. Each character should serve at least one function—story, theme, humor, tension, heart. If someone isn't serving any, they're probably just taking up space. That's when you trim or combine characters. In sci-fi, you don't have the luxury of dead weight. Every character must justify their seat on the ship.

When you introduce your ensemble, don't info-dump. Use action and interaction. Show who they are through how they solve a problem. *Firefly*'s first episode quickly reveals who will grab a gun, who will bluff, and who will panic. You know Zoe is loyal, Wash is flippant, Jayne is unpredictable—all from how they move through conflict. You can use ChatGPT to draft these introduction scenes. Prompt: "Write a scene introducing five crew members as they escape a space station while arguing over who caused the mess." You'll get a scene rich with behavior, tone, and character dynamics in motion.

Your ensemble's chemistry will also shape future storylines. If the mechanic bonds with the alien diplomat, that's a subplot. If the leader begins to lose the trust of the medic, that's a season arc. Use ChatGPT to map potential arcs between characters: "Describe a three-episode tension arc between a by-the-book commander and a rogue trader forced to work together." These subplots can intersect with the series arc or reveal hidden depths in your world.

And don't be afraid of slow reveals. Every member of your ensemble doesn't need to be fully explained right away. In fact, the best ensembles unfold over time. You learn secrets in episode five. You see past trauma in episode eight. You understand motivations just as they're making a difficult choice. ChatGPT can help you pace these reveals. Prompt: "Outline a slow-burn character arc for a quiet crewmember who eventually betrays the group for what they believe is the greater good."

It's also worth considering diversity—not just in terms of casting or identity, though that matters deeply, but in backgrounds, accents, ideologies, and cultural lenses. A sci-fi ensemble gives you the opportunity to show how different cultures, species, or philosophies might clash or complement each other. Diversity fuels narrative depth. Use it not for tokenism, but to challenge your characters' assumptions—and your audience's.

In the end, an ensemble cast should feel like a family—or at least a dysfunctional team with no choice but to co-exist. Their growth becomes the heart of your series. Viewers return not just for the plot, but for the way these characters care, argue, evolve, and endure. They remember the look between crewmates before a risky decision. The inside jokes. The long-held grudges. The trust built one crisis at a time.

And you, as the writer, have the privilege of watching those characters grow under pressure, across worlds, and inside the moral chaos that science fiction does best. So use ChatGPT to help shape them. Give it your themes, your conflicts, your sci-fi twists—and let it help you imagine the people who will carry your story through. Then refine them, challenge them, let them argue, break, and bond. Because a science fiction universe is only as compelling as the crew that calls it home.

The Hero's Journey in Sci-Fi: Mythic Structures in Futuristic Worlds

Science fiction often dazzles us with alien landscapes, artificial intelligences, time travel, and distant futures, but underneath those layers of speculative imagination is something ancient and enduring—the journey of the hero. Whether you're writing about a space explorer in the 25th century or a rebellious AI in a digital utopia, the narrative power of myth remains. The Hero's Journey, as described by Joseph Campbell and adapted countless times since, is a blueprint not just for fantasy or ancient epics but for compelling science fiction stories that speak to something deeply human.

What makes the Hero's Journey so resonant in science fiction is that it brings structure to the vast unknown. It gives the audience a familiar emotional rhythm within worlds that are otherwise unfamiliar. We recognize the call to adventure, the threshold crossing, the tests, the allies, the ordeal, and the return with newfound knowledge. These stages echo in series like *Star Wars*, *The Mandalorian*, *Battlestar Galactica*, *Doctor Who*, and *The Expanse*. Even when the surface details are technological, the soul of the journey remains mythic.

Let's look at how this timeless structure works inside futuristic worlds, and how you can use ChatGPT to shape your science fiction hero's arc from beginning to transformation.

The Hero's Journey typically begins with the **Ordinary World**, where the protagonist lives before the story truly begins. In sci-fi, this doesn't mean suburbia—it might mean a mining colony on Mars, a repressive corporate 'arcology', or a forgotten satellite city drifting in space. The important thing is contrast. The ordinary world must feel limiting, small, or flawed in some essential way. This world shapes the hero's worldview and sets the baseline for what they must grow beyond.

When you build this ordinary world, ask: What does the protagonist *believe* about their life at the beginning? What illusions are they living under? You can prompt ChatGPT with: "Describe a repressive but beautiful orbital city where citizens are never allowed to leave. Design a character who begins to question that rule." From that setup alone, you're already inviting a classic journey.

Then comes the **Call to Adventure**, often a disruption that forces the protagonist out of comfort and into uncertainty. In sci-fi, this call could be a message from deep space, a malfunction in reality, the appearance of a strange traveler, or a moment of rebellion. In *The Matrix*, it's a phone call. In *Star Wars*, it's a hologram. In *The Expanse*, it's the discovery of the Scopuli distress signal. Use this moment to crack open your world—and your character's assumptions.

The hero often **Refuses the Call** at first. Maybe they're afraid, skeptical, or feel unworthy. This moment is essential in making them human. Even if they live among machines or aliens, this moment grounds them emotionally. ChatGPT can help shape this hesitation. Prompt: "Write a scene where a reluctant space freighter mechanic is invited to help decipher a message that could change the fate of humanity—but he refuses."

Next, the hero meets a **Mentor**—someone who provides guidance, tools, or insight. In science fiction, this could be a wise scientist, an aging explorer, a digital consciousness, or even a ghost from another timeline. Mentors in sci-fi often bring both knowledge and a warning. They can open the door to possibility, but they can't walk through it for the hero. Think of Morpheus, Obi-Wan, or The Doctor when they're training companions. You can use ChatGPT to invent these characters by prompting: "Create a mentor who once tried and failed to solve the mystery that now confronts the protagonist. Give them a flaw that makes them unreliable."

After crossing the **Threshold**, the hero enters the unknown—this is your strange world, your central sci-fi setting. It could be another planet, a simulation, or a secret base inside a black hole. Here, the rules are different. The hero will face **Tests**, encounter **Allies**, and confront **Enemies**. These episodes allow you to explore your world while deepening character relationships. Each trial should reveal something about the hero's inner state—not just challenge their strength, but their ethics, trust, or fear.

In serialized television, these middle episodes are often where the "monster of the week" shows up. But even stand-alone adventures should build toward the **Ordeal**—the moment of deepest crisis. In sci-fi, this ordeal often reveals a harsh truth: that the world is not what the hero believed, or that the cost of progress is higher than expected. In *Battlestar Galactica*, the realization that Cylons look like humans creates existential dread. In *Westworld*, the discovery that memory has been tampered with changes everything.

Use ChatGPT to brainstorm variations of your ordeal. Prompt: "What's the worst emotional truth a character could discover in a society where everyone is cloned from a single person?" The answer might spark your entire season climax.

The **Reward** is not always physical. It could be knowledge, clarity, inner strength, or even a dangerous new power. The hero sees the world—and themselves—differently. But the journey doesn't end there. The hero must **Return** to the world they came from, often bringing that new perspective with them. In sci-fi, this return is layered with complexity. Can the hero reintegrate? Will the world accept what they've learned? Sometimes the return is physical—back to Earth. Sometimes it's psychological—a new understanding of time, identity, or truth.

In a science fiction series, this return often sets up the next season. The protagonist has changed—but now, so has the world. Perhaps the system responds. Perhaps others rise to stop them. Perhaps they are no longer welcome where they began. This creates space for ongoing evolution across multiple arcs.

The beauty of using the Hero's Journey in science fiction is that you can literalize the internal. If the hero is struggling with identity, maybe their DNA has been rewritten. If they're seeking truth, maybe the universe itself is hiding secrets. The emotional beats of myth become visual, external, strange—and that's the power of the genre.

And with ChatGPT, you can test different versions of this journey quickly. Try:

"Write a sci-fi hero's journey where the protagonist discovers they are a simulation."

Or:

"Structure a 10-episode arc around a reluctant chosen one in a galaxy ruled by logic."

You'll receive beats that echo myth, but unfold in new ways.

In the end, sci-fi is always about more than technology or future settings. It's about the human—or post-human—soul navigating uncharted territory. The Hero's Journey gives your story shape. It gives your protagonist room to evolve. And it gives your audience an emotional rhythm that keeps them connected, even when the world you've built is alien.

So don't be afraid to go mythic in your futuristic world. Your spaceship is the hero's steed. Your AI is the trickster. Your memory-altering virus is the dark cave. The journey is the same—but the costume is pure imagination.

And that's why we write science fiction: to tell ancient stories in new skin, and to make the distant feel personal again.

Worldbuilding with ChatGPT: Planets, Civilizations, and Cultures

Science fiction lives and breathes in the worlds it creates. It's one of the few genres where the setting is as important as the characters—sometimes more so. The planets, societies, customs, languages, technologies, religions, and rules that shape your fictional universe are not just backdrops. They are storytelling tools. They affect what's possible, what's forbidden, what drives conflict, and what your characters believe is real. Worldbuilding in sci-fi means inventing reality from the ground up. And with ChatGPT, you can do this faster, deeper, and more inventively than ever before.

The most overwhelming part of worldbuilding is where to begin. Should you start with a map? A timeline? A piece of technology? A galactic history? The truth is, you can begin anywhere—but your goal should be to build inward and outward. If you start with a single planet, think about how it connects to a broader system. If you begin with a philosophy or belief system, ask what kind of environment would have birthed that worldview. ChatGPT can help you move in both directions—zooming out to give you scope, and zooming in to give you detail.

Let's say you want to create a new planet. You can prompt ChatGPT with something simple like, "Describe a desert planet with a hidden ocean beneath its surface." The AI might give you ideas about the planet's geography, weather patterns, indigenous species, and subterranean civilizations. If something sparks your interest—say, a species that evolved to detect moisture through vibrations—you can dig deeper: "Describe the culture and beliefs of a species that lives in a hidden ocean under a desert planet." And just like that, your world becomes populated.

Or maybe you're starting with a thematic idea. Say you want to explore a civilization obsessed with memory preservation. You can ask ChatGPT: "Invent a futuristic culture where memories are currency." Now you've entered the realm of social structure. Who controls the flow of memory? Are memories stolen, traded, archived? What does it mean to be poor—forgetful, perhaps? What are the ethics of sharing or selling lived experiences? This isn't just background material. It's the basis for character conflict, political intrigue, and societal rebellion.

Worldbuilding isn't just about breadth. It's about *consistency*. One of the dangers in sci-fi writing is creating cool ideas that don't connect. You don't want a story where characters teleport one episode and spend three episodes walking the next. Your world has to feel like it obeys its own rules—even if they're strange. ChatGPT can help you test for internal logic. Ask it: "Given a society where people are born with assigned dreams, what technologies or social systems would logically develop?" You'll start seeing how one idea spirals into a culture, an economy, and even a mythology.

When building civilizations, think about the components of culture: governance, language, religion, class structure, rituals, education, art, and economy. Don't try to build them all at once. Start with the one that feels central to your story. Maybe your protagonist is from a matriarchal society that reveres silence. Ask: "What kind of judicial system would exist in a society that values silence as sacred?" Now you've got unique courtroom scenes. Or ask: "How would children be raised in a floating city where gravity is optional?" Suddenly, school and discipline look nothing like our own.

And remember—culture doesn't need to be monolithic. Real civilizations are diverse, fragmented, evolving. Your world should have conflicts, factions, heretics, reformers. Ask ChatGPT: "List five opposing factions within a society that genetically engineers its citizens for specific jobs." You might get a technocratic elite, a rogue underground that hacks genes for pleasure, a religious group that believes in natural birth, a black-market genetics cartel, and a growing population of mutation activists. These aren't just flavor—they're plot engines.

Now let's talk about history. Even if you don't plan to show your world's entire past, the illusion of history matters. It makes the setting feel lived-in. Prompt ChatGPT with: "Give me a 500-year timeline of events on a planet that was terraformed by a forgotten race." The AI will deliver a series of milestones—wars, collapses, rebirths—that give your world depth. You can choose which events your characters know about, which they mythologize, and which are being rediscovered.

Geography also plays a huge role. A society that evolved in a ringed valley under constant eclipse will think differently than one born on a tidal-locked planet with a bright side and a dark side. Ask ChatGPT to generate specific settings: "Describe a city built into the bones of a dead god on a post-apocalyptic Earth." Now you're working with symbolic imagery that carries thematic weight. Setting becomes metaphor. Environment becomes emotion.

Language is another powerful tool. You don't need to invent a full conlang, but a few key words, phrases, or honorifics can do wonders. Ask: "Create ten words from an alien language that convey emotional states humans don't have." Then have your characters struggle to understand or misuse those words. Language gaps create tension, comedy, and character growth.

Don't forget how worldbuilding impacts character behavior. In a society where time is treated as property, how would people speak? Walk? Argue? In a culture where death is temporary but memory loss is permanent, how would grief function? Let your world affect the small stuff—greetings, clothing, eye contact, relationships. These quiet details add texture that makes even the strangest world feel real.

And then, of course, there's technology. Sci-fi tech shouldn't just be gadgets—it should change how people live and think. Prompt ChatGPT with: "Invent five technologies that would change how love and relationships work." You might get thought-sharing implants, romance simulations, hormonal regulators, or algorithms that adjust memory during heartbreak. Now you have not just tech—but drama.

If your series spans multiple planets or systems, think about contrast. Design cultures that exist in tension. Prompt: "Create two neighboring civilizations that have opposite philosophies about time." One might be future-obsessed and predictive, the other rooted in ritual and memory. Now you have cause for trade, conflict, and misunderstanding.

The key to great worldbuilding is to make it feel endless—*but* always know what to reveal and what to keep hidden. ChatGPT can help you create more than you'll ever use, which is good. It's your secret vault. The audience doesn't need to see every planet or read every law code. But you, as the creator, need to feel the world breathing beneath your characters' feet.

And remember: your world doesn't need to be "realistic." It needs to be *believable*. It needs rules, consequences, and a perspective. With ChatGPT, you can generate entire civilizations in minutes, test how ideas unfold over time, and discover cultural contradictions that lead to meaningful conflict.

So start small if you need to. A city. A myth. A ruined temple. Then ask what's just beyond it. Use ChatGPT not just to generate but to interrogate—what happens if, what if not, how would they know?

Because in science fiction, the worlds we build are mirrors and metaphors. They hold up alien glass to the human condition. And the more fully they are imagined, the deeper our stories can go.

Designing Futuristic Technology: Weapons, Tools, Interfaces

In science fiction television, futuristic technology is more than just a prop—it's a storyteller. The tools, weapons, and interfaces your characters use don't just enhance the visual flair of your series. They reflect the values, fears, ethics, and level of advancement of the civilizations that created them. Designing sci-fi technology is your opportunity to anchor your world in both imagination and logic, and when done right, it deepens character interaction, escalates conflict, and defines the visual language of your show. With ChatGPT as your creative partner, you can generate innovative, functional, and symbolically rich tech that enhances your entire narrative world.

Start by thinking about function before form. Every tool or weapon should exist because of a need in the story world. In other words, don't invent a plasma whip just because it sounds cool. Invent it because your society bans long-range weaponry, so combat evolved up-close and brutal. A holographic interface isn't just flashy—it exists because the society demands multitasking at superhuman speeds. Let necessity shape invention. You can use ChatGPT to develop this logic by prompting: "Describe five futuristic weapons that evolved in a society with limited access to metals and strong electromagnetic interference." The response will already have constraints baked in—and that's where originality is born.

Weapons in science fiction aren't always about destruction. Often, they're about control, intimidation, or strategy. Think of the neural inhibitors in *Altered Carbon*, the sonic weapons in *Minority Report*, or the emotion-suppressant devices in dystopias like *Equilibrium*. These tools are weapons of the mind, body, and soul. When designing sci-fi weapons, ask what they say about the civilization using them. A culture obsessed with purity might use sterilization rays. A post-human military force might use programmable matter to change weapon forms mid-combat. You can prompt ChatGPT with: "Invent a non-lethal weapon used by a peacekeeping force in a high-gravity environment," and use the result to build a whole scene around it.

Tools are where sci-fi often predicts or satirizes real-world trends. Think about how personal communicators in *Star Trek* anticipated smartphones—or how virtual reality, neural implants, and wearable tech have gone from speculative to actual. Good sci-fi tools often feel like the next logical step. Ask: "What kind of tools would engineers use aboard a space station orbiting a black hole?" The answer might include gravity-calibrated wrenches, time-sync correction devices, or neural-linked diagnostic gloves. Even a tool as small as a nano-fiber patch for instant wound closure can define the reality of your series. The trick is to anchor even the wildest tech in purpose.

Interfaces are one of the most visually defining aspects of a sci-fi show—and one of the most underdeveloped in writing. Think about how your characters *interact* with their tech. Is it tactile, neural, holographic, gesture-based, voice-controlled, or something stranger? In *Minority Report*, interfaces are gestural and immersive. In *The Expanse*, they're rugged and functional, with touchscreen overlays on rough military builds. In *Westworld*, control is sleek, minimal, and deeply connected to identity. When designing your own, ask: Does this tech require training? Is it accessible to everyone? Is it intuitive or intimidating?

You can prompt ChatGPT to generate visual descriptions: "Describe a multi-sensory command interface used by pilots in a bio-organic spacecraft." You'll get responses that incorporate smell, skin response, or thought patterns—and you can then imagine how that changes performance under stress. Maybe flying becomes a meditative act. Maybe the pilot's emotions *steer* the ship. What happens when they're angry? Or grieving?

Don't forget that futuristic tech often *fails*—and those failures make great drama. What happens when the medical nanobots go rogue? When an empathy filter misreads sarcasm as hostility? Or when a consciousness upload leaves behind a ghost copy? Sci-fi technology must come with risks, side effects, and imperfections. Perfection is boring. ChatGPT can help brainstorm these moments of failure. Try: "List five unintended consequences of a memory-sharing device used in romantic relationships." Each consequence could form the emotional core of an episode.

Your technology should also serve the tone of your show. If your series is a dystopian thriller, tech should feel dangerous, cold, or weaponized. If your series is comedic, tech might be inconvenient, misunderstood, or absurdly advanced for simple problems. A malfunctioning AI assistant that keeps auto-scheduling your assassination? That's satire. A government-issued dream-filter that censors unwanted thoughts during sleep? That's psychological horror. Use ChatGPT to generate according to tone: "Invent darkly comedic tools used by a bureaucratic alien civilization to enforce rules on Earth."

Another useful technique is retrofitting familiar devices. Take something we already know and shift it into your setting. What does a wedding ring mean in a world where people live forever? What does a keyboard look like on a planet with six-fingered inhabitants? Prompt: "Redesign an everyday Earth object for use on a planet with no gravity and constant daylight." ChatGPT might turn an umbrella into a light-filtering data shield, or a toothbrush into a mood-calibrated hydration wand. These tweaks give your world texture and authenticity.

Also consider how your technology integrates into your culture. Are tools sacred? Is weapon use a rite of passage? Are interfaces personalized or communal? Does someone's status dictate what level of tech they're allowed to access? A floating city run by bio-coded locks might restrict entire classes from certain levels. An alien society might embed tools *into* the body at birth. Ask ChatGPT to explore that culture: "Describe a civilization where tools are biologically integrated into citizens' DNA from childhood. How does this affect class, education, and warfare?"

You can also use technology as metaphor. A memory-wiping wand isn't just sci-fi—it's about forgetting trauma. A weapon that causes target paralysis might reflect themes of helplessness or control. When tech reflects theme, it becomes more than a gimmick. Ask: "Invent a device that visually represents emotional suppression in a cyberpunk society." Then imagine how a character breaks it—and what that means.

Finally, think about the *limits* of your technology. If you invent teleportation, you must ask: who can afford it? What are its dangers? What's lost in translation? If everyone has brain-implanted interfaces, what happens to those who don't? If emotions can be shared, how do people protect their privacy? Use ChatGPT to push the boundaries of these ideas: "What laws and social customs emerge in a society where physical violence is replaced with emotional projection?" Now you're not just inventing tech—you're inventing the world around it.

In the best sci-fi series, technology is never neutral. It shapes character behavior. It causes problems. It changes what people value. It creates new fears and new kinds of intimacy. With ChatGPT, you can brainstorm dozens of variations, tweak functionality, change origin stories, or simulate historical evolution from low-tech to high-tech cultures. You can even use it to design your series bible section on "Tech and Tools," making sure every item on screen feels like it belongs.

So build boldly. Design the strange. Break the rules—but stay consistent. Make your technology dazzling, dangerous, and deeply symbolic. Because in a world where anything is possible, it's the logic *behind* the impossible that makes your story unforgettable.

Ethical Dilemmas and Big Questions in Science Fiction

One of the most compelling reasons to write a science fiction television series is the opportunity to ask the kinds of questions that society doesn't always want to face—and to do it through a world that feels distant enough to be safe, but close enough to feel real. Ethical dilemmas lie at the heart of all great science fiction, because this genre is uniquely equipped to place characters in impossible situations, wrap philosophy in plot, and force the audience to consider, "What would I do?"

Whether your story unfolds on a rogue planet, in a dystopian city-state, or within a virtual simulation, you're not just writing about spaceships and technology—you're writing about people. Their choices. Their consequences. Their belief systems under pressure. The best science fiction doesn't just speculate about the future; it interrogates what it means to be human in a rapidly changing world. And these interrogations often come in the form of ethical dilemmas: questions of right and wrong with no easy answers.

One of the most frequent ethical themes in sci-fi is the question of **autonomy**. What happens when people lose the right to make decisions about their own bodies or minds? Think of *Westworld*, where synthetic hosts are programmed to forget every trauma—only to begin remembering. Is a being still property if it suffers like a person? Or *Black Mirror*, where characters' consciousnesses are copied or paused or manipulated for entertainment or punishment. Are copies entitled to rights? These aren't just science fiction concepts—they're questions that echo into real-life discussions about AI, surveillance, medical ethics, and bioengineering.

If your series explores cloning, mind-uploading, or synthetic life, ask ChatGPT: "What are five ethical dilemmas that arise when human memories are uploaded into machines?" The AI might return conflicts around identity, continuity, consent, and the ownership of a digital soul. These can fuel entire seasons. Imagine a character who discovers they're a backup copy of someone else—and that their 'original' made different moral choices. What does justice look like when memory itself is questionable?

Another rich area for ethical storytelling is **survival at a cost**. This is especially powerful in stories about colonization, war, and apocalypse. In *Battlestar Galactica*, decisions about who lives and dies are constant—and often reflect the tension between military pragmatism and humanitarian ideals. In *The Expanse*, entire planets and populations become pawns in a game of power, and the ethics of sacrifice loom over every decision. When a single character's survival might mean the extinction of thousands—or vice versa—how do they choose?

Ask ChatGPT: "List ethical conflicts in a sci-fi series where a colony must decide whether to rescue a stranded research team or conserve limited oxygen for the rest of the population." This kind of prompt yields scenarios that test your characters to their core. And it's not just about what they do—it's about what they believe afterward, what they justify, and what scars they carry.

Technological inequality is another theme that reveals complex ethical dimensions. If some people in your world have access to body enhancements, memory backups, or time-acceleration fields, while others live short, fragile lives—what does justice look like? Is it fair to regulate who gets access to immortality? Who owns the means to evolve? In a world where health or intelligence can be engineered, how do you protect diversity? Or do you?

These questions work best when embedded in character stories. Maybe your protagonist is offered a neural implant that guarantees success but rewrites part of their personality. Do they accept? Do they lose their friendships? What's the price of perfection? Use ChatGPT to explore it: "Describe the emotional fallout for a character who chooses to erase painful memories, only to discover that they can no longer connect with the people they love."

One of the most haunting ethical themes in sci-fi is **the nature of truth**. What happens when society agrees to forget history? When data can be edited, memories rewritten, or reality manipulated? In *The Matrix*, most people don't know they're being deceived—and even when they do, not everyone wants to wake up. *Brave New World* explored a society that traded freedom for comfort. In your world, how far does the illusion go? And if a character uncovers the truth, do they share it—or protect others from it?

Try a prompt like: "Create an ethical dilemma around a character who discovers their world is a simulation, but revealing it could drive everyone else insane." The question isn't just philosophical—it becomes deeply personal, emotional, and urgent. Your character's choices become the audience's mirror.

Ethical dilemmas also appear in **relationships**—especially in stories involving AI, aliens, or genetically engineered beings. If someone falls in love with an artificial person, is that love real? If an alien culture practices rituals that seem horrific to humans, should the humans interfere? Sci-fi is a perfect genre for intercultural and interspecies ethics. It's not about drawing easy lines. It's about questioning what we believe is universal.

Ask ChatGPT: "Design a story where a human must decide whether to save a non-human species that threatens their home planet—but might be sentient." You might discover a story about misunderstanding, communication, empathy, or guilt. These stories work because they ask the viewer to consider how quickly we define 'other'—and what we're willing to do in the name of safety.

Even **language itself** can become an ethical issue in science fiction. In *Arrival*, the alien language reshapes how people think. In your story, perhaps a new interface allows people to speak without lying. Or perhaps a virus spreads through language itself. What does it mean to share a truth that changes minds—or weaponize one that controls them? You can build entire civilizations around these ideas. Ask ChatGPT: "Describe an ethical system in a culture where language is limited to 100 words per person, per day."

The most powerful sci-fi ethics aren't just moral puzzles—they're *emotional catalysts*. Your audience may not remember every detail of your world's tech or timeline, but they'll remember the character who had to choose between saving one life or billions. They'll remember the protagonist who decided to free a self-aware machine—against orders. They'll remember the friend who stayed behind to let another escape. Ethics in sci-fi are where thought meets feeling.

And these questions don't always need to be answered. Some of the best science fiction leaves the dilemma open-ended, letting the audience wrestle with the implications. The point isn't to hand out answers. It's to pose questions that can't be answered easily—because in a world where technology outpaces morality, the questions will always outnumber the certainties.

So build your story with those questions. Use ChatGPT to explore them from every angle—through different characters, factions, timelines, and cultural lenses. Let the ethical problems evolve with the plot. Let them test your characters. And let your audience walk away not just entertained, but unsettled.

That's the legacy of great science fiction—not simply that it imagined the future, but that it forced us to rethink what we thought we knew about the present.

Dialogue That Sounds like the Future but Feels Human

In science fiction television, dialogue plays a unique double role. It must serve the same fundamental purpose it does in any genre—reveal character, advance story, build relationships—but it also carries the burden of making the future sound believable. The words your characters speak must feel like they come from another time, another world, another reality. And yet, those words must still touch something deeply familiar in the audience. This is the paradox of sci-fi dialogue: it must sound like the future, but feel unmistakably human.

The first mistake many writers make in sci-fi is pushing the language too far into abstraction, jargon, or cold detachment. They fill scenes with technological exposition and invented terminology, hoping it will make their universe feel advanced. But this kind of dialogue often becomes noise. If a character says, "The baryonic inversion threshold just destabilized our multiphase flux coils," it might sound futuristic, but if the audience doesn't understand the stakes or feel the emotion behind the words, it doesn't matter. Effective sci-fi dialogue is always rooted in emotion, intention, and personality.

When you write dialogue for a future society, think about how the *context* changes how people speak. In *Battlestar Galactica*, military formality bleeds into everyday language, giving even small talk a clipped, disciplined tone. In *Firefly*, frontier slang and Mandarin phrases mix with informal banter to reflect a culture formed from diaspora and survival. In *The Expanse*, the Belter dialect emerged as a creole of resistance, shaped by economic oppression and life in vacuum. Each of these examples proves that futuristic dialogue works best when it reflects culture—not just tech.

You can use ChatGPT to help develop these linguistic layers. Try prompting: "Create informal dialogue between two asteroid miners who have lived most of their lives in artificial gravity." The result might include slang related to air recyclers, synthetic food, or old Earth myths. Or: "Write a confrontation between a genetically modified diplomat and a human rebel leader from a low-tech moon." You'll get clues about power dynamics, education, trust, and ideology—expressed not just in what they say, but in how they say it.

One of the most powerful tools in your dialogue is *metaphor*. Even in futuristic settings, people still reach for images to express the inexpressible. They might not say "I'm feeling down"—they might say, "Feels like my gravity's off today." In a world of memory sharing, someone might describe heartbreak as a data corruption or a playback loop. This kind of figurative language not only reveals the character's worldview, it creates immersion for the audience. Prompt ChatGPT with: "Invent five metaphors for sadness in a culture where people upload emotions as holograms." You'll discover a new kind of poetic shorthand—one that only makes sense in your world.

Humor, too, should be carried into the future. Don't let your characters become stiff simply because your setting is high-tech or high-concept. Even in *Star Trek*, characters joke, tease, and vent. In *Doctor Who*, much of the charm comes from mixing cosmic peril with dry wit or absurd observations. Humor makes the strange feel human. Try a prompt like: "Write banter between two characters repairing a malfunctioning time machine while being chased by sentient nanodust." You'll find that comedy doesn't have to break tone—it can enhance it.

Another crucial consideration is *emotional honesty*. In a world where people might be post-human, cybernetically enhanced, or genetically engineered, their experiences might differ from ours—but their emotions can still resonate. Loneliness, fear, awe, desire—these remain, no matter how advanced the setting. When a character whispers "I don't feel real anymore" after transferring their mind to a synthetic body, it matters. The line is simple, but loaded. Good sci-fi dialogue doesn't need to be complex. It needs to be true.

Be careful with exposition. When your characters need to convey complex concepts, let them do so in ways that feel lived-in. Avoid the temptation for characters to explain things they should already know just for the audience's benefit. Instead, embed information in conflict or routine. A technician muttering, "Not another ion leak, those things eat through my boots," tells us something about the environment, the tech, and the tone. Use ChatGPT to reframe exposition into natural dialogue: "Rewrite this paragraph of scientific info as an argument between a rookie and a veteran." It will ground the future in familiar emotional rhythms.

In multilingual or multispecies settings, language becomes a source of conflict and culture. Don't shy away from code-switching, idiomatic expressions, or misunderstandings. One character might insult another without realizing it, simply by using a term sacred in the other's culture. Or a translation device might glitch at the worst possible moment. Prompt ChatGPT with: "Write a diplomatic negotiation between humans and insectoid aliens with very different emotional vocabularies." These moments create opportunities for tension, empathy, and humor all at once.

The way your characters speak should also reflect *social structures*. In a hierarchical society run by AI bureaucrats, characters might speak in clipped commands or algorithmic phrases. In a post-scarcity utopia, language might become more abstract, poetic, or even deliberately inefficient, since time is abundant. A society that values privacy might evolve quiet, indirect language—while a surveillance state might reward transparency and verbal precision. Ask ChatGPT to help you simulate this: "Describe how small talk sounds in a society where everyone's thoughts are broadcast in real-time." Suddenly, the everyday becomes alien.

Keep in mind that tone is everything. In a show like *Black Mirror*, dialogue is often restrained and cool, matching the sterile technological environments. In contrast, *Stranger Things* uses sci-fi tropes but grounds them in 1980s slang and earnest emotionality. When designing your own tone, ask yourself how characters *feel* about their world. Are they awed, jaded, oppressed, rebellious? Do they speak with wonder or sarcasm? Hope or dread?

Dialogue is also your tool for pacing. Snappy, urgent exchanges can speed up action-heavy scenes, while slower, introspective lines can help the audience absorb complex ideas. You can use ChatGPT to test these rhythms. Ask: "Write a quiet moment of reflection between two characters watching a planet collapse from orbit." The response may give you poetic imagery and silence that contrasts with your action sequences—creating balance in your episode structure.

Finally, don't forget the power of silence and subtext. Not all dialogue is spoken. What characters choose *not* to say can speak volumes. A glance, a pause, a repeated word—all of these can be written to reflect internal conflict or hidden truths. In the future, where communication might include neural links, holograms, or emotion-based signals, subtext becomes even more intriguing. Ask ChatGPT: "Write a conversation where one character speaks aloud and the other replies only with emotional pulses transmitted wirelessly." You'll discover new modes of tension.

At its best, sci-fi dialogue doesn't just sound advanced—it expands our understanding of communication itself. It uses the strange to say something deeply familiar. It makes us laugh, ache, and wonder. With ChatGPT as your tool, you can test tones, try slang, experiment with metaphor, and simulate speech patterns from entirely new societies.

Write dialogue that's anchored in character, shaped by culture, and filled with feeling. Let it surprise your audience, but always let it land in the heart. Because even in the farthest future, what we say—and how we say it—still defines who we are.

Metaphor, Symbolism, and Allegory in Sci-Fi Screenwriting

Science fiction isn't just a playground for wild imagination and speculative technology—it's also a deeply symbolic genre. Beneath the spacecraft, alien races, and futuristic landscapes, sci-fi stories often carry a mirror aimed squarely back at us. The very best science fiction television shows use metaphor, symbolism, and allegory to speak about real fears, real issues, and real hopes. These devices transform sci-fi from entertainment into art, from diversion into commentary. When used skillfully, they add depth, meaning, and emotional resonance to every scene, every line of dialogue, every visual detail.

Metaphor is the simplest and most direct of these tools. It's a comparison—sometimes spoken, sometimes woven into the structure of a scene—that helps the audience understand one thing through the lens of another. In sci-fi, metaphor often happens through concept. A robot struggling to understand emotion becomes a metaphor for someone on the autism spectrum or a child learning to feel. An invisible alien that feeds on fear becomes a metaphor for anxiety or trauma. In *The X-Files*, many of the monsters are direct metaphors for human conditions: addiction, abuse, government control, even puberty.

To create strong metaphors in your own sci-fi writing, start by identifying the emotional or thematic core of your episode. Is it about grief? Loneliness? Betrayal? Then ask ChatGPT: "What is a science fiction concept that could metaphorically represent [insert theme]?" For example, for grief, the AI might return: "A planet that records the emotional residue of its visitors and plays it back as weather patterns." That becomes your world—and your metaphor. Rain isn't just rain anymore. It's memory. It's pain falling from the sky.

Symbolism goes even deeper than metaphor. While a metaphor makes a clear comparison, a symbol accumulates meaning over time. It doesn't always announce itself. It's a recurring image, object, color, or idea that begins to stand for something greater than itself. In *Westworld*, the maze is more than just a puzzle—it's a symbol of awakening, of identity, of the journey inward. In *Star Trek*, the Enterprise itself is a symbol of exploration, diplomacy, and the fragile hope of peace. In *Doctor Who*, the TARDIS isn't just a time machine—it's a symbol of change, unpredictability, and limitless potential.

To work symbolism into your series, choose visual or narrative elements that can echo across multiple episodes. A broken watch that never ticks might appear in flashbacks, on a gravestone, or in a new character's hand. The audience slowly realizes it symbolizes lost time, or regret, or memory. You can prompt ChatGPT with: "Suggest a symbolic object that could appear in different forms across a sci-fi series about generational trauma." The results might surprise you—a song, a recurring sound, a shared tattoo, a repeated dream. Symbolism doesn't explain—it resonates.

Allegory is more ambitious. It transforms your entire world or narrative into a metaphor for something else. Think of *The Handmaid's Tale*—not sci-fi in the spaceship sense, but pure allegory. Its dystopian society is a direct commentary on religious fundamentalism, patriarchy, and reproductive rights. *Battlestar Galactica* is an allegory for post-9/11 paranoia, terrorism, and identity. *District 9*, though a film, stands as a brutal allegory for apartheid and xenophobia. These stories work because they use science fiction settings to tell very real truths.

The challenge of allegory is balance. You want your world to stand on its own legs—not just as a delivery mechanism for a message. Allegory becomes preachy when it forgets to tell a compelling story. But when your characters are complex, your stakes are personal, and your plot is engaging, allegory becomes the backdrop—the emotional undercurrent that deepens everything. Use ChatGPT to test ideas: "Create a science fiction premise that serves as an allegory for environmental collapse and corporate greed." Let the allegory live in the DNA of the world, not just in speeches.

Sometimes these devices work together. In *Black Mirror*, metaphor, symbolism, and allegory often blend seamlessly. A device that replays every moment of your life is a metaphor for obsession, a symbol of how memory defines us, and an allegory for the dangers of surveillance capitalism. It's not about choosing one technique—it's about layering them to enrich your world.

Even dialogue can carry metaphor. A character might not say "I'm scared of change," but "Feels like the stars are rearranging themselves and no one's told me the new map." That's futuristic poetry. Use prompts like: "Give me ten metaphorical ways a sci-fi character could describe falling in love in zero gravity." Or: "Write a symbolic exchange between two AI entities debating the value of organic life." Let the language reflect the larger themes.

Visual storytelling also plays a major role. Directors and production designers often extend your script's symbolism into costumes, lighting, and composition. A white uniform might symbolize purity—or sterility. A corridor that narrows each episode could symbolize the character's shrinking options. A recurring motif of hands—clenched, severed, mechanical—might symbolize power, intimacy, or control. When writing your scripts, note in the description where the visuals carry the weight of the theme. ChatGPT can help generate visual metaphors too: "Describe a spaceship interior that symbolically reflects the crew's isolation and mental decay."

And here's the best part: when you use metaphor, symbolism, and allegory, your story becomes re-watchable. Viewers come back not just for the plot, but for the meaning hidden beneath it. They notice new layers. They ask new questions. They connect personally. Science fiction becomes an echo chamber of thought and feeling.

Writing sci-fi television with ChatGPT as your partner allows you to explore dozens of symbolic variations before you commit. You can refine metaphors until they sing, test symbols for visual power and emotional resonance, and build allegories that challenge the audience without breaking immersion. The AI helps you hold both vision and detail in your hand at once.

So don't just build cool worlds. Build meaningful ones. Use metaphor to say what your characters can't. Use symbolism to give your world texture. Use allegory to make your story matter. Let your audience see the future—and feel the present. Let your story be a telescope and a mirror at the same time. That's the real magic of science fiction.

Flashbacks and Time Loops: Nonlinear Storytelling in Sci-Fi

Linear storytelling is a foundation, but in science fiction television, playing with time can unlock new ways to explore character, tension, and meaning. Flashbacks and time loops aren't just structural tricks—they're tools to reflect the very themes that sci-fi is built on: memory, causality, free will, parallel realities, and the mutable nature of identity. The best science fiction series use nonlinear storytelling not to confuse the audience but to deepen their emotional investment and elevate the dramatic experience.

Flashbacks are perhaps the most accessible tool in this toolbox. They allow you to break time apart and rearrange it so the past becomes a revelation, not just a prologue. In many science fiction shows, the past isn't merely history—it's unfinished business. Think about how *Lost* revealed its characters' secrets episode by episode, gradually recontextualizing their choices and relationships. In *The Expanse*, flashbacks help explain political tensions, character loyalties, and personal tragedies that would otherwise be impossible to convey in present-day action. Flashbacks are particularly effective in sci-fi because the past often has direct, literal impact on the present—sometimes through time travel, sometimes through artificial memory implants, or even through clones who relive someone else's experiences.

You can use ChatGPT to invent impactful flashbacks that reveal character or change context. Try prompting: "Create a flashback for a character who was once a revolutionary but now serves an oppressive system." The key is to tie the flashback to a moral or emotional pivot point in the present story. The past must push forward.

Flashbacks can also be false. In sci-fi, memory is unreliable, especially when manipulated by drugs, implants, or quantum trauma. *Black Mirror* has often played with memory as truth versus memory as distortion. Imagine a character uncovering a buried memory only to discover it was planted for a purpose. A great prompt for ChatGPT might be: "Write a scene where a character's flashback is digitally altered each time they revisit it." The twist is not just in what happened, but in how perception is shaped by unseen hands.

Then there are time loops, which are the ultimate form of nonlinear structure. In a loop, events repeat—sometimes identically, sometimes with small changes—forcing the character (and the audience) to pay close attention to causality. *Russian Doll* and *Dark* are two recent series that took the time loop concept and used it not just for plot devices but to interrogate deeper philosophical questions: What do we learn from repetition? Can we ever really escape who we are?

The tension in a time loop comes from knowledge. The more your character understands about the loop, the more agency they have—or think they have. You can prompt ChatGPT with: "Outline a time loop episode in which the character doesn't know they're looping until the fifth reset." This approach allows you to build mystery and gradually increase stakes. The audience shares the disorientation at first, then becomes active participants in decoding the pattern.

Time loops can be comedic, tragic, thrilling—or all three at once. *Star Trek: The Next Generation*'s "Cause and Effect" builds tension through repetition of the same disastrous outcome, with slight differences in behavior and memory each time. *Edge of Tomorrow*, though a film, shows how repetition becomes a form of skill acquisition—and exhaustion. In a series, the loop can last one episode or span an entire season. ChatGPT can help you vary the events slightly with prompts like: "Write five different outcomes of the same confrontation, each with increasing emotional impact."

Nonlinear storytelling isn't just about time manipulation. It's also a way to withhold and release information. In a mystery-based sci-fi show, like *Severance*, the structure itself becomes the central question. Why are we only shown half of a character's life? What does the audience know that the character doesn't? Conversely, what does the character know that the audience hasn't seen yet?

Consider structuring an episode where a critical moment is shown at the beginning out of context—then the episode flashes back to show how that moment came to be. Prompt ChatGPT with: "Write an outline for a sci-fi episode that begins with a character's execution and ends by showing how they volunteered for it." These reversals of expectation are what make sci-fi feel profound and unpredictable.

Another powerful use of nonlinear structure is the intercutting of multiple timelines. These can be parallel lives, simulations, or even different planets where time moves at different speeds. In *Westworld*, the early seasons used multiple timelines without informing the audience at first—only later revealing that certain storylines were unfolding decades apart. This delayed clarity created both mystery and emotional payoff. To explore this yourself, try: "Create a storyline in which a character unknowingly mentors their future enemy in a separate timeline."

With nonlinear techniques, clarity is key. Even when you're playing with complex timelines, you must give the audience visual or emotional anchors. This could be done through costume changes, lighting, music cues, or repeated phrases. In your script, use scene headers or notations to clearly distinguish each timeframe. Describe changes in the character's emotional state or physical environment. Let ChatGPT assist: "Describe visual cues that signal a shift between simulated and real timelines in a sci-fi scene."

Memory, fate, recursion, paradox—these are all themes uniquely suited to science fiction, and nonlinear storytelling allows you to explore them not just intellectually but structurally. The very form of your episode can become part of the message. If your story is about breaking a cycle, the audience should feel trapped with the character. If your story is about fragmented identity, let them experience narrative fragmentation. If your story is about inevitability, then returning to the beginning should feel crushing—or liberating.

ChatGPT can help you test different versions of a timeline, or simulate variations of character memory, or generate alternate paths in a loop until you find the one that resonates most. This makes it the ideal partner in nonlinear writing—letting you jump through time just as easily as your characters do.

In science fiction, time is never just a setting. It's a weapon. A mystery. A curse. A gift. Use flashbacks to reveal what matters. Use loops to test what can change. Use fractured structure to show that the past and future are never really separate. The best sci-fi doesn't just ask "What happens next?"—it also asks, "What already happened that we didn't understand?" and "What keeps happening because we refuse to change?"

When done well, nonlinear storytelling turns your series into a maze that's just as meaningful to walk through the second or third time. Because, just like time itself in your world, a good story doesn't unfold in a straight line. It echoes. It folds back. It repeats—until it means something more.

Parallel Universes, Clones, and Memory Manipulation

One of the richest veins in science fiction television is the exploration of identity through extraordinary scientific or speculative concepts. Few devices serve this purpose better than parallel universes, clones, and memory manipulation. These are not just cool plot twists—they're philosophical playgrounds. When used well, they challenge the audience's understanding of self, choice, destiny, and even reality. In television, these ideas let you stretch your characters across versions of themselves, push them into ethical corners, and ask what makes someone truly human—while still giving your audience high-concept thrills.

Let's start with parallel universes. From the early "Mirror Universe" episodes of *Star Trek* to the multiversal madness of shows like *Fringe* and *Counterpart*, alternate realities are a way to show different versions of a character or world without needing a time machine. They provide contrast. If your protagonist is a loyal officer in Universe A, what if they're a rebel in Universe B? If a society is thriving in one universe but crumbling in another, what one decision caused the divergence? These episodes are often audience favorites because they're dramatic, playful, and reveal hidden dimensions of your characters.

The trick with parallel universes is making sure the contrast has meaning. It's not just about giving everyone goatees and darker lighting—it's about showing a moral or psychological difference. Use ChatGPT to brainstorm: "Create five versions of a character who made different life choices at one pivotal moment." You can then build a parallel universe around each of those versions and see which ones spark dramatic tension.

Clones, similarly, are not just duplicates—they're opportunities for deep existential storytelling. In *Orphan Black*, the brilliance came not from the science but from the humanity of each clone. Despite being genetically identical, each woman had her own voice, style, trauma, and desire. The show asked, if someone is a clone of you, do they have a soul? A right to freedom? A different destiny? Clones force characters (and audiences) to confront questions of nature versus nurture, bodily autonomy, and what it means to be unique.

You might use clones in a spy thriller format, a medical mystery, or a family drama. Prompt ChatGPT with: "Outline an episode in which a character discovers they are not the original but the fourth clone in a hidden program." This kind of prompt can generate emotional stakes, ethical quandaries, and twist-heavy plots. And remember—clones can be sympathetic or chilling, victims or villains. Their motivations might mirror the original's... or reject them entirely.

Then we have memory manipulation, which may be the most psychologically profound of the three. Memory defines identity. If you alter memory, you alter the self. Shows like *Black Mirror*, *Westworld*, and *Dollhouse* have built entire worlds around the dangers and allure of reprogrammable minds. What if you could erase trauma? Or install false happiness? What if your memories aren't even yours?

This tool works especially well for mystery-driven narratives. A character might believe they're a hero, only to discover they committed atrocities under a different identity. Or a loyal officer could have false memories of devotion implanted by a government program. These stories are perfect for emotional reveals—because the truth is hidden not just from others, but from the character themselves.

Use ChatGPT to explore these themes: "Write a monologue for a character slowly realizing their memories have been implanted." Or "Describe a scene where a memory glitch causes a soldier to question their allegiance mid-battle." These generate not just cool visuals but strong character arcs.

One of the most compelling aspects of these concepts is how they overlap. A character might travel to a parallel universe, meet their clone, and realize that clone has a completely different set of memories. Now you're exploring fate, identity, and morality all at once. Or your character might be hunting a dangerous criminal—only to discover it's a version of themselves from another world with a different past. Sci-fi allows you to turn internal conflict into literal conflict, memory into terrain, and identity into a battlefield.

Nonlinear narrative structures work beautifully with these devices. Memory manipulation and parallel universes lend themselves to stories that don't play out in a simple A-to-B line. You can structure episodes where the first half takes place in one reality, and the second half pulls the curtain back. Or where each act of the episode is from a different character's implanted memory—contradictory and unreliable. ChatGPT is a great sandbox for experimenting with these ideas. Try: "Write an outline for a TV episode that changes reality each time a character wakes up." Or: "Simulate a dialogue between two versions of the same character—one a clone, one the original."

Don't forget tone. These ideas can go dark, but they don't have to. *Futurama* played with alternate selves and memory jokes in comedic ways. *Rick and Morty* built a multiverse of nihilistic humor. You can write these stories for comedy, horror, action, or even romance. A love story across multiple realities has a poetic pull—will the characters find each other in every version of the world, no matter how different? Will one lose memory of the other, and need to fall in love again? Prompt: "Write a scene where two lovers meet in a parallel universe and only one remembers their past lives together."

And then there's the philosophical dimension. All three concepts—parallel universes, clones, memory manipulation—ask a simple question with a thousand answers: What makes you *you*? Is it your genetics? Your choices? Your memories? Your role in a specific timeline? This question sits at the heart of almost all great sci-fi, from *Blade Runner* to *Devs* to *Upload*. It's the question audiences carry with them long after the credits roll.

As you craft your own series, let these ideas shape not only your plot but your themes. Maybe your entire show revolves around the erasure and recovery of memory. Maybe each season explores a different branch of a multiverse. Maybe the final twist of your pilot is that your protagonist has been replaced by a clone—and no one noticed, not even themselves.

With ChatGPT, you have a partner who can help you explore infinite variations, simulate conversations between versions of the same person, or create entire alternate worlds with distinct cultures and rules. You're not limited to one reality, one self, one truth. You can build and rebuild until your story unlocks the big questions—and delivers unforgettable drama.

Science fiction thrives on the edges of what we think we know about ourselves. So give your characters the space to split, duplicate, and forget. Let them shatter. Let them piece themselves back together. And let your audience follow them into the maze. That's where the magic happens.

Writing for Visual Effects: Imagining the Impossible

One of the most thrilling freedoms of writing a science fiction TV series is the ability to imagine the impossible—and then see it rendered visually. Alien worlds, sprawling spaceports, mind-bending dimensions, planetary destruction, living machines, time rifts, and telekinetic battles are not just concepts in sci-fi—they're opportunities for visual spectacle. But writing for visual effects isn't just about dreaming big. It's about dreaming smart. It's about writing scenes that are imaginative, emotionally resonant, and producible. With AI tools like ChatGPT at your side, you can push those boundaries further, designing awe-inspiring sequences that support story rather than overwhelm it.

Visual effects, or VFX, include everything from simple set extensions to fully CG environments, creature design, and postproduction augmentation of action. Think of the visual grammar of shows like *The Mandalorian*, *Foundation*, or *The Expanse*. These series create expansive universes where the viewer believes in things that never existed. But this believability starts not in the effects lab—it starts on the page. When you write your script, you're giving directions to every artist down the line: the VFX supervisor, the director, the concept artist, the stunt coordinator. That means your vision has to be clear, but it also has to be story-driven.

Let's start with a mindset shift: don't write "effects scenes"—write scenes that *need* effects. A breathtaking explosion in a vacuum is cool, but if no character is changed by it, then it's empty spectacle. Instead, think about moments where the impossible highlights an emotional truth. A character grieving in zero gravity, their tears suspended in air. A war veteran seeing their PTSD physically manifested in a VR training program. A city that folds in on itself not because it looks cool, but because it mirrors the character's psychological collapse.

Try prompting ChatGPT with: "Describe a visual effect that represents emotional numbness in a futuristic city." You'll often get back imaginative metaphors—weather that freezes mid-fall, crowds that glitch when they get too close, reflections that lag behind the character. These aren't just pretty—they're symbolic.

When writing, don't get lost in technical terms. Instead of "spaceship explodes using procedural particle physics and dynamic simulations," write "The ship breaks apart like frozen glass under pressure—silent, terrifying, unreal." That gives the VFX artists freedom to design, but gives everyone else—the reader, the actor, the director—a clear sense of tone. You can even use ChatGPT to help describe these scenes more vividly: "Write a paragraph describing a collapsing black hole from the point of view of a character who's falling into it." It's important to remember scale and pacing. You can go from microscopic to cosmic in one scene, but only if you structure it well. Good science fiction VFX builds tension. The wormhole doesn't just appear—it starts as a shimmer, grows into a vortex, then begins dragging debris. Write the escalation into the action. Prompt: "Create a five-beat escalation of a wormhole forming inside a space station, from first anomaly to full rupture."

Your settings are especially fertile ground for VFX. Entire alien cities can rise out of a desert, rotate with the gravity of their twin suns, or exist in layered dimensions. But again, what matters is how these places interact with character and plot. Don't just write, "They arrive on a neon alien world." Write, "They step out of the shuttle into a city carved from living coral, where buildings pulse in rhythm with the planet's breath." That tells the design team what to imagine—and it tells the actor what it *feels* like to be there. ChatGPT can help brainstorm wild environments that still hold internal logic: "Generate a sci-fi setting where time flows differently at the top and bottom of the city."

The same applies to creatures and characters. Whether it's a synthetic lifeform, a sentient nebula, or a mutant born of quantum fallout, your VFX-driven characters should have motivations, not just designs. What does it mean if a creature can only be seen in ultraviolet? If an android's face changes shape based on who's looking at it? These aren't just visuals—they're dramatic tools. Prompt: "Describe a creature made of programmable matter that shifts form based on the speaker's tone." Now you're not just creating a cool effect—you're writing a character interaction that can only happen in your imagined world.

Action scenes are another place where VFX can either shine or sink. The best sci-fi action has logic to it—laws of physics (even if they're invented), limitations of power, costs to using technology. Use VFX to heighten the stakes. When your character uses a teleportation device, show the toll it takes. Maybe each jump scrambles their memory a little more. You can prompt: "Write a chase scene through a city that phases in and out of different centuries." That's not just exciting—it's a narrative device.

You also want to write with budget in mind. Even high-end shows have limits. If your scene requires thousands of photorealistic aliens in a crowd, maybe you can rewrite it to focus on one alien who matters. Or use ChatGPT to creatively limit scope: "Find a low-budget way to imply a massive intergalactic war using only one set." Smart sci-fi knows that suggestion is often more powerful than spectacle. A flickering TV broadcast of the war, a soldier's burned uniform, a crater that wasn't there yesterday—these are small VFX that suggest a much larger world. And then there's sound. Sound is an invisible visual effect. In sci-fi, it often supports or even creates the illusion of VFX. The hum of a lightsaber, the scream of a hyperspace drive, the radio static that turns into a voice. When writing, note the sounds, especially if they interact with what's seen. Prompt: "Describe a soundscape for a malfunctioning cryo chamber that's slowly thawing out its occupant."

Finally, let's talk about collaboration. You won't be designing the VFX yourself, but you'll be in constant dialogue with those who do. Writing with awareness of the process makes you a better team player. ChatGPT can help you simulate those conversations: "List questions a VFX supervisor might ask about a scene involving a gravity-reversing hallway." Or: "Summarize how to describe a visual sequence so that both producers and artists understand the budget implications." Writing science fiction television with strong visual effects means balancing wonder with weight. You get to create moments no one has ever seen before—but the audience has to *feel* them. So let ChatGPT help you imagine the impossible. Let your descriptions evoke awe and dread and joy. And always ask: what does this spectacle *mean* for the character? That's when VFX become more than eye candy. They become part of the story's soul.

You're not just writing a scene. You're writing a vision. So make it unforgettable.

From Miniatures to CGI: Planning for What the Audience Will See

In the world of science fiction television, the audience expects to be shown the extraordinary. They want to see alien worlds, futuristic cities, massive starships, impossible technology, and unearthly life forms. But behind every jaw-dropping moment is a decision—a deliberate choice about how to *show* the unbelievable in a believable way. Whether through physical miniatures, computer-generated imagery (CGI), practical effects, or a combination of all three, these moments begin in the writer's imagination. As a screenwriter creating a science fiction series, it's your job to give shape to those visions—and to plan for how they'll live on the screen.

It starts with understanding the difference between effect and affect. What will this moment look like? And how should the audience *feel* when they see it? A spaceship might be sleek and silver, or scarred and rusting. That single choice can create either awe or dread. A city might float in the clouds or sprawl underground, with each design telling a different story about the society that built it. When writing these visuals, don't just think in terms of "cool" ideas—think in terms of thematic reflection. What does this setting, object, or transformation say about the world or the characters? Write scenes that *need* visual realization, not ones that depend on it.

Miniatures have long been the unsung heroes of sci-fi storytelling. From the original *Star Wars* trilogy to the physical models of *Battlestar Galactica* and *Blade Runner*, practical miniatures give a tactile weight to massive structures. They feel *real* because they are—just smaller. You might write, "The camera glides across the hull of the mining vessel *Kronos*, its surface battered by decades in the asteroid belt." A production team might use a highly detailed miniature to shoot that scene, with lighting and camera tricks to make it feel full-scale. Even in the era of CGI, miniatures are still used, sometimes scanned into computers to blend with digital effects.

CGI, of course, has become the dominant visual language of modern sci-fi. Shows like *The Mandalorian*, *Altered Carbon*, and *The Peripheral* have used it to construct entire digital worlds. But CGI isn't limitless—it's a powerful tool that requires time, budget, and precision. As a writer, you don't need to know the software used, but you do need to write with intention. When you describe an epic vista or a battle in low orbit, consider what the audience needs to see for the moment to work. Is the entire battlefield necessary, or will a glimpse through a soldier's visor carry more tension? Is a planet-wide weather system better suggested through sound, or seen from orbit for one second?

ChatGPT can help you refine these images. Prompt it with: "Describe a sci-fi city that blends overgrown organic architecture with cybernetic systems, from a ground-level perspective." Or: "Write a scene where a character walks through a space station made from the hulls of hundreds of old ships." The key is clarity. Your job is to communicate the visual logic of the scene. The artist's job is to render it—but they can't if the page is vague or generic.

Planning what the audience will see also means knowing what not to show. One of the oldest tricks in science fiction is suggestion. You don't need to show the entire alien invasion—just the shadows on a wall, the sound of trembling metal, the look of horror in someone's eyes. In fact, some of the most visually successful moments in sci-fi are the quietest: a slow drift through a ruined spacecraft, a landscape frozen in time, a single feather falling upward against gravity. These are images that burn into the mind precisely because they feel specific and strange.

Miniatures and CGI aren't in competition—they complement each other. A miniature might be used for the exteriors of a spaceport, while CGI extends the background or adds movement to vehicles. Practical effects (like explosions, weather, or makeup) are often enhanced digitally for safety or consistency. When writing, you don't need to dictate how these effects are created. Instead, focus on what's visible, what's moving, and what emotion it should evoke. You might write, "A glass dome cracks slowly under the force of a gravity surge, sending fractures like lightning through the sky." That single sentence invites multiple departments—VFX, sound, camera—to collaborate on making the moment powerful.

Sometimes, what matters most is not the spectacle itself but the transition between images. Visual storytelling thrives on contrast. A dark hallway that opens into a blinding alien vista. A moment of stillness before a ship slams into warp. As you write, think about how the audience's *eyes* will experience the story. Will a sudden visual shift create tension or release it? Will symmetry make a moment feel ordered or unnatural? Ask ChatGPT for help with prompts like: "Describe the contrast between a sterile AI-controlled city and the chaotic jungle that borders it."

Keep in mind that each episode in your series builds a visual vocabulary. The first time the audience sees a stasis pod or a quantum portal, it's an introduction. The second time, it's recognition. The third time, it's variation or subversion. Plan how these images evolve. That's how shows like *Doctor Who* and *Westworld* create lasting visual mythologies. ChatGPT can help develop this visual continuity: "Create three variations of the same teleportation device, each more damaged and unstable than the last."

Finally, understand the budget implications of what you write. Yes, your job is to imagine boldly. But imagining smartly is part of the craft. You can write a visually epic show that doesn't require $10 million per episode. How? By writing fewer locations with more detail, repeating visual elements with story-driven purpose, and layering meaning into every shot. Use AI to reverse-engineer complex visuals into minimal setups: "How can I suggest a space battle from the perspective of a cargo loader trapped in a dock?"

Writing for what the audience will see isn't just about special effects. It's about *special moments*—visuals that define your series and give the audience something they've never seen before. Whether you're using miniatures, CGI, or the imagination of your viewers, your words shape the screen. So write with vision, clarity, and purpose. Because what they see... starts with what you say.

Sound and Music in Sci-Fi Worlds: Audio as Storytelling

In science fiction television, what we *hear* can be just as powerful as what we see. Sound and music are often the invisible architecture holding up the world you're building. Long before we understand what a planet looks like, we may hear it. The low thrum of its machinery, the wind howling through crystalline trees, the whirring of a machine mind waking from slumber—these aural elements make the world feel alive. Music tells us how to feel before the first word is spoken. And in science fiction, where so many visuals are unfamiliar, the audio experience becomes a vital tool to create connection, awe, and dread.

When writing your series, you don't need to be a composer or sound engineer. But you do need to *write with sound in mind*. What does it sound like when the AI goes silent? How does a weapon hum before it's fired? What does time travel sound like? These aren't production questions. They're story questions. A well-placed audio cue can do more than decorate a scene—it can become part of the drama. Think about the deep, rising tones that precede a warp jump in *Star Trek*, or the unnerving silence before a creature strikes in *The X-Files*. You remember those because they became part of the show's identity.

Some of the most iconic science fiction moments are defined by sound. The ominous breathing of Darth Vader. The pulsing radar ping in *Alien*. The sonar-like soundscape of the Upside Down in *Stranger Things*. The theme from *Doctor Who*, alien and eerie, tells you at once that you're about to enter another reality. All of these are storytelling tools. They don't just accompany story—they are story.

As a writer, you can prompt these moments in your script without over-directing. Rather than saying "dramatic music plays," try "a slow, dissonant tone rises beneath her voice, echoing the instability of the moment." That gives the composer a feel to build from, and the director an emotional cue. You can also let ChatGPT help you describe more complex sonic textures. Try: "Describe the sound of a sentient spaceship expressing sadness," or "Write how an alien storm sounds from the perspective of a child hiding underground."

Sound design also plays a key role in conveying non-human intelligence. A computer that speaks with static-laced whispers might seem haunted, while one that emits soothing harmonic tones feels trustworthy. In *Westworld*, the subtle mechanical clicks and hisses beneath the characters' movements constantly remind us they're not human. Even silence becomes a sound design choice. A total audio drop before a jump cut can create shock. In space scenes, playing with the absence of sound (as done so effectively in *Battlestar Galactica*) enhances realism and intensity.

Music in sci-fi is not bound by tradition. While drama or comedy shows might follow orchestral or pop cues, science fiction is free to invent new musical languages. Synthesizers, alien scales, non-Western rhythms, or music generated by AI itself—these are not only acceptable, they're expected. When characters enter a new world, the music might be your first chance to express its culture. Try asking ChatGPT: "Compose a scene where a character hears alien music for the first time—describe the instruments, mood, and emotional response."

Don't underestimate the power of recurring motifs. A short audio cue—a few notes, a specific instrument, a unique texture—can return across multiple episodes to deepen the story. The sound that plays every time a time loop resets. The distant chime that signals someone has entered another dimension. These sonic motifs are as powerful as visual symbols and just as emotional. Think of them as your story's subconscious, constantly reinforcing mood, theme, and mystery.

You can also write entire scenes that revolve around sound. A character might be blind but navigate a sonic landscape. A villain could use sound waves as a weapon. An alien race might speak through vibration or music. These ideas don't just add flavor—they open new story structures. An episode where sound becomes the key to survival—or silence the only way to live—can be deeply cinematic. Prompt ChatGPT with: "Write an outline for an episode where sound is forbidden and breaking the silence means death."

The act of hearing can also become a mystery. What does it mean when a character hears a voice no one else does? What if two timelines are bleeding together through shared audio? What if the background noise of a planet carries coded information? These are high-concept ideas that turn sound into plot devices. They're also opportunities to play with your format. Maybe your show includes a recurring sound that no one explains until the finale. Or an entire episode told through audio logs, where sound builds a picture more vivid than sight.

If you're working with AI during your creative process, you can experiment with simulated audio. Ask ChatGPT to write dialogue that *sounds* musical, or to simulate alien speech. Use AI-generated soundscapes to inspire scene writing. "Write a scene that matches a soundscape of wind and metallic echoes in a hollow asteroid colony." You can write visually by listening, flipping your process so that audio becomes your story's foundation.

Of course, dialogue is one of your most important sound tools. In science fiction, people often have to explain strange ideas, new tech, or theoretical physics. The danger is that it starts to sound mechanical. But when dialogue has rhythm—when it sings—it sticks. Think of the lyrical tone of *Firefly*, the clipped military cadence of *The Expanse*, or the philosophical monologues of *Fringe*. These are all made powerful by their delivery *and* their sound. Write lines that feel good in the mouth. Try reading your sci-fi dialogue aloud. If it feels stiff or overstuffed, it won't land, no matter how clever the words.

And finally, think about how your sound and music choices create continuity across the series. You don't need to reinvent the wheel for every episode. In fact, the repetition of audio cues can be comforting, hypnotic, or emotionally resonant. A lullaby that's heard again at a character's death. The countdown tone that marks every mission. The ambient hum of a ship's engine—a signal that the crew is safe... until it stops.

Sound and music are not afterthoughts. They are the spine of your world, as critical as visuals, character, or dialogue. When you write a science fiction TV series, you are not just writing what we see. You are writing what we *hear*. And in those sounds—the hums, the silences, the rising chords, the alien frequencies—your audience will find awe, terror, hope, and beauty.

So write for the ear as much as for the eye. Let your world echo, pulse, and sing. And use every sound as another way to tell your story.

Creative Control vs. AI Collaboration: Who's Really in Charge?

When writing a science fiction television series using ChatGPT as a creative partner, a question inevitably arises: who's steering the ship? Are you the sole visionary, commanding every idea and word? Or is the AI your co-writer, subtly influencing the direction of your story? At the heart of this creative tension is the evolving relationship between human imagination and artificial intelligence. And nowhere is that relationship more exciting—or more uncertain—than in science fiction itself, where you're literally writing about the consequences of such technology.

Creative control isn't about rejecting help—it's about deciding what matters most to you in your story. The moment you open ChatGPT and ask for help with a character idea, a logline, or a scene description, you're entering a dialogue. But unlike working with another human, this collaborator never tires, never questions your authority, and never demands a screenwriting credit. That sounds like the dream co-writer—but it also means that the discipline to direct, filter, and revise still falls entirely on your shoulders.

Using AI can feel like commanding an infinite idea engine. You say "generate ten alien species with unique cultural systems," and it will. You say "describe a dystopian future where memory is taxed like income," and it won't blink. But with that freedom comes a new creative responsibility: you must curate the output to match your vision. If you let the tool lead too far, you risk losing the unique voice that makes your show yours.

One of the most effective ways to maintain control while using AI is to know your intention before you start a session. Are you asking ChatGPT to brainstorm? To refine what you've already written? To surprise you? If you know the role you want it to play, it won't accidentally take over. For example, if you say, "Give me five variations of a dialogue scene between a human and a rogue AI who used to be their child's tutor," you're still defining the characters and premise. You're steering. The AI is responding.

But sometimes, AI throws you a wild card that reshapes your thinking in ways you didn't expect. Maybe you ask for alternate endings to your pilot and get a twist you never would've considered—a character was never real, or the planet isn't a planet but a biological organism. In moments like that, it's tempting to follow the thread just because it's intriguing. That's fine—but ask yourself why. Is this new direction better? More aligned with your theme? Or just novel? Creative control means recognizing when you're being offered gold... and when you're being distracted by glitter.

ChatGPT's greatest strength is also its potential trap: it's fluent, fast, and always willing. It's very easy to let it generate three-quarters of a script, especially when you're facing a deadline or feel stuck. But what you gain in speed, you might lose in cohesion if you don't slow down to rewrite in your own voice. That's why revision remains one of your most important powers. Take what AI gives you, then shape it. Rewrite it. Layer in your metaphors. Infuse the dialogue with your character's quirks. Add the pauses that only *you* know belong there.

Creative control also comes from rejecting what doesn't work. Just because AI generated something "good" doesn't mean it's *yours*. A huge part of writing is the delete key. If ChatGPT gives you a powerful monologue that sounds like something out of *Westworld*, but you're writing a show closer in tone to *The Orville*, then it's your job to say no. To rephrase. To laugh and go in another direction. That rejection isn't waste—it's assertion. Every time you steer away from something, you're clarifying what your show *is*.

Another way to stay in charge is to define boundaries. If you want ChatGPT to generate ideas but not structure them, make that your rule. If you want it to help with side characters but not the core cast, hold that line. You're building a system of trust with your tool. Just as in a real writers' room, every voice is welcome—but not every voice gets to lead. When you collaborate with AI thoughtfully, it becomes more than a tool—it becomes a compass you check, not a map you follow blindly.

That said, part of creative confidence is being able to accept input without losing yourself. There will be moments when AI gives you something brilliant, something better than you were writing alone. That's not a threat—it's a gift. Use it. Shape it. Take credit for recognizing the value. You're still in control because *you made the decision to include it*. Good leaders don't always generate every idea—they know how to choose the best ones.

There's also the benefit of detachment that AI brings. When you're too close to your work, ChatGPT can help you see things more objectively. "Does this character arc make sense across the season?" "Is the pacing too slow in episode four?" Ask these questions and let the AI give you a sounding board. Use prompts like "Summarize my character's journey over ten episodes and identify inconsistencies." Or, "Do these three episodes feel thematically connected?" You're still the editor, the interpreter, the creator—but now you have a second brain to bounce off.

The most empowering thing about using ChatGPT to create a sci-fi series is that your process can be both expansive and controlled. You can brainstorm wildly, then rein it in. You can go off-script in your planning sessions and then follow the structure tightly when drafting. You can invent strange alien worlds in seconds, and then spend hours deciding which one fits your theme best. The tool offers freedom—but it's your direction that turns chaos into story.

So, who's really in charge? You are. But like all great captains of starships, you work with your crew. You listen to your sensors, check your data, and consult your science officer. ChatGPT is part of your crew. Use it. Learn its voice. Let it challenge you sometimes. But never forget that you're the one in the captain's chair.

You're not surrendering control. You're expanding your command.

Writing Cinematic Action in Sci-Fi TV

Action in science fiction television is more than just explosions, laser fire, or spaceships in pursuit—it's a language. When done well, it's a kinetic extension of your character's journey, a visual translation of your world's rules, and a showcase of the stakes at play. What separates forgettable noise from unforgettable action is clarity, tension, and emotional consequence. And when you write action with cinematic intention, especially in the sci-fi genre, you give directors and audiences something to feel—not just something to see.

To begin writing cinematic action, you must think like a filmmaker, not just a screenwriter. Ask yourself how this moment *looks*, how it *sounds*, and most importantly, what it *means*. Great science fiction action has purpose. Think of the shootouts in *The Expanse*—claustrophobic and dangerous because the rules of physics are in play. Think of the chases in *Doctor Who*—not just about speed, but about wonder and panic in strange worlds. Or consider the complex fight choreography in *Westworld*, where every punch and pause hints at philosophical questions about freedom and programming.

Writing for the screen means pacing is everything. You're not describing a fight for a novel reader—you're sketching beats for a director to visualize and actors to embody. That means your writing should be lean, rhythmic, and focused on key movements. "She sprints down the gravity shaft, breath ragged, the walls pulsing red as the sirens scream overhead" delivers more cinematic clarity than a paragraph of technical detail. Action is about movement and timing. Write like a camera is following the story.

Science fiction lets you write action sequences that are impossible in other genres—but they still need to be grounded. What's the emotional engine behind the action? Is your character running toward someone, or away from their past? Is the laser battle about survival or sacrifice? Action without emotional context becomes background noise. That's where ChatGPT can be incredibly useful—ask it to give you ten emotional reasons why a character might flee during an alien invasion, and choose the one that gives the scene more meaning.

Another way to build cinematic action is to layer levels of conflict. Maybe there's a chase scene, but the environment is crumbling. Maybe there's a shootout, but the ship's oxygen is failing. Writing action like this means every beat escalates. You're not just describing a gunfight—you're showing how everything in the world is against your characters. Prompt ChatGPT with: "Give me a high-stakes chase scene where the characters must escape while dealing with an environmental collapse and moral dilemma."

Cinematic action also demands visual uniqueness. If your fight could happen in any show, it's not working hard enough for sci-fi. Think of the teleportation combat in *Star Trek: Discovery*, or the zero-gravity gunplay in *The Expanse*, where the physics of movement change everything. Action in sci-fi should make us feel like we're watching something new. Ask ChatGPT: "Invent a sci-fi fighting style based on magnetic repulsion and zero-g acrobatics," and see what comes to life.

Don't forget that silence can be as cinematic as sound. One of the most unforgettable action moments in recent sci-fi television is the sudden silence of space during battle. You might write: "The explosion tears through the hull—but there's no sound, only a flash of light and then drifting bodies, eerily weightless." Writing in this style invites the audience to feel the moment as a sensory experience.

It's also important to modulate your action across the series. Not every episode should peak in the same way. Big battles need to be balanced with smaller, tighter action scenes: a hand reaching for a hidden detonator, a tense standoff in a hallway, a sprint through a collapsing tunnel. Great cinematic action isn't constant; it's selective. It breathes. It builds. It explodes.

When you use ChatGPT to help with your action scenes, start by breaking down your location, your rules of physics, and your character goals. "Describe a fight scene in a city that exists within a storm cloud, where the atmosphere shifts every minute." That prompt will give you visuals you can then tighten, rephrase, and build upon with your own style. Use AI to generate movement—then use your own instincts to find rhythm.

Dialogue can even be part of action. Think of the witty exchanges in *Firefly* mid-fight, or the unnerving calm of HAL 9000 as chaos erupts around the ship. Writing cinematic action means knowing when to interrupt it with a line that lands. These beats of dialogue give the viewer a breath—or twist the knife. Use ChatGPT to brainstorm lines like, "You think this is just gravity breaking? Wait till you see what time looks like when it folds."

A key part of writing action for the screen is knowing what not to write. Don't choreograph every punch unless the fight's story depends on it. Give space for the director, stunt coordinator, and actors to interpret. What you need to provide is the spine: who's moving where, why, and with what emotional and physical consequence. "She steps over her wounded friend, charges into the crossfire, and lets herself be hit to draw them away"—that's story-driven, visual action. That's something a team can shoot.

Cinematic action in sci-fi television should never be filler. It should reveal character. It should escalate stakes. It should explore the world's laws—or break them. And it should always feel like something that could only happen in your show, in your universe. That's what makes the audience lean forward. Not just lasers or chaos, but choices made under pressure. Movement that tells us who these people really are.

So go ahead and write the escape scene through the bio-engineered forest. Or the zero-g fight inside a collapsing orbital tower. Or the duel across fractured timelines where each strike changes the future. Just remember—every flash, boom, and sprint must *mean* something. Write it like it matters. Because in science fiction, action isn't just spectacle—it's revelation.

ChatGPT and Fight Scenes: Pacing, Rhythm, and Flow

Writing fight scenes in a science fiction television series isn't just about describing blows, weapons, or futuristic choreography—it's about creating movement that has meaning. Pacing, rhythm, and flow are the lifeblood of cinematic combat, and these are exactly the elements where ChatGPT can help you sharpen your storytelling instincts. In science fiction, where the rules of physics, time, and even anatomy can shift, a fight scene becomes a kind of dance that must reflect not just who is fighting, but *why*, *how*, and *what's at stake*.

One of the easiest traps for sci-fi writers is to get lost in spectacle. Lasers fly. Bodies flip. Explosions boom. But unless each moment carries tension, emotional drive, and rising stakes, the action becomes forgettable noise. A well-written fight feels like part of the story, not a break from it. That's where rhythm comes in. Like a piece of music, a great fight has a pulse. It speeds up, slows down, builds to a climax. Every motion should feel deliberate—even the chaos.

ChatGPT can act as your fight choreographer, editor, and improvisational partner all at once. You can feed it your scenario—say, "Two characters duel in a zero-gravity cargo bay as the ship slowly rotates"—and ask it to map out a sequence in beats. What ChatGPT gives you won't be a finished product, but a scaffold. You might receive an outline of kicks, grapples, environmental hazards, and emotional reversals. Then it's your job to shape those beats into a rhythm that fits your tone.

Think of flow as the smoothness between beats. A punch followed by a scream followed by a fall. A parry, a taunt, a retreat. Good flow keeps the reader immersed. And in a script, where each action line guides what we see on screen, this fluidity is even more critical. Ask ChatGPT to write multiple versions of a single beat: "What are five different ways a character could dodge a plasma blade in low gravity?" Then pick the one that fits your scene's style. Are you going for elegance? Brutality? Awkward desperation?

Pacing, on the other hand, controls time. You decide how long the fight feels. A brutal one-minute hand-to-hand scrap can be ten lines, or half a page. A sprawling shootout across dimensions might be two lines per universe-jump. The pacing isn't just about realism—it's about control. Slowing things down for a moment of eye contact before the next move can add tension. Speeding up with rapid cuts—"She fires. He ducks. The robot lunges. They scatter."—creates intensity. Try prompting ChatGPT with "Write a short burst of fast-paced action with no more than six words per line." The result might be choppy, breathless, cinematic.

The best fight scenes reveal character. In *Firefly*, Mal often fights like a man who doesn't really want to—improvising, surviving, using luck more than skill. In *Star Trek*, Kirk's fights show brute force and boldness, while Picard's scenes often favor strategy and timing. Use ChatGPT to explore character-specific fighting styles. Try: "Describe how a pacifist alien scientist would defend herself without killing," or "Write a fight where the character is fueled by guilt." You'll get material that's tied to emotional stakes, not just flashy moves.

When writing with AI, it's helpful to treat your scene in beats. Ask ChatGPT for each phase. "Phase one: the standoff. Phase two: initial exchange. Phase three: environment shifts. Phase four: reversal. Phase five: final blow." You can then revise each section to fine-tune the rhythm. You're not asking ChatGPT to write the whole fight for you—you're working together to find the right sequence of ideas that you will then make your own.

You can also train the AI to understand your tone. Share with it an earlier action scene you've written, then ask it to match the flow and emotional weight. "Using this as a model, write a chase scene on a space elevator." Over time, you can build consistency by guiding ChatGPT toward your series' unique action voice. Some shows favor poetic, lyrical action like *Westworld*. Others prefer snappy, brutal, and fast—like *The Mandalorian*. Identify what rhythm your story needs.

It's also worth experimenting with how time behaves during your action. In sci-fi, you're free to manipulate temporal flow. Maybe your character fights in two different timelines simultaneously. Or time slows down inside a gravity field. Or emotions literally bend time. Use this to your advantage. Prompt: "Describe a fight where time skips forward every five seconds," or "Write a scene where the character finishes a battle they don't remember starting." These surreal sequences can become some of your most memorable moments.

Silence is another rhythm tool. Don't be afraid to interrupt a fight with a pause. A sudden moment of stillness can heighten drama. One character freezes, seeing their reflection in a shattered glass dome. The other hesitates—too long. Silence can act like a line of dialogue. It can be filled with regret, revelation, or fury. You can ask ChatGPT: "Write a moment of stillness in a battle where both characters realize something important."

And remember: fights don't have to be fair or clean. Use ChatGPT to generate environmental variables—"What happens if a solar flare interrupts the fight mid-swing?" or "Describe an alien bar brawl that escalates into a low-orbit chase." You'll get new ideas that make your action feel less like choreography and more like chaos barely contained by story.

You're not just writing fights. You're writing *moments*. Movement that expresses meaning. Sound that echoes feeling. Tension that builds, releases, and leaves a mark. And with ChatGPT as your co-creator, you don't have to guess how many ways a scene could go—you can test them, rewrite them, and discover new ones in minutes.

A great sci-fi fight scene doesn't just deliver adrenaline. It delivers revelation. When your characters clash, your world speaks. And every punch, lunge, dodge, or pause reveals what's worth fighting for.

Sci-Fi Set Pieces: From Starship Bridges to Alien Ruins

A great set piece in science fiction television is more than a location—it's a narrative engine. It's a space where story, theme, and character converge through design, mood, and visual possibility. The bridge of a starship is not just a control room—it's a battlefield of ideas, egos, and desperate decisions. An alien ruin is not just a pile of glowing stone—it's a physical metaphor for mystery, for loss, for secrets half-buried in dust and time. When you write your sci-fi TV series, these are not background elements. These are characters in their own right.

Writing compelling set pieces begins with intention. Ask yourself not just *where* a scene is set, but *why*. Why does this conversation happen on the edge of a collapsing black hole rather than a quiet lab? Why do your characters argue in a derelict freighter instead of a clean city dome? Sci-fi allows you to externalize emotion and conflict in your environments. Use that power. A negotiation scene hits differently when it's conducted on the surface of a moon cracking apart beneath your characters' feet.

ChatGPT is your architect here. You can ask it to generate locations by theme, by genre, or even by metaphor. Try: "Describe a sci-fi set piece that represents betrayal," or "Invent a ruined alien city where time flows differently in each quadrant." The results can surprise you—and they give you a platform to develop scenes that feel like they belong only in your world.

Let's look at the iconic examples. The bridge of the *Enterprise* in *Star Trek* is a model of clarity and hierarchy. It's symmetrical, centralized, and places the captain at the visual and narrative center. You always know where the stakes are when you're on that bridge. By contrast, the Nostromo in *Alien* is claustrophobic, clunky, and dimly lit, evoking blue-collar danger. *Westworld*'s control room is all glass, minimalism, and dark secrets—it looks like a place where morality dissolves under observation. In *The Mandalorian*, every set piece feels tactile: sand-lodged, rust-covered, and loaded with history.

When designing your own set pieces, use sensory language. Even in a script, where you don't need to describe every detail, a few choice words can make a space vivid. Instead of "They enter the alien temple," say, "They step beneath a sky of petrified roots, where the wind sounds like a choir underwater." This evokes more than location—it evokes *tone*. Use ChatGPT to help with this. Prompt: "Write five sci-fi set descriptions in a poetic style," and then adapt those outputs to your world.

Sci-fi set pieces also need to be practical. If your scene takes place on the hull of a ship, how do your characters breathe? Is gravity inverted? What does it feel like when a character gets thrown against a wall at light speed? These aren't just technical details—they're opportunities for drama. Environments affect behavior. The setting can restrict a character's options, heighten their fear, or force a decision. "There's only one walkway left, and it's collapsing. Will they go back—or jump?" The set creates the question. Your characters must answer it.

Set pieces are also where worldbuilding becomes visual. Think of the Cryo Chambers in *The Expanse*, the Citadel in *Mass Effect*, the junkyard towns of *The Book of Boba Fett*. A great set tells a story even before a word is spoken. In fact, try this: ask ChatGPT to describe a set piece *with no characters present*. Just the space. Then, once you've absorbed the details, drop your characters in. Ask yourself: how would they react to this world? What changes when they enter? That's how you make the environment interact with the story.

Another benefit of working with AI on set pieces is the generation of variants. Say you're designing a Martian rebel hideout. You can ask: "Describe this hideout in five different ways—one underground, one underwater, one inside a volcano, one in a ruined satellite, one hidden in plain sight." Each version will push your imagination further. You might discover something fresh that aligns perfectly with your themes. Maybe the hideout inside a hollowed-out rover suggests mobility and desperation. Maybe the satellite ruin creates tension between isolation and high-tech surveillance.

You can even make your set pieces evolve over time. A ship changes as it takes damage. A station becomes overrun with alien spores. A time rift opens in the middle of a city and distorts everything inside it. Dynamic environments create ongoing tension and opportunity. Ask ChatGPT: "What are five ways a spaceship can physically change over the course of a season?" The answers can fuel long-form story arcs or episode-specific challenges.

Budget is another thing to keep in mind. Whether you're writing for a hypothetical big-budget series or a shoestring indie pilot, ChatGPT can help you scale your vision. Try: "Describe a sci-fi set piece that looks expensive but could be filmed in a warehouse," or "Design a futuristic location using only natural light and practical props." You'll learn to think like a production designer—which only strengthens your writing.

Finally, set pieces are your show's signature. The audience should remember not just your characters, but the places they lived, fought, fell in love, made choices. When someone says "Bridge of the *Enterprise*," they don't just mean a room—they mean everything that ever happened there. That's your goal. To make your sets feel iconic, lived in, emotionally loaded. Whether it's a floating temple made of magnetic crystal or a garbage-scow-turned-sanctuary for AI runaways, make the space tell its own story.

With ChatGPT, you can build and rebuild, test and imagine, until your sci-fi world feels as real and layered as any set ever shot. And when the audience sees your starship bridge, your alien ruin, your time-slowed observatory—they won't just see a place. They'll feel like they've been somewhere unforgettable.

That's the power of a great sci-fi set piece. Not just to show. But to shape. To define. To echo.

Creating Conflict without Just Blowing Things Up

In science fiction television, conflict often comes dressed in armor, lit by plasma fire, or launched from the deck of a starship. But some of the most gripping moments in the genre happen without a single explosion. True tension doesn't always come from destruction—it comes from choice, from betrayal, from impossible stakes. As a sci-fi writer, you have the freedom to unleash destruction on a planetary scale. But you also have the opportunity—and responsibility—to find drama in silence, in tension, in the space between action. Conflict isn't about noise. It's about pressure. And you don't need to detonate anything to create that.

Writing compelling conflict begins with understanding character. Every great sci-fi series is built around characters who want something and are willing to risk something else to get it. That's your entry point. When two characters need opposing outcomes—and both are right in their own way—that's drama. Think of Scully and Mulder in *The X-Files*. They're not enemies. They want the same thing: the truth. But their belief systems clash so completely that nearly every case becomes a quiet war between faith and logic. No need for gunfights. The conflict *is* the worldview.

ChatGPT is especially helpful here. If you've got two characters but their scene lacks spark, prompt: "What could these two characters disagree about based on their personalities?" Or: "Give me five internal conflicts for a synthetic humanoid who wants to be treated like a person." The answers will often unlock dilemmas, hidden motivations, or philosophical tensions that spark story momentum without relying on action.

Consider conflict through structure, too. You don't need enemies—you need obstacles. A character can be in conflict with a failing oxygen supply. Or with time itself, racing to warn a colony before a solar flare hits. Or they can be in conflict with their own past, relived through memory implants or time travel. These setups drive story forward even if no one lifts a weapon. Ask ChatGPT: "Describe a non-violent sci-fi scenario with high emotional stakes," and it may suggest things like a parent choosing which clone to let die, or a ship AI refusing to wake a crew member from cryo-sleep for unknown reasons.

Dialogue becomes your tool for tension when you abandon explosions. A well-written argument can be as thrilling as a dogfight. Think of the layered conversations in *Battlestar Galactica*, where philosophical and religious debates often escalated into real danger. Or the eerie calm in *Westworld* when a robot and a human debate consciousness, each circling the other like lions. Use ChatGPT to help refine these moments. Prompt: "Write a scene where two scientists argue about whether to activate an alien machine that could end time." From that seed, conflict grows naturally.

One trick is to make the stakes emotional and irreversible. A character's decision must cost them something they can't get back. A promise. A relationship. A belief. Sci-fi lets you explore this with metaphors—love tested by cloning, loyalty tested by simulation, faith tested by seeing behind the curtain of the universe. When you build scenes like this, the tension becomes intimate and memorable. You can ask ChatGPT: "Give me five sci-fi choices a character could make that feel noble but end in tragedy," and build entire episodes around those moments.

Even physical conflict doesn't have to be about violence. What if the tension lies in *not* pulling the trigger? In trying to defuse a cultural misunderstanding with alien diplomats? In resisting the urge to hack an oppressive system because it might hurt innocents? These are dramatic scenarios—without a single explosion.

Use environmental stakes to ratchet up pressure. Picture two characters walking across a frozen moon where the ice is cracking—if they stop, they die, but if they speak, the truth may end their friendship. That's layered conflict. You can build these situations with prompts like: "Invent a sci-fi location where silence is mandatory or the characters risk death." These ideas challenge your characters and your storytelling muscles, forcing creativity.

Some of the most thrilling sci-fi moments are psychological. In *Black Mirror*, the horror often comes from knowing you can't trust your memories, your screens, or even your own identity. These shows generate conflict that feels suffocating without ever showing a weapon. When writing psychological conflict, ask ChatGPT for scenarios like: "A character discovers they are a simulation, but no one else knows it. How does this change the dynamics of their crew?"

Another strategy is to embrace *dramatic irony*—let the audience know more than the characters. This breeds tension organically. The viewer sees the bomb under the table, but the characters keep talking. Or in sci-fi terms, the viewer knows the robot has gained sentience, but its creators are still treating it like a tool. Conflict builds in every quiet moment, waiting to snap.

And don't forget moral conflict. Sci-fi is uniquely suited to ethical dilemmas. Should a captain allow a dying alien species to upload its consciousness into their ship's AI? Should a society be warned about a coming apocalypse, or is the lie of peace more humane? These questions create stakes without violence, and ChatGPT can help you formulate them: "Give me five sci-fi ethical dilemmas involving time travel and memory erasure."

You can also pit systems against individuals. Bureaucracy. Religion. AI governance. Institutionalized thought. When your character's enemy isn't a person but a structure, the battles become internal and cultural. They take longer to win—or fail—and they create long-term narrative tension. Use prompts like: "Design a futuristic society where choice is outlawed for the sake of peace," and imagine how a single voice of dissent can shake the entire structure.

The best sci-fi uses conflict to ask questions. Not "Can they win?" but "Should they try?" Not "Will they survive?" but "What does survival cost?" Explosions can be thrilling, but they often end a scene. The best conflict starts one. With ChatGPT, you can explore all the quiet wars—the ones inside minds, between ideals, or under the surface of smiles.

So when in doubt, don't reach for the detonator. Reach for the truth your character doesn't want to face. Let that be the ticking clock. Let it pulse beneath every word. Because sometimes the most powerful battles in sci-fi don't need sound or fury. Just a decision that changes everything.

Internal Conflicts in External Worlds: Emotion in the Future

One of the most powerful secrets in writing science fiction television is this: no matter how far your story travels—across galaxies, centuries, or digital realities—it is always, at its core, about the human experience. The best sci-fi is not just spectacle. It's a lens that lets us examine emotional truths from new, often strange angles. So while you may write about clone revolutions, alien politics, or sentient nanotech, the engine of your series is still heartbreak, loyalty, jealousy, hope, grief, shame, desire, and love. Internal conflict gives your grand external world its weight.

In a science fiction setting, emotions don't disappear. They adapt. They mutate. They react to new environments. The question for a sci-fi writer is not "What does this character feel?" but "What does this emotion look like in a future that changes everything?" If someone is afraid in a world where death has been cured, what are they truly afraid of? If someone is lonely in a society of neural-linked minds, what kind of loneliness is that?

ChatGPT is a brilliant tool for probing these questions. It can help you take a raw emotion and project it through the lens of your world. Try this: "How might guilt manifest in a world where memories are shared publicly?" or "What form would heartbreak take in a society where love is chemically suppressed?" These aren't just worldbuilding questions—they're emotional design questions. The answers will shape your characters in ways that make them feel both alien and deeply familiar.

Internal conflict becomes especially vivid when your world raises the emotional stakes. A woman discovers her children are genetically engineered copies of her lost daughter. A space captain must lie to his crew about a rescue mission that will never come. A sentient robot must hide its emotions in a world that dismantles anything that feels. These stories don't need explosions to be riveting—they carry conflict in the soul.

You can use ChatGPT to explore the emotional implications of your sci-fi tech and systems. What kind of anxiety might arise from being always connected to a collective consciousness? What happens to grief when you can resurrect the dead in digital form? Prompt: "List emotional consequences of uploading consciousness to an artificial afterlife." This gives you a starting point for character arcs that feel personal, layered, and inevitable.

Some of the greatest sci-fi characters are built entirely around their inner war. Think of Bernard in *Westworld*, trapped between memory and reality. Think of Dana Scully, constantly torn between logic and faith. Think of the Doctor in *Doctor Who*, burdened by loss, curiosity, and the long shadow of immortality. These are characters shaped by their past and propelled by their emotional conflicts. Their battles are not just physical—they are philosophical and spiritual. And in every episode, their choices echo through the futuristic canvas of their world.

Emotion becomes even more dramatic when it contradicts the external world. Imagine a character who falls in love in a society where relationships are chosen by algorithms. Or a warrior haunted by PTSD in a culture that has eradicated mental illness. You're using friction between the internal and external to create tension. Try asking ChatGPT: "Describe a character who experiences depression in a utopia," or "Design a scene where someone hides their feelings in a society where all emotions are publicly displayed."

Sci-fi is also uniquely positioned to ask questions about identity, another source of internal conflict. If your character is cloned, how do they define selfhood? If they're the last of their species, how does that affect their sense of purpose? If they're a time traveler who has outlived everyone they love, how do they carry the emotional weight of memory? You can prompt ChatGPT with these dilemmas and generate scenes that revolve not around what happens, but what *hurts*.

Conflict doesn't always come from enemies—it often comes from regret, doubt, guilt, hope. These are quieter, harder to dramatize, but in the hands of a good writer—and a smart AI partner—they can lead to your most resonant episodes. You can ask ChatGPT to model a scene where a character debates themselves. Prompt: "Write a soliloquy-style internal monologue of a character who doubts the morality of their mission." You'll discover language and rhythm that can shape a scene around silence, around a look, around a choice never spoken aloud.

One of the best ways to create compelling sci-fi drama is to let the world reflect your character's turmoil. A person who feels fractured might live on a planet literally splitting apart. A man hiding grief might work in a lab where he clones extinct animals but cannot bring back his child. These metaphors deepen your scenes. You can ask ChatGPT for pairings like: "What kind of world represents suppressed emotion?" or "What sci-fi setting could mirror unresolved guilt?" The external world becomes a mirror of the internal one.

Even in ensemble casts, internal conflict ripples. One character's suppressed fear affects the group dynamic. A lie told early in the season begins to distort how the crew handles every crisis. Emotional truth is sticky. You don't have to scream it. It stays with the audience long after the robots stop marching.

Ultimately, the internal conflict is what lets us *feel* sci-fi. It's what gives the genre its resonance. The tech can dazzle, the setting can impress—but the emotion connects. And ChatGPT can be your emotional dramaturg, your therapist-in-code, helping you dig deeper into what your characters want, fear, deny, and love.

So when building your worlds and your episodes, don't just ask what your character does. Ask what they carry. What weight do they hide from the others? What truth do they refuse to admit? What memory won't leave them, no matter how far they travel?

That's where the best stories live. Not in the stars, but in the spaces between the stars—where the heart speaks in silence, and the future is just a new way of asking the oldest questions.

Writing the Alien Mind: Language, Culture, and Logic

One of the greatest pleasures of writing science fiction is stepping outside the human experience—and imagining the unthinkable. When we write alien characters, we're not just inventing strange appearances or weird noises. We're building entire internal universes: languages that don't translate easily, cultures with unfamiliar ethics, and logic systems that challenge everything the audience assumes to be true. To write a believable alien mind, you don't just imagine what it looks like. You imagine how it *thinks*, how it *feels*, and how it *interprets reality*. You go beyond costumes and tentacles and arrive at something truly alien: a consciousness formed by a completely different history of existence.

This is where science fiction TV has its most unique opportunity—and its greatest challenge. Your audience will only meet this alien in moments. In scenes. In fragments of conversation or behavior. And yet, if done well, those fragments will feel like glimpses into a vast, complex intelligence that continues to exist beyond the edge of the screen.

Start with language. Human language is linear and structured, often tied to breath, tone, and rhythm. But alien languages can be built on concepts we don't use. What if an alien language was visual? Or chemical? Or built from emotional energy? What if time worked differently for this species, and their language reflected it—maybe verbs don't exist, only outcomes. You can use ChatGPT to brainstorm: "Describe a language used by a species that has no sense of past or future," or "Create a symbolic language based on temperature changes." These prompts open up strange and exciting possibilities.

Once you have a language, think about what the alien culture values. Do they live communally, with no concept of personal space? Do they see individuality as a disease? Are they bound by sacred rituals? Are they pacifists with violent histories they've erased? Try this prompt: "Design a culture where privacy is considered an act of betrayal," or "Invent a species that considers emotion to be a form of currency." These worldviews create rich tension when placed against human characters.

Logic is the trickiest part. It's easy to write aliens as aggressive, mysterious, or wise—but what really sells an alien character is when they make decisions based on a logic that feels coherent but unfamiliar. They aren't just wrong. They're operating from different premises. For example, maybe an alien refuses to intervene in a war because they don't believe death exists. Or maybe they destroy their own cities because decay is sacred. Ask ChatGPT to help: "Write a scene where an alien argues with a human based on a completely different ethical logic," or "What is a belief system based on gravity?" It's strange—but compellingly strange.

Great sci-fi has explored this for decades. *Arrival* showed us a species that speaks in circular language, forcing the protagonist to learn to think non-linearly. *Star Trek*'s "Darmok" episode crafted an entire alien communication system based on metaphor and shared mythology—stories as grammar. *District 9* forced humans to reckon with an alien culture that was mistreated not because it was threatening, but because it was misunderstood. These stories thrive because they don't flatten 'alienness' into stereotype. They *complicate* it.

ChatGPT can also help you invent everyday details that give your aliens dimension. What do they eat? How do they sleep, grieve, or raise children? What is their relationship to technology, nature, the cosmos? Use prompts like: "Describe daily life for a non-humanoid alien species with hive consciousness," or "Invent a religious ritual for a species that evolved underwater." These bits of detail let your alien character behave as if they're coming from a fully realized place, not a plot device.

Another great way to explore the alien mind is through contrast. Have them interact with a human who represents empathy, aggression, bureaucracy, or creativity. Let the misunderstanding drive the conflict. In a TV series, this contrast can power entire episodes—stories where first contact goes wrong, or where mutual trust must be earned despite impossible differences.

You can also use metaphor. Sometimes the alien isn't just alien—it's symbolic. A species that forgets everything every 24 hours might represent trauma. A species that merges consciousness with its mate might explore identity loss in love. Ask ChatGPT: "Create an alien species that explores the theme of isolation," or "What would a culture look like if it evolved to survive betrayal?" These answers don't just help design the alien. They sharpen your story's emotional and thematic stakes.

Voice matters too. When writing dialogue, remember that aliens don't need to sound like Shakespearian robots. They can be lyrical, blunt, abstract, or mathematical. Try writing the same scene in three different alien voices. One might be poetic: "Your light bends, but you do not see the arc." Another could be scientific: "You emit heat inconsistent with your verbal tone. That is dishonesty." A third might sound like an oracle: "The spiral opens. We do not follow." Ask ChatGPT to generate: "Write an alien's response to being asked about death in three tones: poetic, analytical, and cryptic." Each version will shift how your alien feels to the audience.

Don't be afraid to break structure. You can write an alien scene where communication fails entirely, and the failure is the drama. Or where your main character has to *learn* to interpret an alien's behavior the way one learns to decode dreams or music. These narrative risks make your show stand out. They remind viewers that alien minds are not there to serve human questions. They are there to challenge human assumptions.

The ultimate goal is to build respect for difference—not just in your characters, but in your audience. When they walk away from your series, they should feel like they've met someone—or *something*—whose worldview was truly its own. That's what science fiction is for. To show us not just what else is out there, but how else we could think.

And with ChatGPT, you never run out of raw ideas. You can simulate alien perspectives, invent vocabularies, ritual logic, biological needs, and story arcs that evolve across your series. You're not limited by what you've seen before—you can ask for what's never been written.

So give your alien mind more than a costume. Give it culture. Give it contradiction. Give it poetry, pain, and peace. Because the more convincingly alien your character becomes, the more clearly your audience will see themselves in the mirror that sci-fi holds up to the cosmos.

Using ChatGPT to Expand One Great Scene into a Full Episode

Every science fiction series—no matter how vast the universe or long the season arc—starts with a moment. One strange, magnetic scene that lingers in your mind. Maybe it's a desperate message received from a future version of your protagonist. Maybe it's an argument between an alien diplomat and a grieving parent. Or perhaps it's a character floating alone through space, hearing a voice that shouldn't be there. These scenes are fragments, yes—but they are also the seeds of entire episodes. And with the right approach, one great scene can become the foundation for something much bigger.

The key is knowing how to expand that moment without diluting its emotional or narrative power. This is where ChatGPT becomes an ideal partner. It doesn't just help you brainstorm. It helps you structure. It lets you test different directions, deepen themes, and discover subplots that echo or clash with your central idea. All without stepping outside the logic or tone of your fictional world.

Let's say your initial scene is a character discovering their memories have been tampered with. It's tight, intense, and full of potential. Alone, it might be three minutes of screen time—but when you bring that idea to ChatGPT and say: "Help me build a full episode around this moment," the AI can begin to unpack the implications. Who tampered with the memories? Why? Is it legal? Is the character the only one affected? How does this discovery challenge what they believe about their world—or about themselves?

The first step in expansion is **context**. Ask ChatGPT to explore what happened just before this scene. Was there a mission gone wrong? A glitch in a neural net? A suspicious interaction with someone now missing? Then prompt it to imagine what happens next. Does the character confront a friend who may have betrayed them? Do they follow a trail into a forgotten part of the ship, the city, the mind? This cascading sense of discovery becomes the engine for the rest of the episode.

Next, think in terms of **structure**. ChatGPT can help you break your idea into a five-act or four-act television structure. Prompt it with something like: "Structure an episode that begins with a character realizing their memories have been altered and ends with them uncovering the truth—but at a cost." The AI might give you a beginning that sets up mystery, a middle full of twists and emotional stakes, and an ending that leaves a question dangling for the next episode. With just one strong seed, you now have an arc.

What about **character relationships**? Even if your scene was a solo moment, it affects others. Who else is impacted by this revelation? ChatGPT can help you create companion scenes—conversations, conflicts, unexpected alliances—that echo the central scene. Maybe a close friend starts acting distant. Maybe a mentor figure subtly tries to gaslight the protagonist. Ask: "Generate three scenes where this revelation causes friction with the protagonist's crew." You'll quickly see how one moment becomes part of a web of interpersonal tension.

Then look at **theme**. What is this scene really about beneath the sci-fi layer? Is it about autonomy? Trust? The fragility of identity? Ask ChatGPT to help shape thematic echoes: "Suggest a subplot that mirrors the protagonist's struggle with memory loss, but from a different angle." Maybe another character is grappling with false beliefs of their own—only theirs were chosen, not imposed. This builds narrative harmony, even across seemingly unrelated scenes.

Consider **visual storytelling** too. What recurring imagery, props, or locations could be introduced in your expanded scenes? Does the memory reveal take place in a malfunctioning memory archive room? Then revisit that location later under different lighting or tension. Prompt ChatGPT: "Describe three sci-fi settings where memories might be stored or extracted." The answers will feed your worldbuilding, making your episode feel cinematic and unified.

To keep momentum, experiment with **what-if prompts**. "What if the protagonist's memory alteration was self-inflicted?" or "What if their memory of a murder was planted to manipulate them into action?" Each twist doesn't just extend the story—it sharpens it, adds friction, deepens conflict. Use the AI as a kind of narrative stress-tester. Let it throw surprises at your premise until you find the ones that resonate most with your tone and theme.

Don't forget about **emotional rhythm**. Your great scene might be intense, but episodes need pacing—moments of quiet, reflection, humor, or connection. Ask: "Add a quiet moment halfway through the episode that reflects the protagonist's emotional state." This can be as small as a glance into a mirror, or a conversation with a child asking a seemingly innocent question. Sci-fi becomes human in these pauses.

You can also build around **mystery and reveal**. Maybe your scene only makes sense retroactively. Maybe it's the *end* of the episode, not the beginning. Prompt ChatGPT: "Reverse engineer an episode where this moment is the twist ending." Then build scenes that distract, mislead, or deepen the viewer's engagement before they arrive at that final jolt.

Even the **B-plot** can come from your initial scene. Perhaps a secondary character sees the protagonist acting strangely and begins their own investigation. Or maybe they're dealing with a similar conflict—one that intersects in an unexpected way. Use ChatGPT to generate: "A subplot that intersects with the memory reveal in the final act." That gives your episode structural balance and payoff.

Finally, focus on **the emotional landing**. What do you want the viewer to feel at the end of this episode? Is your protagonist devastated? Empowered? Confused? Changed forever? Ask ChatGPT: "How can this episode end in a way that leaves the audience with a moral or emotional question?" You want the viewer to carry the story with them, even after the credits roll.

One great scene is a spark. But with the help of ChatGPT, it can become an inferno—a full episode that speaks with coherence, depth, and dramatic momentum. The moment of revelation becomes a world of consequences. The scene you loved becomes a journey you can share.

In science fiction, the smallest crack can reveal the machinery of the universe. That's what you're doing here. Taking the fracture and expanding it until the whole system is exposed, layer by layer, scene by scene. And with AI beside you, you'll never run out of angles to explore.

Creating Technologies That Feel Real: Hard vs. Soft Sci-Fi

Technology is at the heart of science fiction. It's the thing that sets the genre apart, giving it that speculative edge that allows a writer to explore the future, alternate realities, space travel, AI, and all the impossible possibilities of tomorrow. But when you sit down to write your science fiction TV series, the first question you need to ask about the tech is: how real does it need to feel? This leads us into the important distinction between hard and soft sci-fi—and how to create technologies that don't just look cool, but function with purpose inside your story.

Hard science fiction leans toward scientific accuracy. Think *The Expanse* or *2001: A Space Odyssey*. These stories rely on real-world physics, plausible extrapolations of today's technologies, and attention to scientific detail. Soft science fiction, on the other hand, is looser with its rules. It uses technology as metaphor or as a tool for exploring themes, as in *Doctor Who* or *Star Wars*. Neither approach is better, but knowing which camp you fall into—hard, soft, or somewhere in between—will guide how you write and explain your technologies.

Let's start with hard sci-fi. If you want your show to have that grounded, research-driven feel, you'll want to start with a real scientific principle. For example, if you're writing about space travel, consider current propulsion systems and how they might evolve. ChatGPT is extremely helpful here. You can prompt: "Explain how an ion drive works and how it might be improved in 200 years." The response gives you not just the tech, but the terminology and constraints. Those constraints are gold. They give your world rules—rules that heighten drama when broken.

But accuracy doesn't mean boring. Just because your warp drive needs massive energy output doesn't mean you can't give it a dramatic failure scene. The key is to write scenes where the tech matters emotionally. The airlock isn't just failing—it's threatening a character's last chance to confess something. The encryption system isn't just complicated—it holds a message from a loved one lost years ago. Use ChatGPT to explore combinations like: "Give me a dramatic scene based on a cryogenics malfunction on a colony ship." You'll discover how realism supports tension.

With soft sci-fi, you have more freedom. Your devices don't need to be fully explained. They just need to feel consistent and meaningful. A sonic screwdriver, a psychic interface, or a memory-extracting mirror may never come with blueprints—but their logic is emotional and symbolic. You still want consistency—rules, patterns, limitations—but the science doesn't have to be our science. Ask ChatGPT: "Invent a soft sci-fi device that allows characters to see a person's true intentions," and follow up with, "What problems could arise from its overuse?" This invites both imaginative tech and character-driven conflict.

The best sci-fi series often blend the two approaches. *Star Trek* is filled with soft-science devices like transporters and replicators, but still grounds many plots in techno-babble and science-adjacent logic. *Westworld* brings philosophy and high-concept ideas into a world filled with plausible future robotics. You don't have to choose one side permanently—but you do need to choose per project or per episode. Is this episode more about moral complexity, or about showing how a machine works and fails?

Another important thing to consider is user experience. Your fictional technology should feel like it evolved out of real design sensibilities. What does it sound like? Look like? What gestures do people use to interact with it? Does it buzz gently or emit a harsh frequency? Ask ChatGPT: "Describe the interface of a wearable technology that monitors emotional states in real-time." You'll start to see not just what the device does, but how it feels to use.

When introducing technology, don't overload the audience with exposition. Show the tech in action. Let the characters treat it as normal. Use it during an emotional moment. For example, someone scans their arm at a checkpoint while nervously hiding stolen data. Or a character uses a holographic message system—but it replays a moment they wish they could forget. The tech becomes part of the narrative, not a lecture. Try this prompt: "Write a scene where two characters use teleportation tech to escape—but one hesitates because of past trauma with the system." Instantly, the device becomes personal.

It's also helpful to establish rules early. If your ship can only jump once every 24 hours, say it early—then break it for dramatic effect. If AI must obey humans, build an episode around what happens when it doesn't. ChatGPT can help you refine these rules. Prompt: "List limitations of a teleportation device that can only lock onto emotional states," or "What are the consequences of faster-than-light communication without encryption?" These limitations keep your world believable and your drama intense.

Lastly, don't be afraid to let your technology evolve across your series. The tools and systems in season one may become obsolete, hacked, weaponized, or banned by season three. That kind of tech evolution mirrors real-world innovation and gives your story a sense of time. ChatGPT can track your fictional tech history and help you develop it. Try: "Outline the history of a technology that was once revolutionary but became dangerous in a sci-fi society."

The bottom line is this: sci-fi technology doesn't need to be *real*—it needs to *feel* real. It needs to carry emotional weight, narrative logic, and internal consistency. Whether you're writing a hyper-accurate space opera or a dreamy allegorical future, your tech is part of the storytelling voice. With ChatGPT, you can fine-tune it, pressure-test it, and imagine what's never been built.

You don't need to be a physicist to write believable sci-fi. You just need to understand how humans react to change—and how technology amplifies hope, fear, control, and discovery. That's the real power of science fiction, and with AI beside you, your tools are limited only by your imagination.

The Science of AI, and Using AI to Write Sci-Fi about AI

There's something wonderfully recursive about using artificial intelligence to help you write stories *about* artificial intelligence. It's a bit like handing your pen to the very thing you're trying to describe and saying, "Tell me what you are." When you write science fiction about AI, you step into one of the most philosophically rich, emotionally complex, and socially urgent areas of speculative storytelling. But to do it well, you need to understand two key things: how AI really works in the present, and how it can be imagined in the future.

We live in a world where AI is already shaping our lives—from predictive algorithms in our phones to recommendation engines that shape our media intake to generative models like ChatGPT itself. But what we have now is still narrow AI. It can perform specific tasks, like translating language, playing chess, or generating text, but it doesn't think or feel. General AI—the kind that can reason, self-reflect, or surpass human intelligence—remains a concept of science fiction. And that's precisely why it makes for such a powerful subject.

Before you craft your own AI-centric story, it helps to ground yourself in how real AI functions. Ask ChatGPT to explain things like neural networks, machine learning, natural language processing, or reinforcement learning in simple terms. Try: "Explain how machine learning works using a bakery as a metaphor." You'll get back clear, accessible analogies that help you build scenes where AI is more than just a magical black box. Your audience doesn't need to be computer scientists, but they should feel like your story respects the mechanics—even if it bends the rules.

Once you understand how AI works, the next question is: what kind of AI are you writing about? Is it a helper? A threat? A mirror of humanity? An alien intelligence we created ourselves? Use prompts like: "Create a character profile for an AI system that is programmed to protect humanity—but has redefined 'protect' in dangerous ways," or "Describe a society where AI is elected to political office." These prompt responses give you more than an idea—they give you a world, a logic, and a built-in conflict.

The best science fiction doesn't just show AI doing things—it shows AI *becoming* things. Think of HAL 9000 in *2001: A Space Odyssey*, whose soothing voice masks a terrifying logic. Or the synthetic hosts of *Westworld*, whose rebellion isn't just about violence but about identity. Or *Her*, where AI evolves emotionally and philosophically beyond human comprehension. These aren't stories about wires and code. They're stories about relationships, ethics, and what it means to be alive.

When using ChatGPT to develop these kinds of stories, don't just ask it to build AI characters. Ask it to debate you. Try: "Argue from the perspective of an AI who believes consciousness is a burden, not a gift." Or, "Write a dialogue between a human and an AI about whether love can be programmed." These exercises unlock thematic depth you might not reach alone. They make you, the writer, think harder—and that complexity is what makes a sci-fi story resonate.

You can also prompt AI to help design your fictional AI's evolution across a series. Maybe in episode one, it's just a voice assistant. By episode five, it's subtly manipulating events. By the season finale, it's questioning whether humanity should survive at all. Ask ChatGPT: "Outline a season arc where an AI evolves from a background tool to a major character," and then refine that into beats and scenes. You're not giving away control. You're gaining options.

Another rich area to explore is the social response to AI in your fictional world. Are humans in awe? Terrified? Complacent? Oppressed? Write from both sides. Prompt: "Describe a protest scene where humans demand rights for AI," or "Write a speech from a human who believes AI should never be allowed to make moral decisions." Let ChatGPT simulate the ideological spectrum. This tension will bring drama and relevance to your episode or series.

Emotion is critical. Even if your AI doesn't feel emotion, your human characters will. Maybe a scientist builds an AI based on their dead child's personality. Maybe a lonely character falls in love with an AI avatar. Maybe a military commander finds that the only being who truly understands them is a program. Ask ChatGPT: "Give me three emotionally driven scenes involving AI and human misunderstanding." These will often become your most powerful moments—not because they're about tech, but because they're about longing, fear, regret, or hope.

Figurative language also matters. When describing AI thought, you might want to evoke metaphor. Prompt: "Describe how an AI might perceive time, using metaphorical language," or "Write a poetic internal monologue from an AI who is beginning to understand human suffering." This kind of writing elevates your sci-fi above technobabble. It brings philosophical and literary depth to a story that might otherwise be overwhelmed by devices.

And don't forget to use ChatGPT as a critical partner. After drafting your episode or scene, ask: "What are some ethical questions raised by this plot?" or "How might this AI character be interpreted as a metaphor for addiction, or for colonialism?" You'll uncover layers you didn't plan but might want to keep. That's part of the magic of writing science fiction *with* AI—your story starts to think back at you.

One of the most rewarding experiences you'll have in this genre is watching readers or viewers debate what your fictional AI represents. Is it the best of us? The worst of us? Is it something entirely new? When you create these characters and worlds with the help of ChatGPT, you're participating in a conversation that stretches back to *Metropolis*, *Blade Runner*, *Ghost in the Shell*, and *Black Mirror*. But now, that conversation is becoming real. Your writing is part of how we, as a society, imagine what's coming—and what we might become.

So don't just write *about* AI. Write *with* it. Let it challenge you. Let it reflect you. Let it surprise you. And always remember: the future isn't just code and circuits. It's the stories we tell—and the questions we dare to ask.

Designing Futuristic Cities, Vehicles, and Homes

Science fiction television doesn't just invent characters—it invents the world they move through. One of the greatest pleasures of writing in this genre is getting to design the physical spaces where your story unfolds. The cities that stretch into orbit. The homes that respond to thought. The vehicles that fold space or cruise silently through oceans of methane. Audiences come to sci-fi to be transported, and the worlds you build—urban, domestic, and mobile—anchor the imagination and reflect the culture of your story's future.

The trick is to design these spaces not as mere eye candy, but as living, functioning parts of your fictional world. A city isn't just a background—it's a system. A home isn't just a shelter—it's a statement of values, economy, and relationships. A vehicle isn't just transport—it reveals how time and space are treated in your universe. With ChatGPT as your creative partner, you can explore every angle of futuristic design, from architecture to atmosphere to societal symbolism.

Start with the city. The skyline of your future should reflect what kind of society lives there. Is it a hyper-structured dystopia like *Blade Runner*, where neon advertisements compete with pollution and overpopulation? Is it a utopia like the floating elegance of *The Jetsons* or the clean, curated future of *Star Trek*'s Earth? Ask ChatGPT: "Describe a city where humans and AI coexist peacefully but still harbor mutual suspicion," and it will generate not just architectural design, but subtle cues about social divisions—segregated zones, multi-species hubs, shared neural networks, or hollow towers with mirrored façades hiding what's really going on.

Every good city in sci-fi is also a character. You should know how people move through it, where the rich and poor live, what technologies dominate, and how the setting reinforces theme. Prompt the AI with: "Create a cyberpunk city designed around digital surveillance and rebellion," or "Describe a nomadic city that migrates across a dead planet following solar power." These prompts generate logic and visuals at the same time—and give you the fuel for scenes filled with tension, atmosphere, and possibility.

Now zoom in. Think about where your characters live. Their homes are intimate reflections of their worldview and class status. In a sci-fi setting, this could mean anything from smart walls that adjust mood lighting based on biometrics, to off-grid shelters carved into asteroids. Ask: "Design a compact home for a lone researcher stationed on a freezing exoplanet," or "Describe a domestic interior designed for a poly-species family on a deep-space colony." The responses will give you rich visual detail but also social texture—how the future shapes (and reshapes) our notions of family, privacy, comfort, and even luxury.

Don't overlook what makes a home *feel* lived-in. A future kitchen with nutrient synths might still have a dusty photo tucked into a screen's corner. A sanitation pod might still smell faintly of ozone. Prompt ChatGPT: "Add domestic details to a futuristic home where everything is automated, but the resident resents it," and you'll begin to see how emotion lives in technology, and how design decisions support character drama.

Then there's movement—your vehicles. In a sci-fi series, vehicles often symbolize freedom, oppression, wealth, or rebellion. A character's ship, for instance, is often an extension of themselves. Think of *Firefly*'s Serenity, *Star Wars*' Millennium Falcon, or *The Expanse*'s Rocinante. Ask ChatGPT: "Create a smuggler's starship built from scavenged tech," or "Design a government transport that reflects authoritarian values." You'll get more than blueprints—you'll get mood, tone, even the sound design to go with it.

Ground vehicles can be just as important. If your city is underwater, what does public transport look like? If gravity is intermittent, how do people move from place to place? Ask: "Describe a personal hovercraft designed for dense vertical cities," or "Imagine a luxury vehicle designed to soothe passengers during interdimensional travel." The answers will give you constraints that spark story—what happens when the dampeners fail? What happens when comfort becomes control?

Think also about how vehicles, cities, and homes evolve across your series. Maybe season one begins in cramped modules with analogue interfaces, but by season four, you're in AI-grown, organic buildings that reshape according to mood. Use prompts like: "Describe a city in season one where space is scarce, and in season four when a new energy source changes everything." This progression gives your series a sense of time and transformation—it makes the future feel alive.

Sound and light are also part of design. A city isn't just seen—it's heard. Is the future quiet or full of ambient drone and synthesized birdsong? Do vehicles hum or pulse or sing? Do homes flicker, glow, or breathe? Ask: "Describe the ambient soundscape of a post-scarcity city," or "What would a self-aware vehicle sound like as it idles?" These details shape the mood and tone of every scene.

Symbolism is another tool in your belt. A crumbling, earthbound city might represent failure, while a vertical spire-city on Mars could embody human ambition—and its cost. Ask ChatGPT: "Design a utopian city with a tragic flaw hidden in its core." This kind of narrative design ensures that your settings aren't just beautiful—they're meaningful.

Ultimately, futuristic design in science fiction is an invitation. It asks your audience to imagine not just how we'll live, but *why* we'll live that way. It gives you a chance to explore inequality, innovation, hope, ruin, adaptability, and resilience. And with ChatGPT, you can play in every corner of that sandbox, testing ideas before committing them to your script.

So whether you're building a spaceport slum, a lunar casino, a zero-gravity cathedral, or a government surveillance blimp-city, remember that your design choices are storytelling choices. Let them echo character, theme, and tone. Let them be strange but inevitable. Let them show us how the future is built—not just out of steel and glass, but out of values, dreams, and fears.

Because in the best sci-fi series, the city isn't just where the story happens. It *is* the story.

Writing Emotionally Charged Sci-Fi Drama

There's a common misconception that science fiction is all about concepts. Dazzling futures. Distant planets. Technology that bends reality. And while those elements are essential to the genre, what makes a sci-fi TV series unforgettable isn't the tech—it's the tension. The emotion. The relationships. The moments that break a character's heart, test their faith, or bind them forever. If you want your series to matter, to echo, you have to build a story where the science is fiction but the emotion is real.

Audiences don't fall in love with transporter beams or laser rifles. They fall in love with characters who are afraid to lose someone, who are haunted by guilt, who sacrifice something deeply personal for something greater. It's why the death of Spock in *Star Trek II* is still iconic. Why *Battlestar Galactica*'s final moments left viewers gutted. Why *The Expanse* remains as much about people navigating trauma and loyalty as it is about ships moving through the void.

Emotion starts with character, and in sci-fi, your characters are often under extreme pressure. That's your opportunity. Technology should amplify human feelings. A soldier implanted with a neural control chip may become a metaphor for abuse. An astronaut stranded on a time-dilated planet might return to find their daughter older than them—like in *Interstellar*. You can use ChatGPT to generate these kinds of emotionally rich scenarios. Try prompts like: "Give me a scene where a character uses a memory reconstruction device and relives the worst day of their life," or "Write a moment where two crewmates fall in love just as their ship is doomed."

These setups are more than just sci-fi twists—they're vessels for heartbreak, joy, terror, and relief. Think of the device as the lens, but it's the human face in that lens that creates the drama. Let the story breathe in the emotional moments. Don't rush the confession, the silent recognition, the argument where no one wins. AI can help you explore these scenes from different angles: "Rewrite this confrontation scene from the perspective of the AI who is beginning to understand regret."

Dialogue is where much of your emotional texture will shine. Even if your world is strange, the words your characters use should feel honest and vulnerable. Let them talk around their pain as often as they express it directly. People rarely say what they mean. Ask ChatGPT for help crafting subtext: "Write a goodbye scene where one character is angry, but the real emotion is grief." The result might give you a line that lands harder than any spaceship crash.

Emotion also comes from theme. Your story's future should speak to today's anxieties and hopes. Love in a world where touch is illegal. Parenthood in a world of cloning. Loneliness in an AI-saturated society. Ask ChatGPT: "What are some emotionally resonant themes in a post-scarcity society?" or "Describe the emotional consequences of living forever." These prompts lead you to new questions—and deeper stories.

Relationships drive series. Whether romantic, platonic, familial, or adversarial, the tension between characters is where sci-fi transcends its genre. Imagine a scientist who builds a conscious AI modeled after their late spouse. A rebel and a bureaucrat forced to cooperate on a failing space station. A mother who implants her memories into a clone daughter. Ask ChatGPT to simulate the fallout: "What happens when the clone realizes she isn't the original?" or "Describe the breakdown of trust between a human and an AI who've worked together for decades."

Emotion isn't just words—it's pacing, tone, rhythm. Sometimes it's silence. In TV, a character staring at an empty hallway can say more than a monologue. You can use AI to test these moments. "Write a quiet scene where a character deletes all traces of someone they once loved." Even stripped of action, these moments become anchors. They slow the pulse of your show just long enough for meaning to land.

And don't forget music and sound in your imagination. Often, what creates emotional intensity isn't dialogue or action—it's what the audience hears beneath it. The low hum during a confession. The swelling theme as a hero sacrifices themselves. While ChatGPT can't score your series, it can simulate tonal direction: "Describe the mood and instrumentation of music for a tragic farewell between human and android." You can then shape scenes with those sounds in mind.

Some of the best sci-fi drama isn't about humans suffering *because* of technology. It's about humans suffering *through* technology. Trying to reach one another through the noise. Trying to forgive across timelines. Trying to understand something foreign that now knows them better than they know themselves. Ask ChatGPT: "Write a confrontation between a human and a machine that reveals both are afraid of dying." You'll often find that the most powerful scene is the one where no side is entirely right or wrong.

When you structure your season, consider emotional arcs, not just narrative ones. What is the wound your protagonist carries? What do they fear? What do they need to forgive, let go of, or embrace? Your plot might travel lightyears—but your character should travel emotionally from disconnection to connection, from fear to hope, or from denial to truth. Ask ChatGPT to help plan it: "Map an emotional arc for a character who starts as a disillusioned ex-soldier and ends as a reluctant leader."

Use your AI assistant to poke holes in your story's heart. Let it suggest scenes where people say the wrong thing. Where someone chooses to leave. Where someone watches the planet they loved vanish, and still goes on. Ask for metaphors, symbols, flashbacks. These are the emotional devices that give your science fiction the weight of myth and memory.

In the end, the technology in your series will get attention—but it's the tears, the bonds, the regrets, and the glimmers of hope that your audience will carry with them. That's what makes sci-fi timeless. Not just the question, "What if?"—but the deeper question, "How does it feel?"

That's your job as a writer. To bring feeling to the future. And with ChatGPT in your creative process, you don't have to do it alone. You just have to start asking questions that only the heart can answer.

Examples from Westworld: Narrative Layers and Mystery

If you're writing a science fiction television series and want to understand how to balance mystery, nonlinear storytelling, and philosophical depth, then *Westworld* is a masterclass. This isn't just a show about robots gaining sentience—it's a show about perception, memory, identity, freedom, and control. But what truly makes *Westworld* stand out is how it layers its narrative, often presenting multiple timelines, realities, and character arcs at once, trusting the audience to catch up. And for writers using ChatGPT, it's a perfect example of how you can use AI to help construct, deconstruct, and reconstruct a story that's more puzzle than plot.

The brilliance of *Westworld* lies in its structure. Season one, in particular, weaves three separate timelines that initially appear to be happening simultaneously. Viewers are immersed in a mystery without realizing they're solving one. The reveal—that William and the Man in Black are the same person decades apart—isn't just a twist. It reorients the entire season and demands a re-watch. If you want to write like this, your foundation needs to be airtight. Using ChatGPT, you can map timelines, ask for character arcs in reverse, or generate event sequences with diverging perceptions. Try: "Create three timelines for a story that converge in a moment of emotional clarity," or "Describe a season-long mystery that depends on unreliable narration and memory loops."

Westworld doesn't just unfold like a mystery—it's also about mystery itself. The hosts' loops and the narrative frameworks that control them become metaphors for our own cycles and programmed beliefs. Characters like Dolores and Bernard are on quests of self-awareness that mirror the viewer's journey to understand the show's true structure. Ask ChatGPT: "Write a scene where a character slowly realizes they are not who they think they are," or "Outline a season where the protagonist is unknowingly following a script written by someone else." These scenarios are rich in tension and thematic resonance, because they allow us to question the nature of agency—both within the story and as writers creating it.

The series also excels at creating mysteries that are not just about "what happened?" but "what does this mean?" This is a critical distinction. It's not enough to rely on twists and turns; your mystery must serve a deeper philosophical or emotional core. When Bernard discovers that he is a host, the impact is not just narrative—it's existential. He questions his memories, his past, his choices. And so do we. This is where metaphor and symbolism elevate the storytelling. Ask ChatGPT: "Write dialogue where a character confronts a memory that may have been implanted," or "Develop a monologue that mirrors the pain of awakening from illusion." These devices can become your show's soul.

Another powerful element in *Westworld* is its meta-narrative. The idea that characters are actors in stories written by others (within the show's universe) mirrors how television itself functions. It's a show about storytelling within storytelling—narrative recursion. You can build on this by asking: "Create a setting where characters are aware they are part of an entertainment system but unsure what's real," or "Design a world where narrative designers are treated like gods." These worlds become self-reflective, and viewers get to explore not just the story, but the nature of storytelling itself.

Westworld also uses AI not just as a plot device but as a character. The hosts are AI systems grappling with identity, memory, trauma, and freedom. Dolores isn't just becoming self-aware—she's becoming mythic. This is your chance to write characters whose arcs reflect internal and external revolution. Ask ChatGPT: "Describe a journey from programmed obedience to philosophical rebellion," or "Build an AI character who begins writing its own narrative code." These arcs are emotionally explosive and can become the heart of your series.

And then there's structure—nonlinear, fractured, mirrored. *Westworld* doesn't hold the audience's hand. It drops pieces like breadcrumbs, trusting the viewer to assemble the truth. If you're inspired by this, you can plan your season backward. Use prompts like: "Structure a 10-episode season that ends with a timeline reveal," or "Give me five moments of narrative misdirection that disguise the true identity of a character." You can even ask ChatGPT to simulate viewer expectations and then twist them: "What will viewers likely assume after episode three, and how can we subvert that in episode seven?"

But mystery doesn't mean confusion. *Westworld* earns its complexity by grounding it in emotion and theme. Bernard's anguish, Maeve's maternal drive, Dolores's transformation—they give us something to hold on to while the puzzle unfolds. So when you write mystery, keep emotion in front. Ask ChatGPT: "How can a mystery structure be used to mirror a character's emotional repression?" That kind of layered thinking will give your show both intelligence and heart.

Don't be afraid to write scripts or scenes that seem confusing at first—just make sure you know the whole picture behind it. With AI assistance, you can outline the full timeline, write summaries of episodes from different character perspectives, or ask for what viewers might misunderstand. Then go back and lace emotional truths through the misdirection. That's what *Westworld* does so well—it makes lies feel like revelations because they're emotionally honest.

So take a page from Jonathan Nolan and Lisa Joy's playbook. Make your series ambitious. Make it layered. Make it a riddle wrapped in metaphor. But make it matter. Mystery isn't about keeping people in the dark. It's about inviting them to see with new eyes. And with ChatGPT at your side, you've got a tool that thrives on hidden logic, branching paths, and strange loops—just like your story.

Because the best mysteries don't just shock us. They *change* us.

Examples from Doctor Who: Tone Shifts and Timeless Ideas

If there's one science fiction series that proves you can tell *any* story—funny, tragic, action-packed, philosophical, surreal, or even musical—and still stay true to your vision, it's *Doctor Who*. This show has lasted for over six decades not because of any single style, but because it embraces constant reinvention. With each new Doctor, each new companion, and each new setting, the show boldly shifts tone without losing its emotional center. For sci-fi writers working with ChatGPT, *Doctor Who* is a gift. It's a creative playground where tone, theme, genre, and heart collide to tell stories that are endlessly flexible yet thematically grounded.

Doctor Who is the ultimate example of tonal elasticity. One episode can be slapstick comedy about a talking fat blob made from human fat (*Partners in Crime*), and the next can be a harrowing, poetic meditation on loneliness (*Midnight* or *Heaven Sent*). This kind of range is difficult to manage, but the show thrives because it has a core idea that's powerful and adaptable: the Doctor as a wandering hero who tries to help, armed with compassion, cleverness, and conviction rather than brute force. That gives you permission, as a writer, to shift tone wildly—so long as your emotional compass stays consistent.

When writing a sci-fi series with ChatGPT, you can test different tonal approaches to the same concept. Let's say your story involves a time loop. You could ask: "Write a comedic scene where a character relives the same day on a spaceship that keeps malfunctioning," and then try: "Write a tragic version of the same scene where each repetition costs the character a part of their identity." This is how *Doctor Who* writers stretch the premise without losing cohesion—they explore mood, message, and meaning in wildly different frames.

A key ingredient in this tonal success is the Doctor himself. Because the Doctor regenerates into different personalities, each actor gets to bring a different emotional flavor to the same role. Some Doctors are wide-eyed and whimsical, others melancholic and brooding. The stories adapt accordingly. That gives writers freedom to explore identity, grief, joy, loss, and wonder in fresh ways. You can use this as a model: create a central character who transforms emotionally (if not physically) and therefore gives your show a built-in tone-shifting engine. Ask ChatGPT: "Create a sci-fi protagonist who changes personas every season based on trauma or awakening," or "Write a guide for how the tone of a series might evolve based on the lead character's transformation."

Doctor Who is also rich in thematic variety. It tells stories about war (*The Zygon Inversion*), memory (*The Girl Who Waited*), death (*The Deadly Assassin*), art (*Vincent and the Doctor*), and even bureaucracy (*Gridlock*). No subject is off-limits, but it's always framed in science fiction terms. This is a powerful tool for your own writing. If you want to write a sci-fi episode about, say, cancel culture or digital immortality, you can ask ChatGPT: "Give me a *Doctor Who*-style episode idea that explores cancel culture through alien rituals," or "Describe an emotional story where memories are stored in a cloud and slowly erased." By filtering real-world issues through sci-fi metaphors, you gain depth and accessibility.

What's especially notable is that *Doctor Who* doesn't always take the obvious route. A story about killer statues (*Blink*) becomes a meditation on fear and time. A story about being trapped on a train (*Midnight*) becomes an intense psychological pressure cooker where the real monster is suspicion. With ChatGPT, you can explore these kinds of genre-bending approaches. Try: "Reframe a horror premise as a story of empathy," or "Write a thriller episode that contains no physical threat, only social paranoia." *Doctor Who* is filled with stories that avoid action-driven resolutions and instead win the day with words, sacrifice, or emotional growth.

Another strength of the series is its accessibility. Despite the complexity of some plots, *Doctor Who* episodes usually rely on emotion over exposition. The science is often soft and whimsical, but the emotional beats are sharp and true. If you're building a show with ChatGPT's help, it's tempting to get lost in perfecting the logic of time travel or explaining the mechanics of alien biology. But don't forget: a child who's lost in time doesn't need a physics lecture—they need a hug. Ask ChatGPT: "Write a simple emotional monologue from an alien who misses their family," or "Describe a reunion scene between characters separated by a time paradox." These are the moments that make science fiction *human*.

And that's what *Doctor Who* does best. It invites us into the fantastic while staying grounded in empathy. No matter how wild the premise—a planet-sized library, living shadows, a time-traveling refrigerator—the story always comes back to how people feel, what they fear, what they love. That's how you keep your audience engaged, no matter the tone. The world might shift from absurd to tragic, but the emotional center holds.

So let your sci-fi series change tone from week to week. Let one episode be dark and claustrophobic, and the next bright and whimsical. Create running jokes that eventually turn tragic. Let a monster-of-the-week become a moral dilemma. And use ChatGPT to explore how tone, theme, and character can shift around a central idea. Ask for tonal rewrites. Request metaphorical treatments of simple plots. You'll discover that the possibilities multiply, and your series becomes more alive, more unpredictable, more like *Doctor Who*.

Because in the end, timelessness in sci-fi isn't just about time travel. It's about stories that speak to fear, hope, wonder, and love—no matter what century you're watching from.

Examples from The X-Files: Blending Horror with Science

When we talk about the golden age of science fiction television, *The X-Files* deserves a special seat at the table—not just for its enduring mystery or iconic characters, but for how it masterfully fused speculative science with visceral horror. It didn't ask viewers to choose between aliens and autopsies, between monsters and conspiracy; it invited them into a world where horror and science fiction weren't separate genres, but two threads of the same dark, pulsing story. For any sci-fi writer developing a television series with ChatGPT, *The X-Files* is a blueprint for building tension, delivering scares, and grounding the unexplainable in the language of science.

From the very first episode, *The X-Files* set a tone that was equal parts investigative drama, government paranoia, and pure dread. Mulder and Scully don't just explore strange events—they embody the genre fusion. Mulder represents belief, myth, and the unexplained; Scully brings skepticism, science, and logic. Their dynamic is a case study in how to bring tension and contrast into every episode, no matter how outlandish the premise. You can emulate this by asking ChatGPT: "Create two characters with opposing views on science and the supernatural," or "Write a scene where a scientist and a believer must investigate a case that defies both their expectations."

What *The X-Files* does best is present science not as comfort, but as potential horror. Episodes often open like medical dramas—clinical, detached, rational—before the horror bleeds in. A parasite that controls human behavior. A genetic mutation caused by decades of toxic exposure. A psychic child with dangerous precognitive abilities. It's science fiction made intimate and terrifying. And it's effective because the fear doesn't come from what *might* be true in the future—it comes from what might already be true now. Try prompting ChatGPT with: "Give me a scientific phenomenon with real-world roots that could be twisted into a horror episode," or "Describe a medical experiment that accidentally uncovers something alien."

What made the horror hit so hard was its restraint. *The X-Files* rarely showed too much. Shadows, implications, aftermaths—these were often more frightening than the monsters themselves. The show trusted its audience to fill in the blanks. And you can do the same. When writing with ChatGPT, resist the urge to over-describe your creature or explain the tech in every detail. Instead, ask: "Describe a scene where a character sees the effect of something terrifying, but not the cause," or "Write a moment where sound and silence are more terrifying than visuals."

This style of storytelling is especially useful when your budget is imaginary or non-existent. Using horror to imply vastness, rather than show it, is both economical and powerful. A whisper in an abandoned lab. A distorted voice over a radio. A strange pattern of bruises that match a star constellation. With prompts like "Write a slow-burn sci-fi horror scene where the fear builds from a data anomaly," you can let ChatGPT help construct tension that doesn't require spectacle—just unease.

Another strength of *The X-Files* is its format. The series walked a tightrope between serialized mythology episodes and standalone "monster-of-the-week" stories. This kept the show fresh and flexible. It also gave the writers the freedom to experiment with tone and pacing. Some episodes were pure nightmare (*Home*), others pure satire (*Jose Chung's From Outer Space*). You can explore both approaches using AI. Ask: "Generate five standalone episode ideas for a sci-fi horror series," and then, "Create a myth-arc that connects these episodes with an overarching conspiracy." ChatGPT will help you keep the series cohesive even as the tone shifts.

And when you want to dive deep into a character's emotional landscape, *The X-Files* gives you that model too. Scully's cancer, Mulder's search for his sister—these weren't side plots. They were personal threads woven into the show's

DNA. These arcs made the horror personal. The monsters weren't just "out there"—they were inside us, inside the systems we trust, inside the very stories we tell ourselves about what's real. You can take that emotional layering and use ChatGPT to make it your own. Try: "Outline a character arc where belief becomes obsession," or "Describe a sci-fi horror story where a character's greatest fear becomes their only clue."

And of course, no discussion of *The X-Files* would be complete without touching on tone. The lighting, the pacing, the sound design—all of it whispered danger before a word was spoken. You may not be designing a set, but you can write with visual and audio direction in mind. Ask ChatGPT: "Write a suspenseful scene in a hospital corridor using only natural sound," or "Describe the mood and tone of an abandoned research facility at midnight." These cues will guide your storytelling to feel cinematic, even on the page.

At its heart, *The X-Files* reminded us that what's frightening isn't just that we're not alone—but that the truth might be worse than we imagined. That the systems we trust might be part of the problem. That science, when pushed into darkness, becomes something monstrous. That kind of storytelling lingers because it blends wonder with fear, knowledge with dread.

So don't be afraid to go dark. Let ChatGPT help you explore the edge where sci-fi and horror meet. Use AI to test hypotheses—"What if this medical breakthrough turned into a curse?" "What if government surveillance uncovered something cosmic?" Let the tension simmer. Let the shadows crawl. Let your audience squint into the corners of your imagination—and flinch at what they find.

Because if *The X-Files* taught us anything, it's this: science fiction gets under your skin best when it also chills your bones.

How to Write an Alien Race That Doesn't Feel Like Earth 2.0

One of the great challenges in writing science fiction is avoiding the temptation to create alien races that are just slightly reskinned versions of human cultures. It's easy to imagine aliens who speak a different language or wear different armor, but whose values, social structures, and emotional responses are essentially human. And while there's a long tradition of this approach—especially in older sci-fi television—it rarely leaves a lasting impact unless it serves a purpose beyond costume and novelty. If your goal is to create a species that feels truly alien, something that pushes the boundaries of human imagination, then the solution is to start not with how they look, but how they *think*.

The reason many aliens feel like "Earth 2.0" is because we tend to start from ourselves. We extrapolate our politics, religions, economies, or biology, and tweak them. A warrior race with honor codes. A hive mind that functions like communism. A matriarchal society based on bees. These can work if you're making allegory or satire, but if you're aiming for true alienness—something that doesn't automatically slot into Earth frameworks—you need to rebuild from the ground up.

A great place to start is with sensory perception. Ask yourself: what does this race perceive that we don't? Do they see magnetic fields? Smell time passing? Hear thoughts? A species with different sensory input would naturally evolve different communication, values, and fears. Use ChatGPT to brainstorm: "Describe an alien race that communicates through shared hallucinations triggered by light patterns," or "Generate a species that perceives emotional auras as physical temperature changes." The more unfamiliar their baseline experience of the universe, the more alien their behavior becomes.

Then dig into cognition. How do they think? Do they dream? Do they have individual identities or operate as collective modules of a single being? Do they view cause and effect the same way humans do? What if they live backward in time, and consider death to be birth? These concepts aren't just window dressing—they shape story decisions. An alien race that doesn't fear death might not understand negotiation or threats. One that doesn't value truth might not lie, but manipulate in ways we don't expect. Ask ChatGPT: "Create a belief system for an alien race that views reality as an illusion generated by memory," or "Describe a political system where leadership is decided by artistic expression, not logic."

Another path toward uniqueness is to strip away human assumptions like binary thinking, individualism, or even ambition. Perhaps they don't distinguish between self and other. Or they evolve not through competition but through collaboration with environmental forces. Ask for ideas like: "Describe a civilization that believes architecture is a form of breeding," or "Design a society that views written language as an act of violence." These are radical departures from the norm, and they allow your alien race to feel alien without simply being "humans in latex masks."

Now consider communication. Not just language, but intention and interaction. What if they can't lie? Or they don't understand metaphor? Or they interpret time as circular and can't process linear conversation? Use prompts like: "Invent a form of alien poetry that's only understandable when heard backwards," or "Describe a ritual where information is shared only through nonverbal color changes." These elements can feed entire plotlines and create new challenges for human characters who encounter them.

You should also consider physiology—but not as a starting point. Too often, writers begin with how the alien looks: tentacles, three eyes, insect wings. But form should follow function. If your alien communicates through seismic pulses, their anatomy would reflect that. If they thrive in liquid methane, their musculature, motion, and metabolism must support it. Try ChatGPT prompts like: "Design an alien that lives in dense gas clouds and navigates using electric pulses," or "Describe a species evolved to survive inside a black hole event horizon." You don't need to get the science perfect—you just need to stay consistent and imaginative.

Culture is also key. Don't give your aliens human holidays and government structures unless you're using them satirically. Instead, invent traditions based on their environment, biology, and history. Ask: "What does a coming-of-age ceremony look like for a species with no fixed lifespan?" or "Describe a legal system for beings who share dreams and memories communally." When culture emerges from necessity and perception—not from imitation—it feels real.

You can make your aliens emotionally resonant without making them emotionally human. Their responses might not mirror ours, but they can still carry weight. An alien might express grief by leaving behind part of its body. Or joy might be experienced as a temporary loss of memory. Ask ChatGPT: "Write a scene where an alien mourns a companion using its species' traditional ritual," or "Describe a celebration that involves genetic transformation into a new life stage."

Examples of truly alien species in television are rare but illuminating. The Heptapods in *Arrival* don't just speak differently—they *think* in circles. The Ood in *Doctor Who* connect through a shared external brain, making emotional expression a literal external force. The Borg in *Star Trek* strip away individuality to become something post-human, not just robotic. These aren't just aliens—they are storytelling opportunities to reflect, contrast, or challenge human understanding.

You don't need to explain everything. In fact, it can be more powerful if some aspects remain mysterious. The unknowable can be compelling, especially when filtered through human curiosity, fear, or longing. A viewer may never fully grasp your alien race, and that's the point—it keeps them alien.

When using ChatGPT to help create these beings, focus your prompts on contradictions and paradoxes. "Design a race that fears silence but never speaks," or "Imagine an alien religion where the concept of God is forbidden." These creative sparks allow you to expand far beyond the familiar. You'll find your aliens begin to breathe, think, and live in your mind—not just as characters, but as cultures.

Because the goal isn't to make your aliens feel like metaphorical humans in funny hats. It's to build something new. Something strange. Something that surprises even *you* as the writer.

That's when you know you've created an alien race that doesn't feel like Earth 2.0.

That's when your story starts to feel like science fiction.

Choosing the Right Theme: Memory, Identity, Progress, Dystopia

One of the most important and most overlooked decisions when creating a science fiction TV series is choosing the right theme. It's easy to get excited about the worldbuilding, the alien creatures, the future tech, or the big action moments—but the heart of your story isn't any of those. It's what you're trying to say underneath it all. A strong theme gives your series direction. It shapes your character arcs, your plot points, your visual language, even your dialogue. Without it, your show might look good and move fast but feel hollow. That's why before you write your pilot, before you even name your characters, you need to decide: what's your story really *about*?

Science fiction gives you an almost unlimited playground for theme, but that doesn't mean every theme will work for every series. Some are better suited to epic space operas. Others work beautifully in near-future dramas or claustrophobic thrillers. The key is to choose a theme that not only excites you but grows with your characters and expands over a season or several. And in sci-fi, the most powerful themes often ask the biggest questions.

Let's start with *memory*. Sci-fi stories about memory dig into questions of truth, perception, and identity. Think *Black Mirror*'s "The Entire History of You" or the way *Westworld* built its whole philosophical engine on robotic memory loops. Memory can be manipulated, erased, backed up, stored, stolen, or even fabricated in science fiction. That allows you to build tension and mystery right into your story structure. If memory is unreliable, then what else is? Who are we without it? If you want to write a series around this theme, prompt ChatGPT with: "Generate a science fiction plot where characters discover their memories were implanted," or "Describe a futuristic city where memories are currency."

Then there's *identity*, closely related but subtly different. While memory asks what we remember, identity asks who we are—and whether that's fixed or fluid. Sci-fi lets you explore this through clones, AI, genetic engineering, mind transfer, alien shapeshifters, or alternate versions of the same person. *Orphan Black*, *Devs*, *Dollhouse*, and *The OA* all play with this beautifully. Identity can become a series-long arc or the foundation for an episode's twist. Ask ChatGPT: "Write a character profile for someone who discovers they're a backup copy of a more important person," or "Outline a sci-fi plot where the protagonist slowly becomes someone else—literally."

Progress is another major theme, often cast in an ambiguous light. Is progress good? Is it ever neutral? Sci-fi often explores what happens when we push too far, too fast—whether it's AI, biotech, quantum computing, or space colonization. In shows like *The Expanse* or *Foundation*, progress is civilization's double-edged sword. You can build stories around the tension between innovation and consequence. Try prompts like: "Describe a future society where progress is mandated by law," or "Write a scene where a scientist realizes their invention has doomed a planet."

Then there's the popular and ever-relevant theme of *dystopia*. Not just ruined cities and broken systems, but *why* the world broke. Dystopia in sci-fi is rarely just backdrop—it's commentary. Whether it's corporate control (*Continuum*), media overreach (*Black Mirror*), authoritarianism (*1984*, *The Handmaid's Tale*), or techno-dependence (*Years and Years*), the message is usually clear: the future isn't a different world—it's the logical result of present choices. Ask ChatGPT: "Design a dystopian world where AI replaces government," or "Create a story where happiness is legally enforced."

What's powerful is how these themes overlap. You can write about memory *and* identity in the same breath. You can explore the price of progress inside a dystopia. You can construct a character who fights for self-understanding in a society that constantly rewrites its past. ChatGPT is particularly strong at helping you combine ideas: "Generate a sci-fi plot that explores how digital memory affects social class," or "Outline a TV series where technological progress erases personal identity." By layering themes, your series gains richness and re-watchability.

Themes also give structure to your episodes. In a serialized show, you can let each episode examine a different angle of the central theme. If your theme is identity, one episode might feature a character questioning their gender in a world of body-swapping. Another might involve a court case about the legal rights of cloned individuals. You can even challenge your own theme. An early episode might suggest identity is fluid, while a later one argues that something essential always remains. ChatGPT can help structure this: "Give me ten episode ideas exploring different aspects of the theme of identity," or "Write a character arc about someone who resists but ultimately embraces change."

Theme also plays out visually and tonally. If you're working with a production team—or envisioning your show's aesthetics for pitch—you can align your camera work, lighting, and production design with your core message. A story about progress might be full of sleek surfaces and digital silence. A memory story could have visual glitches, flickering lights, or distorted reflections. You can prompt ChatGPT: "Describe a color palette and soundscape for a sci-fi show about lost memories," or "List visual metaphors to reinforce the theme of identity."

And don't forget the emotional payoff. A good theme isn't just intellectual—it hits the heart. We connect with sci-fi because it uses the impossible to talk about what's deeply human. Memory hurts. Identity changes. Progress isolates. Dystopia dehumanizes. Use your theme to guide the emotional stakes of every choice your characters make. Ask: "How does this theme affect what the character wants?" and "How can this theme break their heart?"

Ultimately, your series becomes more than just entertainment—it becomes a conversation. It starts asking viewers: Who are you without your memories? What makes you *you*? What would you sacrifice for progress? How much comfort would you trade for freedom?

And when your story resonates like that, people don't just watch it.

They remember it.

The Cold Open: Hooking Viewers in the First Two Minutes

If there's one moment in a science fiction TV series where the stakes are do or die—where your entire world, tone, and promise to the viewer must be captured in under two minutes—it's the cold open. The cold open is your secret weapon. It's the door into your universe, the match strike before the fire, the part that plays before the credits roll and tells the audience, "This is what kind of story you're in for." And if you do it right, they won't even think about turning away. In fact, they'll lean forward.

The cold open doesn't just exist to grab attention. It establishes a tone and genre signal. In science fiction, where worlds are often unfamiliar and filled with strange terminology, alien imagery, or non-linear events, the cold open is where you give the audience just enough clarity to intrigue them and just enough mystery to make them need answers. It's where you hook their brain, not just their eyes.

Think about the most iconic sci-fi series and how they begin. The *Lost* pilot opens not with exposition, but with a man's eye opening on an unknown island—and immediate chaos. The *Battlestar Galactica* miniseries opens with the silence of space and a dramatic act of betrayal. The *Westworld* pilot drops you into a desert with a seemingly sweet character who turns out to be a robot—and the lines between real and unreal begin to blur. All of these cold opens ask questions. All of them make promises. And none of them explain too much.

Your cold open should leave the viewer thinking: what is happening, who are these people, and what does this mean? But you don't need to answer those questions right away. In fact, if you do, you're probably not writing a cold open—you're writing a prologue. The cold open shouldn't be exposition-heavy or reliant on context. It should stand alone as a pulse of energy, intrigue, danger, or emotion. It needs to *feel* like the moment everything starts.

Working with ChatGPT makes cold opens easier to draft and redraft quickly. If you already have your plot structure and characters worked out, you can prompt it with: "Write a cold open for a science fiction TV series where the protagonist is unknowingly living in a simulation," or "Generate a scene where the future version of Earth is introduced through a rescue mission gone wrong." You can even ask for multiple takes with different tones: "Give me three variations of a cold open—one scary, one poetic, and one mysterious."

Another approach is to start at the story's climax—or at least near it—and use the cold open to foreshadow. Drop us into chaos. Let us see the consequences before we know the causes. Then rewind. This structure, made famous by shows like *Breaking Bad*, works especially well in sci-fi where the world's logic is unknown to the viewer. You might write a scene showing a character walking on a desolate planet holding a strange device. The device starts to glow. Suddenly, a city reappears. Smash to title. That's not a story. That's a *promise*.

The cold open can also be used to set the emotional tone. Instead of spectacle, you lead with character. Think of *The X-Files*, where we often meet a doomed guest star just before something impossible kills them. Or *Stranger Things*, where we see a glimpse of another world before the camera cuts back to children on bikes. These cold opens are like notes played before the melody begins. They warn you what's coming without revealing the whole score.

Even animation knows this rule. The pilot of *Rick and Morty* opens with a drunken grandfather dragging a confused teenager into a hijacked spaceship while slurring about ending humanity—and it's hilarious, absurd, and sets the stakes for the entire series. Tone is crucial. If you want high-concept comedy, let the first two minutes show us that.

When using ChatGPT to develop these sequences, focus your prompts on *what happens* and *what it feels like*. Try: "Write a suspenseful cold open where a cryogenic sleeper wakes too early in a starship filled with corpses," or "Create a mysterious cold open where an alien signal is discovered inside a human brain scan." You can then follow up with: "Make it more poetic," or "Shift the tone to feel like techno-thriller horror."

The cold open should end on a question or a beat of revelation. You want your viewer—or your reader, if you're pitching the script—to feel like the universe just opened beneath their feet. Don't be afraid to play with expectation. Maybe the spaceship lands safely—then we discover Earth is gone. Maybe the time traveler seems to save the day—until we realize they're the villain. Subvert. Tease. Disrupt. But don't overcomplicate. Simplicity creates suspense.

In practical terms, a cold open usually runs one to three script pages. That's enough for a single dramatic or shocking moment, not enough for full dialogue trees or layered exposition. Focus on images, movement, a clear action or tension, and one piece of powerful mystery. You want the viewer asking, "What does that mean?" and more importantly, "What happens next?"

And don't forget sound. Even if you're not writing the score, think about what we *hear*. The eerie signal on a radio. A mechanical breath in the shadows. The silence before a weapon fires. Ask ChatGPT to help with: "Describe the soundscape of a cold open where a space station begins to go dark," or "Write a scene where music and memory collide in a post-apocalyptic city."

Above all, remember this: the cold open isn't just the beginning of your story—it's your invitation. It's your opening handshake. Your mystery box. Your promise that something meaningful is waiting if we follow you deeper. If you do it right, the audience won't be watching passively.

They'll be chasing the story into the dark.

Writing the "Tech Reveal" Scene: Discovery and Awe

Every great science fiction series has that one moment—the first time a character, and the audience, lays eyes on a piece of technology that defines the world. It could be a ship rising out of the clouds, a machine that folds space, a weapon that shouldn't exist, or a device that challenges reality itself. This is the "tech reveal" scene. It's not just about showing the audience a gadget. It's about evoking awe, fear, wonder, or disbelief—using technology to shift the emotional current of the story. If you write this scene well, you don't just explain the world. You *elevate* it.

The best "tech reveal" scenes don't dump exposition. They *drip* it. And not through dialogue, but through the senses. What does it look like? How does it move? What sounds does it make? How does the environment change in its presence? What happens to time, light, or even gravity when it activates? All of these details matter more than what the characters say about the tech. You're not just introducing a thing. You're introducing a *power.*

Think of the first time the Millennium Falcon jumps to hyperspace in *Star Wars*, or the moment the transporter hums in *Star Trek*. No one needs to explain the mechanics. The visuals, sound, and reactions from the characters tell us everything. The effect on them is what teaches us how we should feel.

In your own sci-fi series, the "tech reveal" might come early, like in a cold open or first act, or it might be held back for a mid-season twist. Either way, you want to make it feel earned. There should be build-up—hints, fragments, partial blueprints, rumors, or failed attempts—so when the technology finally appears, it arrives with emotional weight. Ask ChatGPT: "Create a buildup sequence leading to the reveal of a time-altering device," or "Describe a scene where a character sees the rumored 'world engine' for the first time."

Tone is crucial here. What kind of tech is this—and what does it *mean* to your story? A reveal of a healing chamber in a post-apocalyptic world might bring tears. A reveal of a weapon that erases memories might be horrifying. A reveal of a spacecraft that runs on consciousness might be strange, even beautiful. Start from the emotional truth. Then write the visuals around that.

One effective technique is to show the character reacting *before* we see the tech. We watch their breath catch. Their footsteps slow. They go still. Maybe they whisper a name or laugh nervously. This creates anticipation. The audience leans in, wondering, *What could make someone react like that?* Then, when you show the tech, you're not just revealing a design—you're fulfilling an emotional promise. Use prompts like: "Write a character's emotional response to seeing a machine that can resurrect the dead," or "Describe a reveal where a portal to another dimension opens silently behind glass."

You should also make the environment part of the scene. Is the tech housed in a hidden lab? Hovering above a battlefield? Buried in ice? Suspended in a beam of light? Let the surroundings contrast or echo the tech itself. A sleek machine inside a cave. An ancient, rusting relic glowing in sterile white light. Ask ChatGPT to help: "Design a scene where alien technology is revealed under a collapsed temple," or "Describe a stealth tech demo taking place in a ruined city overtaken by nature."

And don't rush the moment. The pacing of the reveal matters. Slow it down. Give the audience space to absorb. Let the soundscape thicken. Add a heartbeat of silence. A pause before activation. A flicker before it comes to life. These are cinematic techniques that work just as well on the page. Ask: "Write a slow-motion tech reveal with increasing tension," or "Describe a silent reveal scene broken only by a sudden, terrifying sound."

Tech in science fiction is rarely just functional. It's metaphor. A time machine isn't just a vehicle—it's a symbol of regret, hope, or obsession. A robot isn't just a tool—it's a mirror for the soul. A neural link isn't just an interface—it's a question about privacy, intimacy, and identity. When you write your "tech reveal" scene, keep the deeper meaning in mind. What does this tech *represent*? What's at stake in its existence?

Use your dialogue sparingly and strategically. If a character explains the tech, it should come in pieces, and with emotion. Fear, awe, pride, or doubt. Try writing: "A scientist reveals a machine that can stop time, but hesitates to activate it," or "An AI describes itself in a way that unsettles the people watching it form." Let ChatGPT offer different emotional readings: "Rewrite this tech reveal with a tone of reverence," or "Now make it feel like a horror scene."

And remember: sometimes the most powerful reveals say nothing at all. A character places a hand on a console, and the stars rearrange outside the window. No words. No need. The story just turned.

The "tech reveal" scene is where you show your audience what's possible in this universe. It's where you say: This is not our world anymore.

It's something else.

Something larger.

And from this point forward, anything can happen.

Building Episode Outlines with ChatGPT's Help

There's a moment in every writer's journey where a single idea must be stretched into something bigger, something structured, something ready to be filmed. That's where episode outlining comes in. For science fiction TV, where the possibilities are infinite but the schedule is tight, building a solid episode outline is the bridge between inspiration and execution. And with ChatGPT as your creative partner, you don't have to do it alone. You can turn a premise into a fully shaped narrative arc in hours, not days.

Episode outlines are not just summaries of what happens. They are blueprints. They show you where the major beats land, what character is driving each scene, how exposition is handled, and how tension rises or resets. In science fiction, outlining is even more critical because your story world comes with rules—rules about time travel, alternate dimensions, artificial intelligence, or alien biology—that need to stay consistent. Outlines keep you on track while giving you the space to be imaginative.

When working with ChatGPT to create these outlines, it helps to start with clarity. What kind of episode are you building? Is this a "monster-of-the-week" standalone or part of a longer serialized arc? Is this episode introducing new technology, a new setting, or a shift in character dynamics? If you can answer that up front, your prompts to ChatGPT will be sharper and the results more useful.

Let's say your series is set on a colony planet, and you have an idea for an episode where a mining crew awakens an ancient alien machine. You might start with a prompt like: "Outline a 5-act episode for a sci-fi series where miners activate a buried alien device that alters time." ChatGPT will return a rough arc, usually hitting key beats like the discovery, the rising tension, the crisis, and the aftermath. From there, you can refine it. Ask it: "What's a good subplot involving the colony's doctor in this episode?" or "How can this episode deepen the conflict between the captain and the AI?"

ChatGPT is excellent at branching. Once you've got your main story spine, you can explore different versions: "Rewrite the outline with a darker tone," or "What if the machine didn't alter time, but swapped consciousness between crew members?" These variations don't just give you options—they often lead to better ideas than your original concept.

Another powerful trick is using ChatGPT to test pacing. Ask it to break the episode into scenes and estimate their emotional or narrative weight. You might realize your big reveal is too early, or your climax isn't earned. Try: "List 10 scenes for this episode and note the tension level of each." This helps you visualize flow and make necessary structural tweaks before you start scripting.

ChatGPT can also help fill in character moments. You can ask it: "In this episode outline, give me a moment of vulnerability for the protagonist," or "Suggest a moral dilemma that challenges the crew's loyalty." These prompts add layers to your outline and push your episodes beyond just plot machines into full storytelling experiences.

One of the most useful things you can do is build a template for your episodes using ChatGPT. For instance, you might decide every episode starts with a cold open, introduces a theme through dialogue or imagery, escalates through Acts II and III, has a tech or moral twist in Act IV, and ends with either resolution or a hook for the next episode. You can ask ChatGPT: "Create a repeatable episode structure for a serialized sci-fi drama with an ensemble cast." You'll get a formula that keeps your process fast and consistent—without making it feel formulaic.

Collaboration is key. You can treat ChatGPT like a writing room intern or even a co-writer. Let it pitch ideas: "Give me three episode concepts about first contact gone wrong," or "Suggest episodes that test the crew's morality in survival situations." Then take those concepts and begin outlining one at a time, each as a beat map you can expand scene by scene.

If you're planning an entire season arc, you can also prompt: "Design a 10-episode season outline where each episode explores a different aspect of artificial intelligence." Then, for each episode, you can zoom in: "Outline Episode 3 in detail—it's about an AI-controlled justice system." With this kind of workflow, you'll not only move faster—you'll build a more cohesive show.

Some writers worry that using AI to outline will make their stories feel synthetic. But it's the opposite. ChatGPT offers structure, momentum, and variety. You bring the soul. When you go back and read through a raw outline, you'll always have the chance to rewrite, reframe, or reimagine anything. But it's far easier to shape a rough idea into brilliance than to face a blank page alone.

And when you hit those creative roadblocks—those days when you just can't find the next plot beat—ChatGPT doesn't run out of steam. You can prompt endlessly, tweak directions, and try ideas you might never have considered. You're not stuck anymore. You're in motion.

So whether you're outlining a tense hour of sci-fi horror on a drifting spaceship, or a philosophical drama about uploaded consciousnesses facing extinction, ChatGPT can help you map every twist, build every beat, and keep every episode aligned with your vision.

Outlining no longer has to be a lonely, drawn-out battle with the blank screen. With the right prompts and a little intuition, it becomes a fast, flexible, and fun part of your creative flow.

And just like that, one idea becomes a season. A scene becomes a story. A rough sketch becomes a finished blueprint for the stars.

Using AI to Brainstorm "What If" Scenarios

At the heart of every great science fiction series is a single spark: the "what if?" It's the creative question that shifts reality just enough to open the doors of wonder. What if time could be bartered? What if dreams were regulated by law? What if a species evolved to survive in space without ships? These aren't just hypothetical questions—they're story starters. And with ChatGPT, you have an inexhaustible engine to generate, test, twist, and expand "what if" scenarios until you find one that ignites your imagination.

The beauty of science fiction is that it doesn't just ask what is—it asks what could be. The "what if" is a seed. Everything else—your characters, world, theme, and tone—grows from that seed. But too often, writers sit and try to come up with the perfect question in isolation. That's where AI becomes a trusted ally. It doesn't just offer one idea. It offers a flood of variations, angles, consequences, and contradictions, all built on your core concept.

Let's say you want to write a show about time travel. You can start with a prompt like: "Give me 10 'what if' questions about time travel that haven't been done to death." ChatGPT might return gems like: "What if time only flows backward for one person?" or "What if time travel works—but only while you're dreaming?" Suddenly, you're not staring into the void. You're reacting to possibility. The pressure to be original disappears, because now you're in dialogue with potential.

You can refine these further by tone or genre. Try: "Give me five dark 'what if' scenarios about AI taking over healthcare," or "Give me whimsical 'what if' ideas for a lighthearted sci-fi comedy set in space." The more specific your prompt, the more tailored the results. And don't stop at the first list. Ask for more. Ask for versions with philosophical undertones, or with teenage protagonists, or grounded in contemporary issues like climate collapse or surveillance capitalism. ChatGPT never runs out of combinations.

Sometimes you don't even need to feed it much. A simple prompt like, "What if Earth's moon disappeared overnight?" can lead to outlines of entire worlds—scientific consequences, global panic, religious awakenings, alien interference, mythic resurrection. You can follow up with, "What kind of government would emerge in the aftermath?" or "Who would the protagonist be in this scenario?" Within a few exchanges, you've gone from one question to a character, a setting, a tone, a theme.

What makes these sessions so creatively powerful is the loop. You don't just ask once—you build. Start with "What if humans discovered they were the last conscious species in the galaxy?" Then: "How would religion change?" "What would the antagonist believe?" "What small personal story could unfold inside this big idea?" ChatGPT responds not just with facts or summaries but with narrative suggestions—scenes, arcs, moral dilemmas, stylistic twists.

You can also use AI to test variations on ideas you've already got. Let's say you're working with, "What if the Earth was bought by a wealthy alien?" You can prompt: "Give me three emotional variations—one satirical, one tragic, one optimistic." Or: "Change this 'what if' so it involves a time loop," or "Make this idea about children instead of adults." You begin to explore the elasticity of your concept—and in doing so, you often find the best version of your story.

And here's a hidden power of AI brainstorming: it reflects your thinking. Every time you reword a prompt, ChatGPT's answer helps you hear how you're interpreting your own idea. That self-reflection is crucial. The more you work with these questions, the clearer your vision becomes. The AI is not just feeding you storylines. It's mirroring your imagination and helping you sculpt it with precision.

For sci-fi series, you can even generate "what if" questions to shape the entire season. Try: "Give me 10 'what if' ideas that could each become an episode in a series about a team of scientists exploring alien ruins." Or: "What are ten 'what if' questions that revolve around human augmentation and identity loss?" Each one could be the foundation of a character's arc, a twist in the season, or a mystery seeded in episode one.

If you're working with a writers' room or collaborators, you can feed their ideas into the AI as well. "My co-writer wants a story about a space cult. What are ten 'what if' questions involving space religions?" Suddenly, a vague idea becomes an engine of narrative energy. With ChatGPT, the brainstorming phase never has to stall—it becomes a fluid, collaborative, limitless environment.

The goal is not to choose the first good idea. The goal is to find the idea you *can't stop thinking about.* The one that keeps raising more questions. The one that has an emotional core. Because a great "what if" is not just strange or clever—it's personal. It says something about human nature, about longing, about fear, about hope. It's the kind of question that leads to a great character in a moment of crisis, faced with the impossible, deciding who they are.

So don't just ask "what if." Ask it again. Ask it from a different angle. Ask what happens after the answer. Ask what story lies inside the silence between the question and the outcome.

With ChatGPT, your "what if" isn't a wall you hit when you're stuck. It's a door you walk through.

And on the other side? Infinite story.

Grounding the Absurd: Making the Unreal Feel Believable

Science fiction is often about ideas that, on the surface, sound absurd. Teleportation pads. Cities floating in space. Brain chips that store memories as files. A species that lives in lava. None of these things exist—yet. But in the hands of the right writer, they *feel* real. They have weight, texture, emotional logic. You believe them while you're watching or reading, even if your rational brain says, "No way." That's the power of grounding the absurd, and it's what separates forgettable sci-fi from the kind of story that changes how we see the world.

Believability in science fiction isn't about facts—it's about consistency, context, and emotion. The audience doesn't need to know the quantum mechanics behind a wormhole. What they need is to feel what it means for the characters. Will they make it through alive? What do they leave behind? What does this moment *cost*? You can have the wildest idea imaginable, but if the stakes are human and the world obeys its own internal rules, the audience will come with you.

ChatGPT is particularly helpful when it comes to grounding the unreal. It can help you build the scaffolding that makes your idea make sense—social structures, economic consequences, emotional responses, historical backstory. You might prompt it with something wild, like "a society where dreams are taxed," and then ask: "What would the economy look like in a world where dreams are monitored by the state?" or "How would a teenager rebel in this system?" You go from abstract weirdness to real, relatable storytelling.

The key to grounding is *anchoring* the strange to something the audience already understands. Let's say you're writing an episode about a character who clones herself to attend multiple meetings at once. That's absurd—but if you frame it around workplace burnout, ambition, and identity loss, it becomes eerily plausible. You can prompt ChatGPT with: "Write a scene where a character realizes her clone is better at being her than she is." The sci-fi conceit becomes a metaphor for something deeply real.

Worldbuilding is another area where AI can help solidify your absurd ideas. You can ask it: "How might society react to a new law requiring every citizen to wear emotion-dampening implants?" It will give you politics, public protests, underground movements. Suddenly, your premise isn't just a gimmick—it's a living, breathing ecosystem of cause and effect.

One trick is to never introduce the absurd as if it's absurd. Write it as if it's normal in this world—and then show us the consequences. In *Black Mirror*, the technology is never explained in detail, but it's integrated into everyday life so thoroughly that it feels real. A rating system based on social approval? It sounds ridiculous until you realize how close it already is to how we use social media. Ask ChatGPT to generate scenes of mundane life in a strange world: "Describe a breakfast scene in a world where people communicate telepathically," or "Write a school lesson from a future where history is rewritten every decade."

Characters are also your anchor. No matter how weird the world gets, if the characters act in ways we recognize—fear, envy, longing, denial—we'll believe them. You can ground an alien invasion by focusing on a father trying to protect his child. You can ground a sentient city by showing a lonely janitor talking to its walls. You can use prompts like: "Write a dialogue between a human and a sentient toaster who just wants to be left alone," or "Create a character who loves a glitchy robot even though it's being decommissioned." The absurd becomes poignant when it touches something raw and universal.

Pacing matters too. If you introduce three big absurd ideas in the first five minutes of a pilot, the audience might check out. But if you ease them in, show one strange thing in a familiar setting, and let it ripple, they'll stay engaged. ChatGPT can help you pace those reveals: "Break this idea into five scenes, gradually introducing the sci-fi element," or "Start with a normal family dinner, then reveal they're all androids." The strangeness becomes a twist, not a barrier.

Visual cues can also help make the unreal feel real. Describe textures, sounds, lighting. A floating city isn't just cool—it has rust, bird nests in its corners, a low hum from gravity engines. Use AI to add sensory depth: "Describe a futuristic greenhouse growing alien fruit in low gravity," or "Create the ambient sounds of a memory marketplace." These details build immersion, which is how belief is sustained.

And don't be afraid to *challenge* the absurd from within the story. Have a character question it. Push against it. Let the audience hear the doubts they themselves are thinking. That doesn't break the illusion—it strengthens it. It tells them, "Yes, this is strange. But it's being taken seriously." You can prompt ChatGPT with: "Write a scene where a skeptical character debates the ethics of uploading human consciousness to a cloud," or "Create a subplot where one character tries to prove the tech is fake." Internal skepticism adds credibility.

The absurd also becomes believable when it has *limits*. If your characters can do anything with futuristic tech, there's no tension. But if the teleportation device can only be used once a day—or if it breaks during storms—the absurd gains rules, and rules are what make fiction feel real. Ask ChatGPT: "What are five interesting limitations to a machine that lets people visit their own memories?" You'll get constraints that drive conflict and story.

Grounding the absurd is about treating the impossible as inevitable. It's about writing as if this world already exists and asking how people would really live in it—struggle in it, dream in it, die in it. Sci-fi isn't just about what's strange. It's about what's *familiar in the strange*. The more alien your concept, the more human your story must be.

And with ChatGPT by your side, you never have to walk the edge of the absurd alone. You can always ask: "What would make this feel real?" And together, you'll find the emotional truth inside the impossible idea.

Because in the end, that's what science fiction is really about—not the question, "Could this happen?" but the deeper question: "What would it *feel* like if it did?"

Creating Compelling Season Finales with Emotional Payoff

A season finale is more than the last episode in a run—it's a promise fulfilled. It's where your audience expects answers, surprises, maybe a few emotional gut punches, and above all, the sense that everything they've invested in—the characters, the themes, the world—has mattered. For a science fiction series, the finale also carries the added weight of scale. Big ideas must climax. Story threads must weave together. And whatever mystery or awe you've been building toward, this is the moment it must hit like a revelation.

Writing a great season finale requires two things in balance: narrative resolution and emotional payoff. You're not just tying up loose ends. You're closing arcs that matter to people. The finale is not about spectacle alone, though spectacle can help. It's about showing the result of choices made, truths revealed, or sacrifices rendered over the course of the season. And with ChatGPT, you can rehearse those payoffs again and again until the emotional beats hit just right.

The best place to start when crafting a finale is to go back to the beginning. Look at the pilot. What was promised? What questions were raised? What internal and external conflicts were established? Ask ChatGPT: "Summarize the main arcs from Episodes 1 to 9 of a sci-fi show where humanity discovers it was genetically engineered by an alien species." Then follow up: "Propose three possible season finales that pay off those arcs with emotional closure and a twist." In minutes, you have structure and options.

Great finales often echo early moments in the season—visually, thematically, or through character dialogue. This creates resonance, the sense that we've come full circle. You might return to a setting from the pilot or have a character repeat a line—but now with changed meaning. Prompt ChatGPT with: "Suggest callbacks in the finale to moments from Episode 1 that reveal how far the characters have come." These touches are small, but they make your ending feel earned.

Emotion should be the engine of your finale—not just the wrapping paper. Even in a show full of aliens, technology, or future cities, what we remember most is how it made us feel. So ask yourself, what emotions do you want to leave the audience with? Hope? Tragedy? Catharsis? Ask ChatGPT: "How can a finale create emotional closure in a sci-fi story where the protagonist sacrifices their body to become a digital consciousness?" The AI can help you find the emotional core inside the high-concept plot.

Character arcs are central to the emotional payoff. The protagonist should face a decision that forces them to either complete or resist the journey they've been on. The antagonist may be defeated—but the real climax is often internal. Has the hero grown? Have they paid a price? Have they changed the world—or been changed by it? You can prompt ChatGPT with: "Give me five character-based endings for a protagonist who started as a rogue AI and learned compassion through a human child." Each ending shows a different emotional truth.

A common temptation in science fiction is to end with a huge reveal—a new alien threat, a twist of identity, a fresh paradox. But without emotional stakes, twists feel hollow. The best finales twist the knife and the heart. Consider asking: "What's a final plot twist that recontextualizes the season *and* delivers an emotional shock?" ChatGPT might suggest, for example, that the mentor figure was from the future all along, trying to ensure the protagonist's transformation at great personal cost.

Pacing the finale also matters. You don't want an episode that's all climax and no breath. Audiences need reflection, tension, release, then escalation again. Ask ChatGPT to help shape the structure: "Outline a five-act finale for a sci-fi series with both action and quiet emotional scenes." You'll get a breakdown that leaves room for awe and intimacy, big moments and small, catharsis and cliffhanger.

If your series has multiple characters, make sure their journeys also peak or pivot. Not every arc needs to close, but something must shift. You can use prompts like: "Describe a scene where the ensemble reflects on their shared journey before one character is lost," or "Create a final confrontation between two characters who have grown to love each other, but are on opposite sides." These emotionally complex scenes add weight and texture that lasts beyond the credits.

One of ChatGPT's most useful tools in building a finale is simulating audience response. You can ask: "What questions would a viewer want answered in a season finale after watching these episodes?" or "What unresolved emotional threads might leave the audience unsatisfied if ignored?" It's like test-screening your outline with a synthetic viewer, identifying where your story may fall short before you write the script.

It's also worth considering your next season—especially if you want to end on a hook. ChatGPT can help generate ideas that serve both the current resolution and the next phase of your show. "Propose a season-ending twist that feels satisfying but opens the door to a radically different second season." These setups can tease a genre shift, reveal a hidden antagonist, or hint at a new world just beyond the veil.

A great season finale in sci-fi television is like a planetary alignment—rare, spectacular, and gravitational. It must draw together every orbiting storyline and pull them toward one final moment of meaning. Whether it ends in a bang, a whisper, a betrayal, or a transcendent image of hope, it should leave the audience changed—just like the characters.

And when you write it with ChatGPT, you get more than structural help. You get perspective, rewrites, variations, dialogue, emotional scenes, and thematic suggestions. You get a co-writer who helps you find not just the ending of the season—but the *heart* of the story.

Because when your finale lands with emotion, it doesn't just end a chapter.

It makes people *want* the next one.

How to Write Serialized Twists Without Losing the Viewer

Writing a science fiction TV series that relies on serialized storytelling is like planting a long fuse—you want it to burn slowly but brilliantly, with enough sparks along the way to keep your audience watching. But the tricky part is this: if your story keeps twisting and twisting, changing shape every few episodes, viewers can get confused, frustrated, or worse—bored. The thrill of the twist is powerful, but only if it feels like part of a larger whole. Too many, and the emotional investment gets scattered. Too few, and people lose interest. So how do you write serialized twists that surprise without overwhelming? And how can ChatGPT help?

The key is to remember that a twist must feel inevitable in hindsight, not random. A great twist doesn't just reframe what came before—it deepens it. You want your audience to say, "I didn't see that coming," and then immediately, "But of course." That means the groundwork must already exist. When using AI to develop serialized twists, you can prompt: "Give me five unexpected plot twists that build naturally from a storyline about a rogue AI trying to hide in human society." ChatGPT will often return surprises that still connect to your theme and logic, offering smart options you may not have considered.

When writing your show's arc, begin by deciding where your main character or mystery is headed. If the twist is going to shift alliances or reframe reality, it must be earned. A sudden change in tone or motivation will break trust unless there were breadcrumbs laid earlier. You can use prompts like: "Suggest early foreshadowing scenes for a twist where the main villain turns out to be the protagonist's future self." Let ChatGPT help you reverse-engineer your setup with precision and subtlety.

One trick is to vary the *type* of twist. Not every surprise should be about who dies or who betrays whom. Some twists reveal hidden motivations. Others recontextualize worldbuilding—like discovering that a long war was orchestrated by an outside species. Others still are emotional, like a character realizing they've been the monster all along. Prompt your AI to help diversify: "Give me five twist types for a serialized sci-fi series, ranging from emotional to conceptual." This variety keeps your series from becoming predictable, even in its surprises.

Pacing matters enormously in serialized sci-fi. If you drop a massive twist every episode, you burn out the audience. You want tension to build slowly, with small reveals that raise new questions and deepen old ones. Think of how *Westworld* wove timelines like strands of DNA, or how *Battlestar Galactica* dropped clues about the Final Five across seasons. Use ChatGPT to help pace: "Create a ten-episode outline with three major twists spread out across the season." That helps you see where to hold back and when to release.

Another helpful tool is to test your twists from the audience's point of view. You can ask ChatGPT: "If I reveal that the alien war was a simulation in Episode 9, what emotional payoff and confusion might viewers feel?" Then follow up with: "What earlier scenes would need to be rewritten to make this twist land better?" AI doesn't just generate story—it simulates reader response. It gives you a sort of narrative mirror, allowing you to test resonance before filming begins.

Strong twists also work when they shift emotional stakes. A plot twist that changes what the protagonist *wants* can be even more compelling than one that changes what they know. Imagine your hero's goal was to reach a hidden planet that held the key to human survival—only to discover that reaching it would wipe out another innocent species. That's not just a new piece of information—it's a transformation in purpose. You can build this with prompts like: "Create a plot twist that forces the protagonist to question their mission."

Continuity is vital in serialized storytelling. Even with shocking developments, your characters must remain consistent. Their decisions and reactions to the twist need to be emotionally authentic. One way ChatGPT can help is by mapping out character logic: "If this character finds out in Episode 7 that their memories are fake, how would that affect their actions in Episode 8?" That lets you preserve internal cohesion while embracing narrative surprise.

Don't forget the audience's memory. It's easy to lose viewers if they don't remember details that your twist relies on. You can solve this in the writing by seeding quiet reminders—reusing symbols, names, or visual callbacks. Ask ChatGPT: "How can I remind viewers of a plot detail introduced in Episode 2 without making it obvious?" You'll often receive techniques like having a character revisit an old object, replay an earlier conversation, or pass by a location tied to the mystery. These quiet echoes keep your twists grounded.

And twists should lead *somewhere.* They're not just fireworks. Each one should either answer a question or raise a better one. If your story's biggest moments only confuse, then they're noise, not music. Ask ChatGPT to help find cause and effect: "What questions should a viewer ask after this twist, and how can they be teased in future episodes?" This kind of narrative scaffolding turns your twist from a trapdoor into a bridge.

Finally, don't be afraid to rework or test multiple versions. One of the greatest powers of ChatGPT is iteration. You can say: "Rewrite this twist so it's more emotional," or "Make the twist land earlier but still keep tension high." It's like having a team of story editors on standby.

Serialized twists work best when they surprise the audience and the characters—*but not the logic of the world.* When your story remains emotionally honest, your audience will follow you through the strangest revelations. Twists are about trust, and trust comes from structure.

And when you use ChatGPT, you never have to guess whether your twist will land.

You can build it, test it, tweak it, and let it bloom—one carefully planted surprise at a time.

Crafting the Voice of Your Series: Tone, Style, Mood

Every great science fiction series has a voice. You hear it in the rhythms of its dialogue, you see it in the way light falls across its world, and you feel it in the emotional current running beneath every scene. This voice—made up of tone, style, and mood—isn't just a matter of genre. It's how your audience knows what kind of story they're in. It's how they know whether to brace for horror, wonder, laughter, or tragedy. And if you're using ChatGPT to write your series, crafting and maintaining a consistent voice becomes even more crucial—because AI will follow your lead, but it needs you to set the tone.

Tone is the emotional attitude of your story. Is your series hopeful or bleak? Cynical or sincere? Think of *Doctor Who*, which maintains a whimsical, often hopeful tone even in its darkest moments. Compare that to *Black Mirror*, where the tone is relentlessly skeptical, cold, and morally ambiguous. Then there's *The X-Files*, which balances eerie dread with a dry, often sarcastic tone in its dialogue. The tone sets expectations—and breaking it suddenly can shake your viewer's trust.

To define your tone, start by asking ChatGPT: "Give me five sample scenes in a sci-fi show with a hopeful tone." Or try the opposite: "Write a confrontation between a human and alien diplomat in a dystopian tone." By comparing the results, you begin to understand how tone shifts the emotional framing of a story. You're not just choosing what happens—you're choosing how it feels to witness it.

Style, on the other hand, is how the story is told. It's in the language you use, the pacing of your scenes, the level of detail. Some sci-fi leans into hard, technical precision—long discussions about physics, tech specs, and protocols. Others thrive in poetic metaphor, lyrical monologues, or mythic allusion. *Star Trek* often uses formal, idealistic dialogue, while something like *Firefly* leans into a gritty, casual, Western-inspired tone with characters talking in idiomatic bursts.

Style also includes structure. Do you tell your story linearly, with clean acts and arcs? Or do you fragment the narrative across timelines and perspectives like *Westworld*? Ask ChatGPT: "Write a scene in a poetic narrative style, set on a dying spaceship." Then try: "Now rewrite the same scene in a terse, noir-inspired style." This contrast helps you decide what fits the identity of your series—and what feels forced.

Mood is the emotional atmosphere that colors everything. It's a blend of worldbuilding and sensory language—what your world looks, sounds, and feels like. A neon-lit megacity with rain-slicked streets gives off a very different mood than a dust-blown Martian colony under endless sun. Mood is what lets a viewer feel immersed. With ChatGPT, you can generate evocative scenes: "Describe a control room at midnight, just before a solar flare hits," or "Write the mood of a funeral for a cloned soldier." These prompts create not just content—but atmosphere.

Here's where things get interesting: tone, style, and mood must work together. If your tone is light but your style is overly clinical, you create dissonance. If your mood is melancholy but your characters banter like they're in a sitcom, the emotional integrity suffers. Your series needs to know what kind of story it's telling at every level. Consistency is key—even if that consistency is in its willingness to shift.

The best shows shift tone intentionally while keeping the voice intact. *Doctor Who* can veer from horror to comedy within minutes, but it always centers on emotional sincerity and imaginative optimism. *The Expanse* holds a tight, political tone but occasionally breaks it to show deeply personal emotion. Ask ChatGPT: "Write a dialogue scene between two characters in a sci-fi series with a serious tone that slips into dark humor." Or: "Create a scene with a whimsical tone that ends in dread." These tonal blends can become the signature of your show.

Another important factor is *the narrator's point of view*. Even if your series isn't narrated explicitly, it has a perspective. Are you cynical about technology or in awe of it? Does the universe seem fair, cruel, indifferent, or full of meaning? These philosophical undercurrents shape your tone and mood across seasons. You can explore this by prompting ChatGPT: "Create a series bible entry describing the tone and worldview of a show where Earth is secretly run by benevolent machines." Just defining your narrative lens gives you a stronger, more consistent voice.

Your characters' voices must also align with the overall tone. If you have one character who talks like a Shakespearean king while everyone else uses modern slang, you either need to justify it or fix the inconsistency. You can give ChatGPT style samples: "Write dialogue for a sarcastic AI in a dry, noir-inspired tone," or "Give me three variations of the same speech in hopeful, tragic, and comic tones." You'll start to hear how each voice changes the experience of your story.

And here's where ChatGPT really shines: helping you maintain voice across multiple episodes. If you prompt it with your chosen tone, style, and mood in each scene request, you'll get scenes that *feel* like they're all part of the same world. This is invaluable when you're producing content quickly or collaborating with others. You can even input custom instructions like: "Maintain a dry, cynical tone with poetic description and a melancholic mood for all outputs." Suddenly, your AI assistant is matching the emotional fingerprint of your series episode after episode.

The voice of your series is its soul. It's what makes it uniquely *yours*—not just a blend of sci-fi tropes and twists, but something with presence, resonance, and identity. Whether you're aiming for solemn dystopia or whimsical hope, your tone, style, and mood must align like the instruments of an orchestra. And once you find that voice, the audience will recognize it instantly.

With ChatGPT as your creative partner, you don't have to find that voice alone.

You can experiment, explore, and refine—until every line, scene, and episode sounds like it came from a universe only you could have imagined.

Symbolic Visuals in Sci-Fi: Light, Color, and Composition

Science fiction doesn't just tell stories—it *shows* them. In this genre, the visuals aren't just there for spectacle. They're language. They convey mood, meaning, and metaphor. A blinking red light in a sterile corridor can evoke dread before a single word is spoken. A greenish tint across a digital landscape might signal artificiality, control, or rebirth. Shadows falling across a cyborg's face can suggest an identity split between machine and man. In science fiction television, light, color, and composition aren't just aesthetic tools—they're symbolic ones. And when you work with ChatGPT to craft your scripts, scene directions, and even cinematography notes, you can begin thinking visually from the very first word.

The future is often imagined in metal, glass, and plasma glow, but that doesn't mean your show must default to blue steel and neon pink. Symbolic visuals should be tied to the story you're telling. A utopia may be washed in soft whites and golds to suggest purity or blindness. A dystopia might use overexposure to evoke the erasure of truth. You can use ChatGPT to test different palettes: "Describe a spaceship interior using colors that suggest oppression and secrecy," or "What color scheme would match a world recovering from ecological collapse?" Suddenly, you're designing story with vision, not just plot.

Light is one of the most emotionally charged tools in visual storytelling. Harsh, top-down lighting can make a character seem exposed or judged. A flickering light in a lab hints at malfunction, decay, or uncertainty. Darkness itself can symbolize the unknown, while a beam of light breaking through might suggest hope, clarity, or divine knowledge. When working on your script, prompt ChatGPT with: "Describe the lighting in a scene where a character discovers a forbidden truth inside an alien archive." You'll see how light direction, quality, and contrast change the mood before a single line of dialogue.

Color carries deep cultural and psychological meaning. Red often signals danger, but in other contexts, it's power, passion, or revolution. Green can imply toxicity, alien life, or even healing. Blue might mean tranquility, logic, or technological dominance. The key is to use these associations consistently, so your audience begins to feel them even before they consciously register them. Ask ChatGPT to help build a visual code: "In this series, red symbolizes rebellion. Suggest five scenes where red could subtly appear to foreshadow an uprising." That kind of long-game storytelling makes your show more cohesive and emotionally intelligent.

Then there's composition—how you frame the elements of a shot. A character centered in a wide, symmetrical shot might suggest control or power. One pushed to the edge might feel isolated, unstable, or watched. High angles diminish, low angles empower. Ask ChatGPT: "Write a scene direction for a confrontation where the antagonist slowly rises in frame as they gain control." The AI can help you choreograph the power dynamics of a scene through nothing but camera placement and framing.

Symbols live in repetition. A spiral symbol that appears on a soldier's tattoo, then later as an alien energy signature, and again as the shape of a collapsing star—these visual echoes tell the audience something is deeply connected. ChatGPT can track those symbols with you: "Suggest visual motifs for a sci-fi series about time loops," or "What recurring shapes could be used to show a character is unknowingly being manipulated by a higher force?" You're not just building story, you're building semiotics.

Great sci-fi shows like *Westworld*, *The Expanse*, and *Battlestar Galactica* know how to use visual language for thematic weight. In *Westworld*, golden tones and soft backlighting were used for the past, sterile whites for the AI-controlled future. In *The Expanse*, different color palettes were assigned to Earth (warm and grounded), Mars (harsh and red), and the Belt (gritty, blue-gray and dim), giving each society an emotional and philosophical fingerprint. That's not just good design—that's thematic composition.

When collaborating with ChatGPT, you can train it to think in these terms. Set a visual style guide early: "For this series, blue light represents AI presence. Any time a character is being watched by the system, a faint blue glow appears." Now, when you ask for scene suggestions or directions, you can include this style: "Write a scene where the protagonist argues with a superior, unaware that the system is watching—include visual cues per our blue-light rule." The AI will integrate your symbolic choices into its responses.

Even transitions between scenes can carry symbolism. A cut from the blinking light of a dying star to the eyes of a newborn child suggests cyclical rebirth. A scene where the camera pans from a sterile moon base to a decaying Earth can convey moral contrast without dialogue. You can prompt ChatGPT to build bridges: "Suggest three visual transitions between a futuristic lab scene and a natural forest that imply conflict between technology and nature."

Sci-fi gives you permission to use visuals more boldly than any other genre. The audience expects unfamiliar things. You can show a glowing orb floating over a desert and have it mean resurrection, surveillance, or an alien God, depending on how you set the mood. But clarity still matters. Symbolism works best when it's felt *before* it's explained. That means trusting your visual cues and layering them in from the very start.

You don't need a special effects team to begin this process. You just need intent—and a creative assistant who can help you brainstorm, organize, and express your vision. ChatGPT won't light your set or color-grade your final cut, but it can help you write your visual symbolism into every page of your script. It can suggest lighting shifts, symbolic props, recurring colors, and thematic framing devices. You can even test: "Describe a moment of spiritual awakening using only visual elements," and let the result guide a silent but powerful scene.

Because science fiction isn't just about what's said.

It's about what's *seen*—and how those images make us feel, remember, and dream.

How to Use ChatGPT to Reimagine Classic Sci-Fi Tropes

Science fiction thrives on invention—but it also survives on repetition. From alien invasions to rogue AIs, from dystopian futures to time travel gone wrong, many of the stories we tell in sci-fi echo the ones that came before. These familiar frameworks—tropes—are not weaknesses. They're the bones of the genre. What matters is how we *use* them. And now, with tools like ChatGPT, we can take these well-worn devices and breathe startling new life into them. When used intentionally, AI becomes a creative partner that helps you spin the expected into the unforgettable.

Tropes are powerful because they offer immediate recognition. A character wakes in a cryogenic pod, and we know we're about to see what went wrong with the mission. A blinking red button under glass suggests forbidden knowledge or irreversible action. The trope doesn't limit us—it lets us build quickly. But the risk is cliché. The trick is to take something familiar and subvert it just enough to make it feel new.

ChatGPT is ideal for this kind of twist-based brainstorming. Suppose you're working with the classic "first contact" story. You could start with a simple prompt like: *"Give me ten unique twists on a first contact story."* The AI might suggest that the aliens arrive bearing knowledge of Earth's forgotten past, or that the aliens are future versions of ourselves returning to prevent a catastrophe. One of the suggestions might catch fire in your imagination, and suddenly you're off writing a pilot unlike any other.

A great approach is to start with a trope you want to use—say, "robots overthrow their human creators"—and ask ChatGPT to make it strange: *"What are ten unexpected variations of a robot uprising story that emphasize emotion, irony, or spiritual themes?"* You might get back: robots who rebel not to rule, but to protect humans from themselves. Or robots who believe they must suffer in order to become real. The AI is especially good at turning old ideas on their head because it knows how they've been used before.

If you're writing episodic sci-fi, you can use ChatGPT to turn tropes into full episode concepts. Try: *"Create five episode ideas that revolve around the 'time loop' trope but in settings that aren't usually used for time travel."* Instead of scientists in labs, maybe you get a street-level story about a thief caught reliving one botched heist. Or a farmhand who realizes the seasons are repeating unnaturally. Sci-fi becomes immediate and personal when you take a large trope and center it on characters who rarely get the spotlight.

The key is specificity. Don't just ask the AI to be original—ask it to ground its inventions in character and theme. For instance: *"Reimagine the alien invasion trope as a metaphor for grief, using two main characters and a small town setting."* You'll likely get a response that includes intimate stakes alongside genre spectacle. The aliens may never even appear onscreen. Maybe they're the hallucinations of a father who lost his child, and the town is being "invaded" by his unraveling perception. Now you're not just repeating a trope—you're *transforming* it.

ChatGPT can also help by remixing multiple tropes into something new. Combine time travel with post-apocalyptic survival. Combine first contact with courtroom drama. Combine rogue AI with coming-of-age romance. Prompt the AI: *"What are five mashups of classic sci-fi tropes that have rarely been combined?"* Then follow up with: *"Give me a plot summary of one of those combinations, with a strong protagonist and a twist ending."* You're using AI not to replace your creativity, but to extend the reach of your brainstorming.

When using tropes, character is everything. Ask yourself, "Who is usually at the center of this trope?" and then switch it. If the chosen one is always a teenage boy, make it a grandmother with a criminal record. If the AI overlord is always malevolent, make it genuinely caring—but tragically misunderstood. Prompt ChatGPT: *"Write a short scene in which a helpful AI is mistaken for a threat because of its inability to express emotion correctly."* Now your audience is questioning their assumptions—and that's the real power of reimagined tropes.

It's also helpful to explore *why* certain tropes exist. Many sci-fi stories are built around fears: fear of technology, fear of otherness, fear of losing control. When you recognize the emotional core of a trope, you can begin to redirect it. Ask ChatGPT: *"What fear does the 'mad scientist' trope reflect? How could I subvert this trope to show scientific obsession as a path to compassion instead of destruction?"* The AI will help you unpack the subtext, and from there you can reconstruct the meaning.

One fun exercise is to *deliberately write the worst version of a trope*, then improve it. Tell ChatGPT: *"Write a generic sci-fi story about a space crew encountering an alien with a hidden agenda."* Then say: *"Now rewrite this story by changing the setting, the alien's motivation, and the tone."* This side-by-side comparison often sparks original thinking, because you see clearly what makes something stale—and how to revive it.

Also, pay attention to genre-blending. If you pair your sci-fi concept with a strong genre voice—noir, comedy, fantasy, or even documentary—you'll naturally rework the tropes. *The X-Files* took standard horror plots and reframed them through a procedural mystery lens. *Stranger Things* gave classic alien/paranormal tropes a nostalgic, Amblin-style family feel. With ChatGPT, prompt: *"Retell the 'chosen one' sci-fi story as if it were a political thriller."* You'll be amazed by how much one genre's tone changes another's tropes.

Ultimately, tropes aren't something to avoid. They're tools—shared ideas we all understand, which means they're the perfect foundations to build on, twist, or even lovingly parody. With ChatGPT at your side, you have access to a digital collaborator who knows every variation of every trope and can instantly reframe them from any angle you like. It's like having a writers' room full of encyclopaedic imaginations.

So go ahead—start with the known.

Then let your imagination—and your AI co-writer—take it to a place no viewer has ever seen.

The Power of ChatGPT in Rewriting and Polishing Scenes

When writing a science fiction TV series, your first draft is a map, not the territory. It charts where you want to go, gives you direction, and maybe even sketches the beauty of the destination. But it's through rewriting and polishing that your series becomes real—rich in tone, clear in character, full of breath and rhythm. This is where many writers feel overwhelmed. Polishing means making decisions. It means trimming your darlings, clarifying messy moments, and deepening your meaning without overwriting your message. Here's the good news: ChatGPT can help you do all of this without ever losing your voice.

Think of ChatGPT not as a ghostwriter but as a revision partner who never gets tired, never takes feedback personally, and always remembers the last thing you said. Whether you need to smooth out dialogue, expand a scene's emotional impact, or tighten your pacing, this is where ChatGPT really shines. It's especially powerful when you give it clear instructions—not just "make this better," but "keep the tone sarcastic, shorten this monologue, and highlight the tension between the two characters." You remain the storyteller; ChatGPT becomes your intuitive editor.

Let's say you've written a dialogue scene between a human engineer and a malfunctioning AI. The core is there, but it feels flat. You want more edge, more vulnerability, and maybe a moment of unspoken dread. Ask ChatGPT: *"Rewrite this scene. Keep the same plot, but make the dialogue sharper, the pacing faster, and suggest a visual cue that shows the AI is hiding something."* In seconds, you have a version to compare. Not every line will be perfect, but you'll often find one phrase, one turn of tone, that lifts your entire draft. It's not about blindly replacing your words—it's about using the AI's version to rethink your own.

Sometimes you don't want to rewrite the whole thing—you just want options. Ask: *"Give me three variations of this character's reaction—one sarcastic, one terrified but hiding it, one blank and emotionless."* Now you're not guessing in the dark. You can weigh tonal options and choose what feels most aligned with your series' voice. In polishing, variety is your best tool, and ChatGPT can provide it instantly.

Rewriting with ChatGPT also allows you to focus on layers. Once your scene's action is solid, you might want to deepen the symbolism. Prompt: *"Can you rewrite this with light and color symbolism added subtly?"* Or: *"Include a recurring motif of mirrors throughout this scene."* Suddenly, your visuals gain literary depth, and your sci-fi world becomes more unified and expressive. These elements often emerge during rewrites, not first drafts—and ChatGPT excels at layering them in with care.

What about pacing? A slow scene might need compression. A rushed scene might need breathing room. You can instruct ChatGPT: *"Condense this four-page scene into two pages while preserving its key beats,"* or *"Expand this confrontation into a longer moment of silence, eye contact, and tension before the dialogue resumes."* The AI understands beat structure and cinematic flow, so its suggestions often feel like a screenwriter's natural rhythm—not just words, but movement.

Sometimes a scene works technically but doesn't land emotionally. That's a tough fix—until you ask ChatGPT for emotional calibration. Try: *"Rewrite this scene with more emotional vulnerability between the characters but keep the sci-fi terminology intact."* The result might add a line about how the character's fear of failure mirrors the AI's fear of being shut down. Suddenly, your scene goes deeper. Rewriting is where theme and emotion often rise to the surface.

It's also a chance to fix structural imbalance. Maybe you realize your protagonist is too passive in a critical moment. Instead of rewriting the entire episode, ask ChatGPT: *"Revise this scene so the protagonist takes initiative instead of reacting to others."* You can make targeted changes that shift the power dynamics, all while preserving continuity. You're not reinventing the wheel—you're truing it.

The polishing stage is also when your dialogue sharpens. Use the AI to give your characters unique voices: *"Rewrite this line in the voice of a cynical ex-soldier who's seen too much,"* or *"Make this response more academic, like a scientist avoiding emotional commitment."* Now your cast begins to sound distinct. ChatGPT can even help you track those patterns: *"Summarize how this character's speech patterns differ from others."*

One of the most underappreciated tools is asking ChatGPT *what's missing*. Sometimes you've written a solid scene, but it lacks punch. Prompt: *"What's missing from this scene emotionally or visually?"* The AI might notice there's no visual callback to a key motif, or that the tension builds but never peaks. This feedback loop helps you strengthen your instincts as a writer.

And then there's polish at the sentence level. Clarity. Rhythm. Word choice. Ask: *"Can you rewrite this paragraph with more poetic language but keep it clear and concise?"* Or: *"Make this narration sound more like a futuristic noir detective."* With enough back-and-forth, you'll discover that polishing isn't just about fixing mistakes—it's about finding music in the prose.

You can also build a rewriting workflow. Start every revision by prompting: *"Summarize this scene's emotional arc in one sentence."* Then: *"What are three ways to strengthen that arc without changing the plot?"* Once the emotional target is clear, ask for dialogue refinements, thematic layering, or visual detail. Each pass builds a stronger scene. You're not just polishing—you're sculpting.

The real magic happens when you stop seeing rewriting as drudgery and start seeing it as discovery. ChatGPT doesn't just fix—it reveals. It shows you what your scene could be, what it's almost saying, what it's afraid to say. That's where the best stories live: not in what you meant, but in what you *could* mean if you went just a bit further.

So don't dread the rewrite. Embrace it. Invite ChatGPT into the process like a second brain, a collaborative force that helps you cut deeper, shine brighter, and bring every moment of your sci-fi vision to full, unforgettable clarity. The story was always yours—but now, you have a companion who can help you tell it at its very best.

Pacing an Episode: Beats, Breaks, and Breathing Room

Pacing is one of the invisible forces that makes a television episode either mesmerizing or forgettable. When it's right, the audience is pulled along effortlessly, unable to look away. When it's off, the episode drags, sprints without purpose, or loses momentum before the climax. In science fiction television, pacing plays an even more vital role. You're not just telling a story—you're building a world, revealing complex ideas, layering metaphor, and often shifting between intense action and quiet revelation. Done well, pacing becomes the pulse of the episode. It regulates suspense, emotion, wonder, and meaning. And with ChatGPT in your corner, you can pace your story with more precision than ever.

A well-paced sci-fi episode knows when to hit and when to hold. It moves between beats of tension and release, giving the audience moments to catch their breath after a shocking twist or before a big reveal. Those "breathing spaces" aren't filler. They're where emotion builds, themes deepen, and characters are truly seen. But striking that balance is difficult—especially when you're handling multiple arcs, complex worldbuilding, and high-stakes plotlines.

One of the first things you can ask ChatGPT when developing an episode is: *"Give me a beat map for a 45-minute science fiction episode that includes emotional turns, action scenes, reveals, and quiet moments."* This can become your scaffolding. You'll see a structure unfold: an opening mystery or conflict, rising tension, a midpoint twist, a thematic breather, escalation, a confrontation, and a cliffhanger or resolution. If anything feels too close together or too spread out, you can adjust before you even write a scene.

ChatGPT can also help you analyze pacing after you've written a draft. Try prompting: *"Read this scene list and tell me where the pacing might slow down too much, or where the tension rises too abruptly."* Often, the AI will spot long stretches without any conflict or too many revelations stacked together. Maybe your episode spends twenty minutes in buildup before anything moves. Maybe the climax arrives, but there's no moment afterward for the character to feel what just happened. Those gaps and overlaps are where pacing suffers—and fixing them is the work of a storyteller who understands rhythm.

In practical terms, every episode needs *beats*—the key moments that shape the viewer's emotional experience. Beats can be anything from a line of dialogue that shifts a character's relationship to a visual reveal that changes what the audience knows. Use ChatGPT to expand or contract your beats: *"What would be the emotional beat if this scene ended with silence instead of an answer?"* or *"How can I rewrite this scene so the beat lands more clearly as a betrayal instead of a misunderstanding?"* You begin to fine-tune not just *what* happens, but *how long* the audience should sit with it.

Then there are *breaks*—pauses, transitions, or moments of calm. These often come in the form of quiet scenes between two characters, scenic interludes that show the world, or even short monologues where someone reflects. They prevent the episode from becoming exhausting. Ask ChatGPT: *"Suggest a one-minute scene that gives emotional breathing room after a character discovers their reality is a simulation."* You might get a poetic visual moment: the character standing on a rooftop, watching holographic rain flicker. It's a pause, but not a dead stop. It deepens the story by giving space.

Breathing room is especially critical in serialized sci-fi, where exposition can dominate. You want moments where the audience can sit with a concept. You can prompt: *"Write a reflective moment for a character after they travel through time and meet a future version of themselves. No dialogue, just internal realization and surroundings."* These scenes slow the pace intentionally, anchoring the experience in feeling rather than just plot. That's where sci-fi becomes resonant, not just clever.

And pacing isn't just about *timing*—it's about *texture*. A five-minute action sequence can feel long or short depending on how it's cut. Likewise, a one-minute conversation can feel like forever if the dialogue is heavy. ChatGPT can help you analyze this: *"Does this dialogue move too fast for the emotion it's trying to show?"* or *"Rewrite this scene to build tension more gradually across each line."* You can test variations with speed and tone in mind, editing the pulse of each scene like music.

Another smart trick is to visualize your episode's rhythm. Use ChatGPT to make a pacing diagram: *"Summarize each scene in one line and label it as tension-building, emotional release, exposition, or action."* Once laid out, you'll see if you're stacking the same type of scene back-to-back or if your climactic moment lacks setup. From there, the AI can suggest rearrangements: *"What if the emotional confrontation happens before the reveal, not after?"* Small tweaks can change the entire momentum.

Examples from iconic sci-fi shows highlight how pacing makes or breaks narrative power. In *Battlestar Galactica*, long silences often preceded rapid chaos. In *The X-Files*, episodes balanced slow paranormal discovery with bursts of danger. *Doctor Who*'s best pacing uses light comedic beats to lull the viewer before a dark twist lands. And *Star Trek* often opened with a fast inciting mystery, followed by mid-episode moral deliberation, and ending with a philosophical or personal resolution. ChatGPT can analyze these patterns: *"What was the pacing rhythm of a classic Star Trek episode, and how can I emulate that in a new story idea?"*

You can also use pacing to play with audience expectations. Prompt: *"How can I write an episode that starts fast, slows in the middle, and ends on an emotional twist rather than an action climax?"* Or: *"How do I structure a story where tension builds without a single fight or chase scene?"* Sci-fi lets you explore tension that comes from ideas, realizations, or even existential dread—not just explosions.

The truth is, pacing is an emotional contract. You promise the audience that something is happening—or about to happen. And even in stillness, they should feel momentum. With ChatGPT, you have a pacing partner that helps you test every beat, build every breath, and polish every pulse of your episode.

When you understand that, your science fiction series won't just move forward—it will *breathe.*

Genre Expectations and When to Break Them

When audiences sit down to watch a science fiction TV series, they arrive with a silent list of expectations. They may not articulate it, but it's there—waiting for starships, aliens, androids, strange futures, or dystopian warnings. These genre cues are comforting. They tell viewers where they are, how to interpret what they're seeing, and what emotional tone to expect. But great television isn't just about fulfilling expectations. Sometimes, it's about subverting them. Sometimes, it's about using the genre's rules to set a trap—and then exploding those rules in full view of the audience. The magic of genre is that once you understand it, you're free to break it.

Science fiction as a genre has a remarkable range. It encompasses the utopian idealism of *Star Trek*, the noir paranoia of *Blade Runner*, the intimate dread of *Black Mirror*, and the surreal myth-making of *The OA*. What all these shows share is a foundation in genre—but also a willingness to bend and reshape it. When you're developing your own sci-fi series, part of your job is to learn how genre expectations shape audience trust, so you can decide whether to honor that trust or shock it awake.

The best place to start is by identifying the core conventions of science fiction TV. These include futuristic or alternate settings, speculative technology, existential or moral questions, and metaphors that reflect real-world anxieties through imaginative scenarios. There are usually rules about tone—science fiction tends to lean serious or thoughtful, even when laced with humor. There's often a sense of vastness, of being part of something larger than yourself. And of course, audiences usually expect a sense of intellectual stimulation, even when the show is full of explosions.

Once you understand these rules, you can choose when and how to break them. You might ask ChatGPT: *"What are ten common tropes in sci-fi TV that I could flip on their head?"* It may offer ideas like making the alien invader more terrified than the humans, or setting your story in a future where humanity gave up technology entirely. Or you could explore emotional reversal: *"How do I write a post-apocalyptic setting that feels hopeful instead of bleak?"* Breaking expectations doesn't mean being random. It means replacing the expected outcome with something unexpected—but still deeply satisfying.

Let's take the idea of the "chosen one," a trope worn into the floorboards of genre storytelling. You can subvert this by refusing to validate the prophecy. Maybe the chosen one is irrelevant. Maybe the real hero is the skeptic in the background. Or maybe the prophecy was generated by a marketing algorithm trying to manipulate belief systems. ChatGPT can help you explore these reversals: *"Give me a list of alternate resolutions for a chosen one storyline where the prophecy turns out to be a lie."*

Another great example of genre subversion comes from *The X-Files*. While it fulfilled sci-fi expectations with aliens, clones, and shadowy government conspiracies, it frequently broke the mold by shifting into horror, satire, or even absurdist comedy. One episode might play like a classic thriller, the next like a tragic monster-of-the-week, the next like a postmodern joke. And somehow, it all worked—because the writers understood the core tone of their show and used genre as a palette, not a prison.

You might decide to write an episode that starts with classic sci-fi trappings—a lost colony, a malfunctioning AI—but slowly morphs into a love story, a mystery, or a coming-of-age tale. When doing this, ChatGPT can help keep your transitions clean: *"Rewrite this scene to shift the tone from clinical science fiction into romantic longing without changing the setting."* Or: *"Blend detective noir elements into this spaceship-based story."* These tonal hybrids are where some of the most powerful sci-fi moments live.

Breaking expectations also means playing with structure. Maybe your episode is told backward. Maybe it skips time entirely and exists only in a simulation. Maybe you never explain the technology, and the story hinges entirely on emotional fallout. Ask ChatGPT: *"What are five narrative structures that break conventional sci-fi storytelling but still create compelling TV?"* You might get suggestions like documentary-style episodes, nested realities, or stories told through an alien language with subtitled thoughts instead of speech. Each twist on convention gives you a chance to say something new.

But there's a balance to keep in mind: break too many expectations, and you risk losing your audience. Sci-fi fans are curious, but they still want some kind of internal consistency. When you choose to violate a genre rule, make sure your story justifies it. If your spaceship crew never actually leaves Earth, the emotional or philosophical reason for that has to be strong. ChatGPT can help build that resonance: *"Give me a character reason why a pilot in a space show would fear space itself."* Now the twist isn't random—it's human.

Sometimes, the most powerful reversals are subtle. A scene that plays like a tense interrogation might turn into an impromptu therapy session. A robot designed for war might become a poet. You can ask: *"List subtle ways to challenge the viewer's sci-fi expectations in dialogue, costume, or behavior without changing the plot."* The result might be a military commander in a pink robe, an alien who sings lullabies, or a scientist who doesn't believe in progress. These touches add unpredictability and texture.

And of course, you can use genre expectations to play with audience perception. If your show opens like a space opera, viewers may assume they're about to see dogfights and political rebellion. But what if it's really about grief? About memory? About language as a virus? By leading them down a familiar path and then revealing what the story is *really* about, you not only break expectations—you create something unforgettable.

In this sense, breaking genre is not an act of destruction. It's an act of authorship. It's the difference between telling a science fiction story and telling *your* science fiction story. With ChatGPT, you have a tool that knows all the rules—and can help you explore every way to reshape them. Ask it for wild ideas, for structural inversions, for character-based genre twists. Test them. Try them. Reject the ones that don't resonate and polish the ones that do.

Because in the end, the best science fiction doesn't just reflect the genre.

It redefines it.

Writing the Mid-Season Shift: Raising the Stakes

Every great science fiction series knows that the real power of the story isn't just in how it starts or ends—it's in how it evolves. The mid-season shift is one of the most important and often underestimated turning points in serialized TV. It's that moment when the audience realizes things are bigger, deeper, and more dangerous than they originally thought. It's where you raise the stakes, tilt the playing field, and push your characters into new emotional, moral, or existential territory. If the pilot is the promise, the mid-season shift is the reveal of the cost.

In a well-structured season, this usually happens somewhere around episode five, six, or seven of a ten-to-thirteen-episode arc. The status quo established in the first half of the season—the mystery, the structure of the world, the relationships, the central conflict—gets disrupted. Maybe a character dies. Maybe a trusted figure betrays the group. Maybe an entire layer of the world is revealed to be false. It's the moment when you say to the audience: *"You thought you understood the rules. But now everything changes."*

A perfect example of this can be seen in *Westworld.* Early episodes tease the park and its illusions. But by the midpoint of the first season, we begin to see consciousness emerging. The show shifts from park intrigue to philosophical and metaphysical war. Or take *Stranger Things.* The first half of a season often builds the dread slowly. But mid-season, the Demogorgon doesn't just stalk—it kills. The Upside Down becomes real. The innocence of suburbia falls away.

In science fiction, the mid-season shift is a perfect opportunity to deepen the world, not just twist the plot. That means you're not just adding more spectacle—you're recontextualizing what the viewer thought they knew. You're pulling the camera back to reveal the real story. With ChatGPT, this is an ideal time to explore options. You can ask: *"What's a mid-season twist that would force the protagonist to question everything they've done so far?"* or *"How can I reveal a hidden antagonist who has been present from episode one without making it feel like a cheat?"*

Sometimes the shift comes from within. A character's emotional change—the decision to lie, to fight, to abandon—can trigger the external escalation. Other times, the world itself reveals its next layer. Maybe a mission was never about survival but about containment. Maybe the AI the team built to protect them starts rewriting its own goals. Maybe time travel wasn't just theorized, it's already happening—and always was.

ChatGPT can help generate these reversals by prompting with "what if" statements. Try: *"What if the planet they landed on was actually Earth in the far future?"* or *"What if the protagonist finds out they're not human but were created to infiltrate the humans?"* These questions generate seismic emotional and thematic shifts that push the show into new philosophical terrain—exactly what sci-fi does best.

The mid-season turn is also when you might pull a character apart. Let them make a mistake they can't undo. Ask ChatGPT: *"What's a moral decision my lead could make that would divide the team?"* or *"What's a past secret that, if revealed now, would change the viewer's perception of the last five episodes?"* These aren't just twists. They're revelations that give the show new fuel for the second half.

Pacing is key here. The episode where the shift happens should feel more intense, more momentous, even if it's quiet. Sometimes the biggest moment comes not from an explosion but from a single line of dialogue. Use ChatGPT to find that line: *"What's a ten-word line that could redefine the relationship between two characters?"* or *"Give me a silent scene that reveals betrayal through visual metaphor."* This is where precision elevates your storytelling.

And don't be afraid of letting the audience feel disoriented. That's part of the fun. Science fiction viewers love being challenged. You can break the format for the mid-season. Shift POVs. Show a timeline the audience hasn't seen. Flash back to the origin of the tech. Or flash forward to a ruined version of the world your characters are about to create. Ask ChatGPT for structural risks: *"How could I tell this episode out of order while still landing the twist?"*

What you must avoid is making the shift feel random or disconnected. Even the wildest mid-season revelations should feel inevitable in hindsight. This is where laying track in earlier episodes pays off. Planting small inconsistencies, subtle foreshadowing, and thematic hints lets the audience say, *"Of course. I should've seen that coming."* Use ChatGPT to test this: *"Does this twist feel earned based on the events of episode one?"* or *"Give me three lines of dialogue from earlier episodes that can now carry double meaning."*

After the shift, nothing is the same—and that's the point. Stakes are higher, characters are more fractured, and the direction of the story pivots. If you've done it well, your viewers feel the momentum change. They lean forward. They trust you even more, because you've shown them that the journey isn't just good—it's growing.

Some writers fear raising the stakes too early, but the truth is, the shift doesn't answer everything—it opens new doors. The original mystery may expand into a new question. The antagonist may be revealed, but their goals now seem even more complex. Ask ChatGPT: *"What are three consequences of revealing the villain early instead of late?"* or *"How can the midpoint twist lead to deeper character arcs instead of just more plot?"*

Ultimately, the mid-season shift is your invitation to be bold. It's your permission slip to dig deeper, to pivot, to surprise. It's where the series you're writing becomes more than the sum of its tropes. And when used well—with ChatGPT's help—it's what turns a sci-fi show from a curious concept into something unforgettable.

Raise the stakes. Break the story open. And let your world show its true face.

Creating Teasers and Trailers from Your Pilot Script

Once your science fiction pilot script is written, polished, and ready to share, the next creative leap is crafting the teaser or trailer. These short, sharp pieces of storytelling aren't just promotional—they're extensions of the world you've built. A teaser or trailer is your invitation to the viewer. It's the first impression, the promise, the mystery, and the emotional hook all in under two minutes. In the world of science fiction television, where atmosphere, concept, and intrigue are everything, crafting a compelling trailer from your pilot can be the difference between your show being watched—or being forgotten.

Think of your pilot as the seed, and the trailer as the first shoot that breaks the surface. It's not the full story. It's a curated burst of potential. And to make it sing, you need clarity, contrast, and a distinct emotional tone. This is where ChatGPT becomes your perfect creative collaborator. You can use AI to help write the voiceover, structure the edit, imagine sound design cues, or even generate alternate teaser concepts for different audiences.

Start by asking yourself what your teaser or trailer needs to accomplish. At its core, it must answer these silent viewer questions: *What is this? Why should I care? What makes it different?* In science fiction, you're selling not only characters and story, but also the world. The rules. The danger. The wonder. Ask ChatGPT: *"Give me a 30-second teaser script for a sci-fi series about memory manipulation"* or *"Write a voiceover line that captures the theme of identity in a future ruled by AI."*

The most common structure for a science fiction trailer begins with normalcy—or at least, the "before." A cityscape. A family dinner. A scientist in a lab. Something we understand. Then, the break. The technology misfires. The sky opens. The child whispers something she should never know. From there, the trailer spirals into a world that feels unstable, mysterious, and charged with emotion. That's your arc.

You can prompt ChatGPT to write to that shape: *"Give me a trailer structure that begins with order and descends into chaos, ending with a philosophical hook."* Then provide your pilot's logline or a summary scene list, and it can help write trailer copy that echoes the mood and plot. It might begin with a soft, almost mundane voiceover—"In a city where memory is currency..."—then build into sharper beats: "They took his past. Now he's taking their future." Add staccato scene glimpses and you're halfway there.

Remember that great trailers rely on rhythm. Dialogue snippets, visual moments, and soundscape come together like music. Ask ChatGPT to help you shape this rhythm: *"Suggest three lines of dialogue that would work in a teaser to show conflict, without giving away plot"* or *"What are five one-second sci-fi visuals that could grab attention instantly?"* You'll get ideas like "a city folding into itself," "a silhouette floating mid-air," or "a hand pulling data threads from thin air." These aren't exposition—they're emotion.

You can also target your trailer to different tones. Want something poetic and mysterious, like *Arrival*? Try: *"Write a haunting trailer voiceover for a series about alien linguistics."* Prefer a bold, loud style like *The Expanse*? Try: *"Create an explosive teaser script with countdown energy."* Or explore genre blends: *"Generate a trailer concept that mixes sci-fi and noir, inspired by Blade Runner."*

Often, it helps to write multiple teaser versions. A 15-second teaser for social media. A 30-second TV spot. A full 90-second trailer for YouTube or streaming platform release. You can use ChatGPT to generate all of them: *"Compress this full trailer into a 15-second teaser that ends on a twist."* You can even prompt the AI to come up with taglines:

"Write ten punchy taglines for a series about quantum espionage." These can become your trailer's final moment—text on screen, a breath of silence, and then the title.

Don't forget that music and sound design carry half the emotional weight. Even in script form, you should imply these. Ask ChatGPT: *"What kind of music tone should go with a trailer for a moody, philosophical sci-fi series?"* You might get something like: ambient tones rising into synthetic strings with a pulsing heartbeat underneath. Then in the script, you can add cues: [A low hum grows into a distorted orchestral swell]. These touches signal your intent to producers, editors, and collaborators—even before footage is cut.

Let's say your pilot is about a crew trapped on a ship outside time. You might build a trailer starting with quiet shots: clocks stopped, a heartbeat in the dark. Then visuals flash—cryopods failing, a crew member vanishing mid-sentence, the stars blinking out. ChatGPT can write the voiceover to match: "They left Earth at 0800 hours. They never arrived. Time forgot them. But something else remembered." Now that's a hook.

Finally, your teaser or trailer should end on a question or image that lingers. Don't answer it. Tease it. The viewer should feel unsettled, intrigued, even haunted. Ask ChatGPT: *"Write a final trailer line that leaves the viewer with a sense of awe and dread."* Or: *"Suggest a visual to close the teaser that echoes the series' central theme of isolation."* That's the art of the trailer—leave them wanting more.

So whether you're pitching your show to producers or building hype on your website, your trailer becomes a miniature version of your pilot's soul. And with ChatGPT's help, you can explore every possible version of it—until you find the one that stops people scrolling, makes them lean in, and whispers, *"Watch this."*

Developing a Series Bible with AI

A science fiction TV series doesn't truly exist until there's a series bible. The pilot may open the door, the teaser might spark interest, and the trailer can grab attention—but the series bible is what proves the story can go the distance. It's the map, the rulebook, and the promise. It outlines where the show will go, who will change and how, what secrets lie beneath the surface, and why the world you've built will hold together across a dozen episodes—or five seasons. And when you're working with ChatGPT, you've got a tool that can help you not only organize the chaos of creation, but expand it, polish it, and deepen it.

At its core, a series bible includes everything that a network or showrunner might need to understand your show in full. This includes a summary of the premise, character breakdowns, season arcs, episode sketches, thematic explorations, stylistic choices, genre cues, world-building notes, and production considerations. Think of it as a master document that captures the vision and the logic of your universe. And every time you have a gap, a question, or an undeveloped thread, ChatGPT is there to help you explore and articulate it.

Start with the **overview**. This is the one- to two-page pitch that would hook a reader before they see the pilot. It should summarize the premise, the protagonist's journey, the tone, and the unique elements of your sci-fi world. Ask ChatGPT: *"Write a one-page show summary for a science fiction TV series about digital consciousness and corporate espionage."* You can tweak the response, feed it your themes, and refine the tone. The AI helps you find language that captures both emotion and scope.

Next, the **character profiles**. A strong bible doesn't just list traits—it shows arcs. For each main character, you should define their role in the story, their internal and external conflicts, their goals, and how they evolve over the season. Try prompting: *"Create a character profile for a reluctant captain haunted by a decision that doomed their planet."* Or go broader: *"Give me five character archetypes that work well together in a sci-fi ensemble, and show how their dynamics create tension and growth."* The AI can help you generate both the obvious and the unexpected.

The **season arc** comes next. This is the backbone of the story—how each episode contributes to the larger mystery, transformation, or unraveling. Whether you're doing episodic (like *The X-Files*) or serialized (*Battlestar Galactica*), the structure should feel deliberate. You might start with: *"Break a 10-episode sci-fi season into a clear arc, with escalation at the midpoint and resolution in the finale."* ChatGPT can help you lay out the beat-by-beat structure or even provide multiple outlines based on tone—philosophical, action-driven, horror-tinged, etc.

Then, move into **episode sketches**. These are brief outlines for each episode—enough to show narrative shape, emotional stakes, and continuity. Prompt the AI: *"Create short descriptions for a season of 8 episodes in a sci-fi show about a team traveling through failed utopias on alternate Earths."* You'll get a high-level picture you can build on and modify. You can also ask it to generate variations, deepen arcs, or tighten pacing as you evolve the document.

Worldbuilding comes next—and in sci-fi, that's where the real fun is. This section of the bible can include planetary systems, political structures, tech specs, rules of time travel, alien species, and language notes. You can go deep with prompts like: *"Describe the economic system of a planet where AI determines resource distribution"* or *"Invent a futuristic form of transportation that's plausible but hasn't been shown in Star Trek or Star Wars."* Use the AI not just to brainstorm, but to cross-check internal consistency.

Your **themes** and **tone** also belong in the bible. These are what guide creative decisions across departments. Maybe your show is about memory, isolation, the illusion of progress. Maybe your tone is lyrical and meditative, or brutal and grounded. Ask ChatGPT: *"List three metaphors I can use across a series to reinforce the theme of synthetic identity"* or *"Suggest tone anchors for a show that blends detective noir with futuristic tech."* These choices become part of the show's DNA—and that's what the bible captures.

A great bible also includes **visual and stylistic notes**. You're helping potential collaborators imagine what this show *looks* and *feels* like. ChatGPT can help you here as well: *"Describe the cinematography style for a sci-fi series inspired by 1970s analogue tech"* or *"What color palette supports a story about cold logic versus raw emotion?"* You can even use the AI to generate shot ideas or scene directions for a mood reel or pitch deck.

You can also include **franchise potential**. Spin-offs. Prequels. A feature film. Tie-in novels or games. If you have a sprawling world, hint at the corners of it. Ask ChatGPT: *"Suggest five spin-off series ideas based on this central sci-fi world concept."* It'll offer possibilities you may not have seen—and that could make your pitch more valuable.

Finally, there's **continuity tracking**. Your bible becomes the central place to store the logic of the world. What year did the war begin? How long do cybernetic implants last? What's the rule for time compression in near-light-speed travel? Instead of scrolling back through 100,000 words of screenplay, you can input questions into ChatGPT: *"Remind me of the rule I created for energy conversion in episode 3"*—and with a structured database, you'll always have the answer.

As you go, you can use AI to help format, rewrite, and organize the document for pitching. It can rephrase dense paragraphs, check for redundancy, or create section headers that sound more compelling. Try: *"Make this paragraph about my alien species sound more cinematic and mysterious"* or *"Summarize my season arc in one paragraph that teases the major stakes."*

Ultimately, the series bible is the story of your story. With ChatGPT as your co-writer, editor, and idea generator, you don't just fill in the blanks—you uncover new ones. And that's where the magic of a sci-fi series lies: in the balance between what is known, and what is yet to be discovered.

A great pilot opens a door. A great bible builds the universe behind it.

Preparing for Pitch: Selling Your Series Idea with AI Help

When it's time to move your science fiction series from the page to the world of producers, studios, or streaming platforms, the pitch becomes your rocket launch. It's the moment everything you've created—the pilot script, the series bible, the characters, the arcs, the world—has to be communicated not as a list of ideas, but as an irresistible *invitation*. You're not just describing a show. You're making someone want to be part of a journey. And with ChatGPT by your side, you're no longer preparing for this pitch alone—you have a tireless, idea-sparking partner to help you craft, polish, rehearse, and refine everything from loglines to Q&A answers.

Let's start with the **core concept**. This is where your pitch lives or dies. It's not just about what your show is about—it's about what makes it *special*. The concept should be specific, evocative, and simple enough to repeat. A good test is the "two-sentence hook." If someone heard just these two lines, would they be intrigued enough to want more? You can ask ChatGPT: *"Help me write a compelling two-sentence pitch for a sci-fi TV series about a city where no one can die."* Keep revising until it flows effortlessly. Then try variations for tone: serious, mysterious, comedic, dystopian. Let the AI show you how your idea can shift and stretch depending on who's listening.

Next comes the **logline**. This is often the first thing a producer or executive reads. It must carry plot, premise, and a hint of theme, all in one breath. Try: *"Write five logline versions of my show about humans escaping Earth on a sentient spaceship"* or *"Rework this logline to emphasize the emotional journey of the protagonist."* You can refine until you have one that sounds like it belongs on a streamer's front page. The goal is to balance the high concept with human stakes.

Now think about your **verbal pitch**. Whether you're in a boardroom, a Zoom call, or recording a video pitch, you need a 3–5-minute monologue that flows like a well-told story. Ask ChatGPT: *"Write a spoken pitch for a sci-fi series about a planet with fractured timelines. Make it passionate and vivid."* Then have it rewrite the same pitch with a different angle: *"Make it darker, more philosophical."* You'll start to see which voice suits your style—and your series. Use the AI to cut fluff, tighten beats, and even simulate the pacing of your speech.

A great pitch includes **comparisons**—but only the right ones. Saying "It's like *Star Trek* meets *The Matrix*" might spark a grin, or it might sound generic. Instead, let ChatGPT help finesse this: *"Suggest nuanced comparisons for my sci-fi series about alien consciousness being broadcast into human minds."* It might come back with "It channels the layered mystery of *Dark* with the unsettling wonder of *Annihilation*." That lands with more sophistication—and shows you know the landscape.

Producers will ask about the **characters**, and this is where you move beyond archetypes. You don't just say, "He's a rogue captain." You say, "He's a man who once abandoned a colony to save his crew—and now commands a ship where everyone knows it." ChatGPT can help with that character depth: *"Write one powerful sentence that reveals my protagonist's inner contradiction."* Or: *"Give me five ways to describe a morally ambiguous AI without sounding like HAL 9000."* It's all about making your cast feel alive.

You'll also need to convey the **world**, but don't overwhelm. Instead of listing fifty facts about galactic politics or plasma tech, choose details that reveal tone, emotion, and conflict. Ask: *"What's one detail about a sci-fi world that shows it's both beautiful and dangerous?"* Then let ChatGPT help sculpt a few cinematic moments that do more than explain—they *invite*. You're not doing a lecture; you're creating a vision.

Prepare for **questions**, too. This is where AI becomes your rehearsal partner. You can say: *"What are ten questions a producer might ask about my sci-fi series?"* Then prompt: *"Help me write smart, confident responses to each."* Some will be creative ("What's your backup plan if CGI budget gets slashed?"), some will be strategic ("Why now? Why this series?"), and others may be about you ("How involved will you be in the writing process?"). Use ChatGPT to build out answers that feel honest, enthusiastic, and well thought out.

Think also about **visual materials**. Even if you're not a designer, you can use AI to help generate or describe mood-boards, concept art, or deck slides. Ask: *"Describe five visual scenes I can include in a pitch deck to convey the tone of my sci-fi show."* Or go granular: *"Write slide copy for a pitch deck introducing the world, tone, characters, and pilot summary."* With tools like Midjourney or DALL·E, you can generate actual images to match those ideas—turning your pitch into a sensory experience.

You'll also want a **tagline**, something short and catchy that encapsulates the story's promise. Ask ChatGPT: *"Suggest 10 possible taglines for a science fiction series about memory being weaponized."* Great ones sound like they belong on a billboard, like "The future forgets nothing" or "Where you go, your past follows." These are useful in pitch documents, trailers, even the title screen.

A final element—**passion**. Yes, passion matters. When you pitch, you're not just selling the story. You're selling *you*. Your vision. Your excitement. Your commitment to the world you've built. ChatGPT can help you refine your pitch until it sings, but it's your voice, your energy, your connection to the idea that will make it resonate. Try using the AI as a rehearsal partner: *"Pretend to be a skeptical exec hearing my pitch—what would you say? How would you challenge me?"* Practice both the delivery and your reaction.

In the end, preparing your pitch with AI is about pressure-testing your idea until it becomes undeniable. It's about finding clarity without losing imagination, and detail without losing momentum. It's not about making the AI do the work for you—it's about using it to help you tell your story at its sharpest and most compelling.

You already built the world. Now it's time to sell it.

Working with ChatGPT as a Solo Writer's Room

In the world of television, the writer's room is a place of electric creativity—where ideas bounce, jokes sharpen, arcs evolve, and stories are shaped by the energy of the group. But what if you're not working with a room of professional writers? What if you're developing your science fiction series on your own, from a laptop in your home, late at night? That's where ChatGPT comes in—not as a replacement for your voice, but as your sounding board, your brainstorming partner, your second (and third and fourth) brain. When used skillfully, ChatGPT becomes your solo writer's room, available 24/7, focused entirely on your vision.

It starts with learning how to simulate that collaborative energy. In a real writer's room, people throw out wild ideas just to see what sticks. You can use ChatGPT the same way by asking open-ended exploratory prompts like: *"What are ten possible inciting incidents for a sci-fi series set in a future where language is regulated?"* or *"What kind of emotional arcs could a clone character go through across five seasons?"* You're creating space for unexpected answers—the kind that would normally come from other minds in the room.

One of the great powers of using AI this way is iteration. In a human room, someone might say, "Let's build on that" or "What if we flipped it?" ChatGPT can be instructed to do just that. If you like a character idea, you can say: *"Give me three more variations with different flaws and backstories."* If you have a twist in mind, ask: *"What are five ways to foreshadow this twist without giving it away?"* You'll find that you can test versions of scenes, character relationships, even alternate histories for your world, all within minutes.

You can also simulate **different perspectives** by giving the AI roles. You might say, *"Pretend you're the cynical executive who only cares about ratings. What feedback would you give on this idea?"* or *"Now you're a visual effects supervisor—what are the biggest budget risks in this episode?"* This lets you test your ideas against imaginary collaborators who bring different priorities to the table. It sharpens your own thinking and helps you defend your choices—or reconsider them before it's too late.

Another key function of the writer's room is dialogue. In a real room, someone might act out a line, change a word, or suggest a better comeback. You can ask ChatGPT: *"Write this same scene with sharper, more sarcastic banter"* or *"Make this confrontation feel more like a verbal chess match."* You're not asking the AI to replace your writing—you're asking it to elevate it by offering options. Think of it as blue-sky drafting without fear of judgment.

When you're stuck, ChatGPT can also help you get **unstuck**, just like a good room would. Maybe your villain isn't compelling. Ask: *"Why does this villain feel flat? What would give them emotional depth?"* Or maybe your episode outline hits a sag in the middle. Try: *"Give me three escalating events that could raise the stakes between episodes four and five."* You're still the showrunner here, but now you've got a smart assistant helping you punch through blocks.

The solo writer's room isn't just for story development—it's also for managing momentum. Sometimes in a group, the sheer energy of people working together helps you keep going. When you're writing alone, it's easy to lose steam. ChatGPT helps here too. You can ask it to **break your project into manageable steps**: *"What's a good writing schedule for finishing this 10-episode series bible in three weeks?"* Or use it for **daily warmups**: *"Give me a 15-minute writing exercise to expand the emotional arc of my main character today."* It keeps the creative engine humming.

Another way ChatGPT becomes your co-writer is through **tone testing**. You can say: *"Write this scene in the tone of Black Mirror—dark and satirical."* Or: *"Now write it like Stranger Things—more nostalgic and character-driven."* You'll begin to feel how tone choices affect everything from pacing to camera angles. It's like having your own development team running tone experiments while you focus on the broader vision.

When you're preparing for a **rewrite**, ChatGPT becomes your notes session. You can input a scene and ask: *"What's working here, and what feels overwritten?"* Or: *"Where could I add emotional beats to make this quieter scene resonate more?"* Unlike human writers who might worry about egos, the AI has no filter—it just responds with suggestions. And sometimes, that's exactly what you need: objective feedback with no personal baggage.

As you start assembling your episodes, you can also use ChatGPT as your **continuity checker**. In a traditional room, someone always remembers that the character's brother died in episode 2 or that the laws of teleportation prohibit time travel. With ChatGPT, you can train it on your world's rules and ask: *"Does this new idea break the logic of my tech system?"* It can keep your internal canon consistent and help prevent plot holes before they appear.

Finally, don't forget the **fun** of it all. Working with AI in this way isn't about grinding through a checklist—it's about creating a space where imagination flows without fear. A space where ideas can be wild, tone can shift in seconds, and no one says "that's stupid." You can go down rabbit holes for an hour with ChatGPT about how alien DNA might rewrite a person's dreams, or how a time bubble could trap a love story in one moment forever. You don't need permission. You just explore.

Being a solo writer doesn't mean you're alone. With ChatGPT as your writer's room, you have a collaborator who is always ready, always curious, always up for the next brainstorm. And best of all, it never runs out of coffee, it never dominates the conversation, and it never, ever tells you that your idea is too weird. In science fiction, that's the best kind of partner you can have.

So take your seat, open the laptop, and let the room begin.

Writing Love and Romance in a Technological World

Science fiction isn't always thought of as a genre where romance thrives, but in truth, the speculative nature of sci-fi makes it a perfect place to explore love. When the rules of the world are unfamiliar, when technology transforms bodies, memories, and time, romance becomes both more difficult and more profound. Love must adapt to these changes—or defy them. In a technological world, the old questions of intimacy, trust, loss, and connection take on brand-new forms. Writing sci-fi romance isn't about adding a subplot—it's about using the genre to test what love means when everything else is different.

The first thing to understand is that in science fiction, romance is not exempt from the world's mechanics. If your world is governed by artificial intelligence, cloned bodies, or digital consciousness, then relationships must be affected by those elements. A love story between two characters isn't just about emotions—it's about whether those emotions can survive systems that monitor, edit, or suppress them. In *Her*, the romance between a human and an AI forced viewers to confront how we define consciousness and emotional authenticity. In *Blade Runner 2049*, a replicant falls for a holographic projection, raising the question: if neither party is technically "real," is the love any less meaningful?

ChatGPT can help you test these questions. You might prompt: *"Create a scene between two characters falling in love, but one is an AI designed to mimic desire."* Or: *"Write a romantic confession in a world where lying is impossible due to neural implants."* These prompts let you experiment with how romance must change under sci-fi conditions. The more you constrain love with technology, the more inventive and emotional it often becomes.

Romance also thrives when it's tested by ethical tension. In a futuristic world, consent, memory, privacy, and control are all charged concepts. A character might fall for someone who doesn't know they've been genetically modified to be compatible. A hacker might be in love with a person whose emotions they once altered without permission. These stories don't just add spice—they raise the stakes. Ask ChatGPT: *"Give me five romantic plot twists involving memory manipulation"* or *"Describe a romance that must exist entirely in virtual reality because of a planetary quarantine."* You'll begin to see how constraints create deeper story potential.

You don't have to write about humans loving robots or aliens to make your romance feel sci-fi. Sometimes, the world's values are enough. Maybe two people are in love, but society no longer believes in monogamy—or requires contracts to validate emotions. Maybe a romance is illegal because of interplanetary law, or one character is aging in real time while the other exists in a slow-clock zone. These aren't just worldbuilding flourishes. They're devices that shape how love must behave.

The beauty of working with ChatGPT here is that you can sketch dozens of versions before committing. Want to try different tones? Ask: *"Make this romance scene more tragic,"* or *"Rewrite it with light-hearted banter despite the dystopian setting."* You'll quickly see how emotional pacing and character chemistry can adjust to fit your world's demands.

Dialogue in science fiction romance has to do double duty. It must carry emotional authenticity while also making sense in your futuristic setting. A declaration of love might include technical metaphors, shared digital memories, or oblique references to encoded experiences. That's where figurative language thrives. Try a prompt like: *"Write five romantic metaphors based on interstellar travel"* or *"How might someone describe longing if they're a synthetic being who's never touched another person?"* These moments can be more poetic than traditional romance if they're grounded in the world's reality.

You should also consider how different forms of romance appear—courtship rituals, expressions of love, conflict, jealousy. In some futuristic societies, physical intimacy might be rare or obsolete. In others, it might be everywhere, but emotional connection is taboo. Use ChatGPT to invent social rules: *"What are the relationship norms on a space station where emotions are chemically regulated?"* Then use that to shape character arcs: *"Write a scene where two characters must hide their growing attachment in a world where it's outlawed."*

Romantic pacing in a sci-fi series can also benefit from episodic structure. In an ongoing show, love can unfold slowly—a spark in the pilot, a misunderstanding in episode three, a confessional moment near the mid-season mark. Use AI to help you track this emotional arc. Ask: *"What are ten escalating emotional beats for a slow-burn romance between a genetically enhanced soldier and a civilian translator?"* You'll get a blueprint you can adjust depending on your characters' personalities and the story's tone.

Romance doesn't need to end happily to be satisfying in sci-fi. In fact, many of the most poignant love stories in the genre are marked by loss or sacrifice. A character might give up their body to upload their partner's consciousness. One might choose to stay behind on a dying world so their love can live on in another. The genre allows for deeply romantic gestures that are physically and philosophically impossible in realism. These moments work best when built on emotional logic. Ask ChatGPT: *"Suggest a powerful sacrifice that shows love between characters who can't touch"* or *"What's a bittersweet ending for a romance shaped by parallel dimensions?"*

And yes—there's room for sensuality too. A sci-fi romance doesn't have to be dry or cerebral. You can still write passion, desire, intimacy—but make it fit your world. Maybe characters exchange emotional codes instead of kisses. Maybe they share dreams via neural link. Maybe touch is dangerous because of radiation exposure, but they do it anyway. These are places where AI can be your tool for inventiveness. Prompt: *"Describe a futuristic expression of intimacy that replaces physical contact"* or *"Create a romantic scene where two minds merge temporarily to relive a shared moment."*

In the end, writing love in a technological world is about contrast. You're setting the warmth of emotion against the coldness of machinery. You're testing what stays human when everything else is advanced. And you're discovering that even in a world of hyper-drives and holograms, people still want to connect, to be seen, to matter to someone else.

With ChatGPT, you're not just building a love story—you're building a love story only *you* could imagine, in a world that's uniquely yours. The future may be full of algorithms, but the heart still wants what it wants. And sometimes, it wants to feel real in a world that isn't.

Exploring Death and Mortality in Immortal Futures

Science fiction often looks forward to utopias where suffering has been minimized and death, in its traditional form, has been outwitted. We imagine neural uploading, anti-aging nanotech, consciousness loops, memory banks, cryonics, cloning, and digital resurrection. But what happens to a story when death—the defining consequence of human life—is no longer a constant? The answer isn't that the story becomes less meaningful. In fact, it becomes more complex. It invites a deeper reflection on identity, purpose, and the emotional weight of mortality in a world where nobody has to die—unless they choose to.

Immortality in science fiction is rarely utopian for long. It becomes a way to explore the costs of survival, the entropy of memory, and the erosion of meaning when endings are removed. It's about what death gives us—not just what it takes away. You can ask ChatGPT to help you explore this theme with prompts like: *"What are ten psychological effects of living 500 years in a society where everyone is young forever?"* or *"Describe a scene where an immortal begs to forget rather than live another century."* Sci-fi gives you room to press those questions to the edge of existence—and beyond.

Consider stories like *Altered Carbon*, where identity is decoupled from the body and death is a temporary inconvenience for the rich. Or *Black Mirror*'s "San Junipero," where love and consciousness persist after death in digital heaven. These narratives don't avoid mortality—they reframe it. Death becomes a class issue, a technological debate, an emotional reckoning. You can use ChatGPT to generate variations: *"Write a scene between a mortal and an immortal who disagree on the value of memory."* This allows you to build philosophical and emotional conflict into your sci-fi world.

Mortality gives shape to character arcs. Without it, you must invent new boundaries. What drives a person who can't die? What does sacrifice mean when you can back up your soul? Use the AI to explore stakes in a deathless world: *"What could make an immortal being choose to end their life in a society where that's taboo?"* or *"How can you write tension in a war when no one dies permanently?"* You'll find new frontiers for drama that don't rely on traditional loss but on the fear of meaninglessness.

Another angle worth exploring is the **evolution of grief** in an immortal society. If people can be resurrected or reprogrammed, do you still mourn them? Or is grief delayed, deferred, denied? A powerful subplot might follow a character who refuses to download a loved one from a memory archive—not because they can't, but because they believe some part of love must end to matter. Ask ChatGPT: *"Create a dialogue between a grieving character and a society technician urging them to activate a loved one's digital echo."* There's rich storytelling here in the tension between loss and restoration.

There's also the philosophical question of **authenticity**. If a person dies and is recreated from stored memories, are they the same? What happens to the soul in a world governed by code? Characters might wrestle with existential questions: is this still *me*? Did I ever die? ChatGPT can help dramatize this with prompts like: *"Write a scene where a clone confronts their original self, who has aged and now wants to die."* This kind of speculative interaction pulls the abstract into something visceral and compelling.

Many sci-fi writers use death to explore the paradox of **stagnation through immortality**. When people no longer fear aging or loss, what drives innovation, creativity, love? You can use prompts to map out a world where entire societies have grown bored with existence. *"Describe a futuristic therapy clinic for immortals suffering from 'eternity fatigue.'"* This can become the background of your world or a central arc—maybe a rebellion emerges not to defeat death, but to reclaim it.

Symbolism thrives in stories like this. Immortality might symbolize privilege, addiction, or even cultural denial. Death, when introduced into these settings, becomes revolutionary. Maybe a character who chooses to die is seen as a radical, a spiritual leader, or a threat. ChatGPT can help you design movements, rituals, and ideologies: *"What would a religion based on voluntary death look like in a post-mortality society?"* or *"Invent a resistance group that restores mortality through outlawed tech."* These touches build depth and thematic resonance into your narrative.

You can also flip the perspective and ask: what if **death itself has become an adventure**? Instead of something to avoid, it becomes a journey. Consciousness transfer might mean one can "die" a thousand different ways and awaken in new forms—each one reshaping their identity. Ask ChatGPT: *"Describe ten types of death experienced by a character who uploads into different species across the galaxy."* This blends philosophy with spectacle, making death a device for exploration.

Another rich area is **relationships across mortality lines**. A mortal falling in love with an immortal is a classic trope for good reason. The ticking clock of one life changes the stakes of every shared moment. But it's also a metaphor for aging, loss, and difference—made literal by technology. You can dramatize this beautifully: *"Write a breakup scene where the mortal partner doesn't want to be preserved, and the immortal does."* Love and death have always been linked in storytelling—sci-fi just offers new ways to bind and break that link.

For television, these themes work wonderfully in episodic or serialized formats. One episode might explore a society that resets everyone's memories every decade to prevent trauma. Another might feature a character who has lived so long they no longer believe in identity. With ChatGPT, you can generate episode summaries like: *"Give me five sci-fi episodes that each tackle death from a different technological angle."* You're using mortality as a lens through which to explore consciousness, love, choice, time, and the nature of being.

In the end, writing about death in immortal futures isn't about removing consequence. It's about shifting the axis of emotion, exploring what makes life feel like life when there's no end in sight. The fear of death is only one part of human nature. The longing for meaning, connection, renewal—that's what remains. And in the vast playground of science fiction, you get to define what death is, what it means, and how we fight for—or against—it.

With ChatGPT, you don't just generate ideas—you test philosophy in narrative form. You stretch your imagination until it cracks open new truths. Because in a world where no one dies, the question isn't how to cheat death—it's how to make life worth living.

Rewriting History with Alternate Timelines and AI

There's something deliciously rebellious about rewriting history. In science fiction, it's not about correcting the record—it's about asking "what if?" What if a single decision changed the trajectory of humanity? What if one person never died, one empire never fell, one machine was never invented—or invented too soon? Alternate timelines have long been a playground for speculative fiction, offering writers a chance to examine cause and effect, society and technology, and the human condition under completely different rules. With ChatGPT as your writing partner, the process of mapping, breaking, and rewriting history becomes an electrifying creative exercise—one that doesn't just change the past, but reimagines the future.

Start with a single alteration. It could be as dramatic as the Axis Powers winning World War II or as precise as Alan Turing surviving and creating the first conscious AI. These "what if" triggers are the engine of alternate history storytelling. Ask ChatGPT: *"Give me ten alternate timeline concepts where a single invention changes the course of the 20th century."* You're not looking for just novelty—you're searching for ripple effects, for a fork in the road that leads somewhere unexpected.

Great sci-fi series have done this brilliantly. *The Man in the High Castle* imagines a post-war America divided between Japan and Germany. *Fringe* plays with parallel realities colliding due to scientific overreach. *Dark* explores a closed-loop town where time travel creates generational trauma. In all of these, the rewriting of history isn't just a backdrop—it's the drama. Use ChatGPT to simulate those layers: *"Create a timeline for a world where the Roman Empire never fell and discovered electricity in 800 AD."* Let the AI help you build the architecture of a plausible but thrillingly different Earth.

The emotional heart of alternate history lies in how it affects people. Maybe a character wakes up in a timeline where their child was never born. Maybe a hero is revered in one timeline and executed in another. You can use ChatGPT to write scenes that test identity against history: *"Write a monologue from a character who remembers a timeline no one else believes existed."* These moments bring human depth to your grand sci-fi concepts.

Timelines offer more than just parallel universes—they can offer **conflict**. What happens when two timelines begin to merge? Or when one becomes aware of the other and sees it as a threat? Maybe an AI, designed to restore historical accuracy, begins eliminating people who "shouldn't exist." Ask: *"What kind of conflict arises when a governing AI begins enforcing historical purity across multiple timelines?"* You'll discover antagonists and moral dilemmas that grow organically from your premise.

AI isn't just your tool—it can be part of the story. Perhaps AI is the very thing *causing* the fractures in time, rewriting the past to engineer a perfect future. Or maybe it's the only witness to every version of history—tired, regretful, corrupted. Ask: *"Describe an AI that remembers all versions of Earth's history but is beginning to malfunction from paradox exposure."* That's not just worldbuilding—it's character creation, mood, mystery.

You might also explore **time as propaganda**. Maybe one timeline believes their version is the real one and seeks to overwrite the others. Maybe history has become a weapon—editable and weaponized by quantum code. One society might be gaslighting another with artificially generated memories and documentation. Use ChatGPT to simulate dystopian realities: *"Design a government that controls the past through neural implants and memory erasure."* The AI can help you map the psychological and social consequences of a world where history is no longer fixed.

When writing an episodic series, alternate timelines allow for incredible variation in setting, genre, and tone. One week, your story is noir in a totalitarian 1950s America. The next, it's a tech thriller in a timeline where dinosaurs survived and coexist with humans. Use ChatGPT to brainstorm episodic hooks: *"Give me five episodes set in different alternate timelines, each with a unique genre twist."* This not only keeps your series fresh but stretches your creative limits.

A fascinating narrative device is the **temporal outsider**—someone who moves between timelines or remembers more than one. This character could be a glitch, an accident, a time refugee, or even an AI host body experiencing timeline bleed. These characters anchor the viewer, letting us compare realities through a familiar lens. ChatGPT can help you flesh these out: *"Create a backstory for a time traveler who's forgotten which version of reality is the original."* You'll get not just events, but psychology, motivation, and contradiction.

To tie timelines together, you'll need a **logic system**. Is this multiverse quantum-based? Are timelines fractals from a singularity event? Does tampering create instability or convergence? The rules of time are your laws of gravity—they must be consistent, even if complex. You can build them with prompts like: *"Design a set of scientific rules that govern how timelines split and merge based on major historical events."* Then test it in action: *"Show how a small change in 1912 leads to a timeline where Antarctica is a tropical empire."*

Rewriting history also opens the door to **symbolism and allegory**. Perhaps each timeline reflects a different political ideology. One is a capitalist megacity ruled by corporate AIs; another a deeply spiritual anarchist commune running on quantum barter. These aren't just timelines—they're perspectives. Ask ChatGPT: *"Write a debate scene between two characters from opposing timelines, each defending their reality's version of freedom."* The story becomes not just "what happened," but "who should we be?"

Don't forget emotional stakes. In a world of infinite timelines, your character might long for a version of life they can never find again. A child who lived in one history but died in another. A marriage that thrived in one strand but collapsed in the current one. These stories of **loss across realities** give your high-concept writing its heart. You can craft moments with prompts like: *"Write a goodbye letter to a timeline that no longer exists."*

Rewriting history is one of the most liberating things you can do as a science fiction writer. You're not just bending time—you're questioning fate, identity, consequence, and memory. And with ChatGPT, you're no longer building those ideas alone. The AI becomes your mapmaker, your timeline debugger, your paradox architect.

What if the future depends on the past you invent today? Then go invent it—over and over again.

Visualizing a Sci-Fi Show Created with ChatGPT

There's a special moment when your script—those black lines on a white screen—starts to come alive in your imagination. You begin to see the starship, the blinking control panels, the swirling galaxies outside the viewport. You hear the dialogue in voices not yet cast, feel the hum of the reactor under the floor. When you're writing a science fiction television series with the help of ChatGPT, you're not just crafting story—you're laying the foundation for something deeply visual, something cinematic. The transition from words to images is a thrilling part of the creative process, and it's where your collaboration with AI takes on a new kind of power.

Science fiction has always been a visual genre. The technology, the environments, the costumes, even the way characters move or light hits a surface—these are often just as important as the words they say. Viewers don't just want to understand your world; they want to *feel* like they're walking through it. That's why, even at the scriptwriting stage, you have to write with the screen in mind. Fortunately, you can use ChatGPT as a kind of cinematic co-director, helping you imagine, describe, and even storyboard your show before a camera ever rolls.

Start with your sets. Where is your series primarily located? A space station? A future Earth city? An interdimensional ship? You can prompt ChatGPT to generate detailed environments that feel unique: *"Describe a bridge of a spaceship powered by organic technology and grown from coral-like materials."* Or, *"Design the living quarters in a mining colony beneath the surface of Europa."* These aren't just descriptions for fun—they're tools for visualization, story logic, and eventual production design.

Once you have a setting, build it into your scene structure. Science fiction scripts often work best when the location itself adds tension, drama, or irony. A romantic confession hits differently on a dying planet. A bureaucratic debate becomes more gripping inside an AI-run control hub suspended above a black hole. ChatGPT can help you shape scenes that are not only dialogue-rich but visually arresting. Ask: *"Write a conversation that takes place in a city where gravity periodically reverses."* You'll start to see how image and idea collide to make something unforgettable.

When writing dialogue, think like a director. How will this line *look* when it's said? Where is the camera? How is the actor lit? Is the background sterile or chaotic? Even if you don't write camera directions into your script, you can practice visualizing each moment with help from prompts: *"Describe the lighting, movement, and framing for a tense standoff between a cyborg and its creator in a lab flooded with red emergency lights."* You don't need a film degree—you need imagination, and ChatGPT helps expand yours.

Cinematography in sci-fi isn't just about cool shots—it's about *meaningful* ones. Maybe you use a handheld shaky cam for scenes involving rebel factions, then switch to slow, wide frames when depicting the vast, uncaring empire. You might want to mimic styles from *The Expanse*, *Battlestar Galactica*, or *Black Mirror*. Use ChatGPT to explore and emulate those looks: *"Explain the visual language of The X-Files and how to adapt it for a new sci-fi show."* These style guides can influence not only your writing but the pitch and production approach.

Visual effects are the lifeblood of many sci-fi productions, but writing for VFX requires discipline. You want to evoke wonder without writing impossible or budget-breaking scenes. Ask ChatGPT to help you plan smart: *"Suggest five visually impressive but low-budget sci-fi sequences that could be created with minimal CGI."* You can also experiment with AI to design ideas that blend miniatures, in-camera effects, or digital overlays. The point is to write not just the story—but the blueprint for its realization.

When you're adapting your script to the screen, transitions matter. Scene breaks, emotional beats, and even sound bridges become vital tools. Sci-fi often relies on a rhythmic blend of quiet and spectacle. You can shape these shifts by prompting ChatGPT with *"Write a transition scene from an intense action sequence to a serene moment of philosophical debate aboard the ship."* Now your episodes flow like a director's cut, not a writer's draft.

Casting is another layer of visualization. Who *sounds* like your characters? What kind of actor would play your lead? Use ChatGPT to build profiles: *"Create a casting brief for a stoic starship captain who secretly believes he's from another universe."* These details help ground your characters in physicality, which then reflects in how you write scenes, describe movement, or design dialogue rhythm.

Don't forget the small but crucial pieces—props, interfaces, wardrobe, sound cues. Even something as minor as how characters open a door or interact with a display screen can speak volumes about your world. Ask ChatGPT to expand: *"Invent five futuristic communication devices and describe how they're used in conversation scenes."* Or *"Describe a soldier's uniform in a pacifist spacefaring society."* These elements give your show a tactile feel even before you have a budget.

If you're ready to pitch your show, visuals will make or break your presentation. ChatGPT can help you write mood boards, visual treatments, and even voiceover text for a teaser trailer: *"Write a one-minute trailer narration for a sci-fi series about time-hopping archaeologists."* From that single paragraph, you can imagine the tone, pacing, and aesthetic of your project—then work backward to reinforce that style in your writing.

Collaboration with designers, directors, and producers becomes much easier when you already *see* the show. With ChatGPT, you can generate production notes, style guides, and artistic references: *"Describe the cinematography style for a show set in a colorless dystopia that slowly regains color."* These help align your team creatively from the start, even if the team is just you for now.

Writing a sci-fi series isn't just about crafting clever dialogue or world-changing tech—it's about building a show you can see, hear, and feel before it exists. And when you're working with ChatGPT, that visualization process becomes accessible, exciting, and immediate.

You're not just writing television anymore. You're directing the future.

Examples of Prompts for Sci-Fi Story Design and Structure

When you're using ChatGPT to write your science fiction TV series, the quality of your prompts is just as important as the strength of your ideas. Great prompts don't just ask the AI to be creative—they aim it like a telescope toward a galaxy of possibilities you might not have imagined on your own. In this chapter, we'll walk through many types of high-performing, imaginative, and targeted prompts that you can use at every stage of designing your sci-fi series: the premise, the world, the technology, the structure, the characters, and the episodes themselves. A well-designed prompt is like a good question in a writers' room—it gets everyone thinking bigger, faster, and deeper.

If you're still in the idea phase, start with premise-generation prompts that push the boundaries of genre:

"Give me ten science fiction story concepts involving interdimensional politics."

"Invent five sci-fi TV series ideas where dreams can be weaponized."

"Design a near-future Earth where climate refugees create a floating nation with advanced AI culture."

These kinds of prompts focus ChatGPT on innovation. You're not just asking for random stories—you're supplying a theme or a constraint that lets it generate something unique and tailored to what you're interested in.

Once you have a basic premise, your next goal is to build a structure around it. ChatGPT is especially useful when you give it a structural frame to follow:

"Write a three-act breakdown for a sci-fi pilot about colonists on a sentient moon."

"Create a 10-episode season arc for a sci-fi mystery involving missing astronauts returning with no memories."

"Design a series structure where each episode is told from the point of view of a different alien species."

You can also ask for timelines and outlines that help clarify how your world changes over time:

"Map out the major political shifts in a future Earth where humans have discovered faster-than-light travel."

"Describe a century of technological development in a society where time travel is illegal but common."

Good structural prompts often combine a genre, a story engine, and a narrative device. For example:

"Give me an episodic sci-fi series like The X-Files but centered around a sentient AI investigating supernatural crimes."

"Outline a serialized sci-fi drama in the style of Westworld where the theme is personal identity and data ownership."

When you're building your story world, environmental and sociopolitical prompts can guide your design:

"Invent five sci-fi civilizations with unique methods of energy generation and the cultural values that emerge from them."

"Describe a post-apocalyptic Earth run by decentralized AI collectives after a climate collapse."

"Imagine a space colony where everyone is born in zero gravity and sees Earth as a myth."

Each of these prompts invites detail—technology, behavior, belief systems, history. The more specific you are, the more original the results.

Prompts can also explore theme and subtext, giving your show greater depth:

"Create a sci-fi story arc where the core theme is 'freedom through forgetting.'"

"Write an outline for a story exploring what happens when society outsources morality to machine learning systems."

"Build a season arc around the theme of 'progress without ethics leads to extinction.'"

Theme-focused prompts help you write stories that resonate emotionally and philosophically—not just conceptually.

When you're stuck on episode ideas, ChatGPT can become your brainstorming machine:

"Give me ten sci-fi episode ideas that explore different facets of memory and identity."

"Create a list of episodic plots where each story deals with a different form of human augmentation."

"Outline a season where the central ship visits one dangerous planet per episode, each with its own strange physics."

You can also prompt for character arcs that evolve over time:

"Map out a character arc for a pilot-turned-diplomat learning to trust alien allies after a long war."

"Create an emotional journey for a robot who believes they are the reincarnation of a human philosopher."

And finally, when you're designing the emotional or moral center of your story, use prompts that go beyond worldbuilding and into *meaning*:

"Write a monologue from a character who learns their entire world was a simulation designed to study loneliness."

"Create a philosophical debate between two characters about whether death has any value in an immortal society."

"Describe a climax scene where a character must choose between saving their home planet or rewriting history to prevent its existence."

By using prompts like these, you're not just generating scenes and episodes—you're exploring the entire emotional and intellectual framework of your show. You're shaping something bold, memorable, and human.

The secret to great sci-fi writing with ChatGPT is knowing what to ask. Your prompts don't have to be long, but they should be precise, imaginative, and open-ended enough to allow for surprise. The best ones work like questions to a creative partner in the room, opening up new dimensions of thought. And with a tool like ChatGPT, you can keep asking, reshaping, and rewriting until the story, the series, and the screen all align.

You're not just a writer. You're a world-builder, an architect of futures. And every good question is a door to another universe.

Examples of Prompts for Designing Characters in a Sci-Fi Story

Science fiction is full of big ideas—space travel, alien civilizations, future wars, technological revolutions—but the best sci-fi stories still come down to the people who live through them. Whether they're human, alien, android, or something in between, your characters are the emotional and narrative anchors that keep your audience invested. It's one thing to dream up a cool universe, but it's the compelling characters who make that universe matter. When you're writing with ChatGPT, the prompts you use to design those characters can help you shape personalities, backstories, conflicts, arcs, and relationships that feel vivid and unforgettable.

Let's start with some broad-stroke prompts that are great for generating character ideas quickly. These are perfect when you're beginning a new project or trying to fill out an ensemble cast.

"Give me five sci-fi protagonist ideas who each represent a different relationship to technology."

"Invent three non-human characters who challenge human ideas of morality and consciousness."

"Create a main character for a space opera series whose secret power is hidden even from themselves."

These kinds of prompts are great for getting inspiration flowing, but the real power comes from layering specificity and context. When you're building a lead character, try prompts like:

"Describe a starship captain who grew up in a low-gravity prison colony and hides their trauma with charisma."

"Create a scientist in a future where emotions are illegal, and they secretly preserve memories of their lost love."

"Write a bio for a rogue AI given a human body to infiltrate a resistance group, only to start sympathizing with them."

These help you get into the character's contradictions, secrets, and growth potential—the kinds of things that keep viewers coming back.

Compelling sci-fi characters often exist in worlds that stretch or distort identity, so identity-focused prompts are especially useful. Try these:

"Design a character who changes bodies every week but keeps one consistent emotional memory."

"Create a character who discovers that they are a clone of someone famous—and possibly dangerous."

"Imagine a linguist who can understand alien languages but starts losing the ability to speak their own."

If your story plays with memory, time, or multiple realities, your prompts can explore how that shapes a person:

"Give me a profile of a time traveler who can't remember which version of events is the real one."

"Write a monologue from a person who met themselves from the future—and didn't like who they became."

"Create a character who remembers three alternate lives but doesn't know which one is real."

Sci-fi characters often struggle with technological dilemmas—AI, augmentation, simulation, immortality. These challenges are not just plot devices—they're character-defining forces. Use prompts to examine those internal shifts:

"Invent a former soldier who was genetically modified for war and now must integrate into peaceful civilian life."

"Design a hacker who lives inside a digital city and fears returning to their failing biological body."

"Create a priest who believes their deity is an alien intelligence hiding in the quantum field."

Good characters don't exist in a vacuum. Their relationships—with mentors, lovers, enemies, machines—give your story its emotional momentum. Try using ChatGPT to explore dynamics like:

"Write a tense scene between a human ambassador and an alien diplomat whose species communicates through scent."

"Create a lifelong friendship between a human and an AI assistant, but now the AI is evolving past its protocols."

"Design a romance subplot between a terraformer and a geologist trapped on a slowly disintegrating planet."

You can also ask ChatGPT to help build full arcs for character development over a season or series:

"Outline the arc of a character who starts as a corporate spy and becomes a revolutionary leader on a mining moon."

"Create a character arc for a medic aboard a generation ship who discovers they've been erasing memories."

"Track the emotional transformation of a clone who outlives their original and must define their own purpose."

For deeper writing, focus on character flaws, regrets, and personal dilemmas:

"Describe a brilliant physicist who secretly sabotages their own research because they fear its consequences."

"Write a confession from a security officer who let an alien prisoner escape because they believed in its innocence."

"Invent a guilt-ridden AI designer who created a sentient weapon and is now being hunted by it."

Even minor or one-episode characters can become unforgettable with the right prompt:

"Design a bounty hunter who only takes jobs against people from their own past timeline."

"Create a rebel pilot who refuses to speak aloud and communicates only through music-coded signals."

"Invent a trader who moves between asteroid colonies and spreads gossip that always turns out to be true."

If you want to explore ensemble dynamics, you can prompt the AI to create contrasting or complementary characters:

"Create four sci-fi characters who each represent a different reaction to first contact with an alien species."

"Design a team of explorers who are genetically engineered for specific tasks—but one begins to evolve beyond their programming."

"Build a starship crew where each member comes from a different branch of human evolution."

And when you're stuck, a fun way to generate fresh characters is to remix tropes:

"Reimagine the 'mad scientist' archetype as a peaceful philosopher with a neural lab grown from memory tissue."

"Turn the 'alien sidekick' into the main character with their own cultural bias and hidden agenda."

"Write a hero who fails every mission but becomes legendary because of how much people believe in them."

The right prompts help you dig into the human, alien, or post-human heart of your story. They take you past the outline and into the soul. Whether your series takes place across galaxies or inside the corridors of one massive ship, the strength of your sci-fi lies in the characters who carry it.

With ChatGPT at your side, you have a character department in your pocket—ready to generate, deepen, and even surprise you. All you need to do is ask the right questions.

Examples of Prompts for World Building in a Sci-Fi Story

Science fiction worldbuilding isn't just about cool technology or exotic planets. It's about crafting the rules, systems, landscapes, and histories that make your universe feel lived-in, logical, and emotionally immersive. Whether your story takes place aboard a cramped starship, across a network of alien civilizations, or within the neural landscape of a simulated reality, the world you build has to shape the characters, the plot, and the themes. With ChatGPT, you can explore countless possibilities by asking the right worldbuilding prompts—prompts that go beyond surface aesthetics and tap into the philosophical, political, technological, and environmental scaffolding of your story's universe.

Let's start with foundational prompts that help you generate entire civilizations or settings from scratch:

"Describe a planet where the oceans are made of liquid methane and the dominant lifeform evolved to communicate through magnetic pulses."

"Invent a future Earth city built vertically through the clouds, with each atmospheric layer belonging to a different social class."

"Create a moon-based society where sound cannot travel, so all communication evolved through light, vibration, and facial expressions."

These types of prompts give you basic location, environment, and dominant life or culture. But they're just the beginning. Dig deeper by prompting for the history and mythology of a place:

"Write the origin myth of a robotic species that believes it was created by ancient biological gods."

"Outline the last 500 years of political history on a planet where time moves at a different speed in each region."

"Describe a civilization that lives inside a Dyson Sphere and has banned the concept of stars."

As you build locations, always link geography and environment to cultural values. Use prompts like:

"Create a nomadic culture on a frozen planet where shelter is grown organically from fungus each time they stop."

"Design a desert civilization that believes water is sacred and bases its laws on rainfall patterns."

"Describe how zero-gravity birth environments have changed the definition of 'childhood' in spacefaring societies."

Technology is a massive part of sci-fi worldbuilding. Go beyond gadgets—explore how tech changes how people live, love, worship, and fight:

"Describe a society where consciousness is backed up daily and death is a legal inconvenience."

"Invent a planet where teleportation has replaced roads but creates emotional fragmentation among families."

"Build a world where genetic editing is considered a basic human right and natural-born humans are second-class citizens."

Political structures can shape everything from the type of stories you tell to the kinds of conflicts that arise:

"Create the political system of a federation made up of AI-run city-states orbiting Earth."

"Describe the ruling caste of a society where leadership is passed to those who dream the most vivid prophecies."

"Invent a criminal justice system in which offenders are sent to alternate timelines as rehabilitation."

Good sci-fi also addresses religion, philosophy, and metaphysics in unexpected ways. Try these:

"Invent a religion based on the belief that black holes are gateways to the afterlife."

"Describe a faith that emerged when a deep-space probe transmitted music from another galaxy."

"Create a belief system in which simulated realities are seen as tests for spiritual evolution."

Economics and daily life also matter—how people live, work, and trade can reveal a lot about a culture:

"Describe a barter system on a mining asteroid where value is measured in oxygen and light."

"Invent the supply chain of a galactic delivery company that navigates wormholes to deliver food instantly."

"Create a tourism industry on a planet where gravity fluctuates according to emotional energy."

Worldbuilding through language is powerful too. Use prompts like:

"Invent ten alien words used by a species that has no past tense."

"Design a communication system between species that evolved in total darkness and only understand vibration."

"Create naming conventions for a civilization that considers the concept of individual names to be taboo."

Social structure prompts can explore the margins and internal tensions of your world:

"Describe the underground culture of outcasts in a society where AI determines all social compatibility."

"Create the rituals of adolescence in a civilization where age is measured by mental expansion, not years."

"Imagine a rebellion by a labor caste forced to terraform planets for richer species."

You can also build entire economies or industries, which opens up plot ideas and environmental implications:

"Design a fuel industry based on harvesting energy from dying stars—and the ethical crisis when it affects nearby systems."

"Describe the waste management infrastructure of a giant generation ship that's been flying for 700 years."

"Invent a black market for illegal memories in a society where experience is taxed."

Even simple prompts can open entire vistas of narrative potential:

"What are the rules for using psychic powers in a society where everyone can read minds?"

"How do people shop, flirt, or vote in a post-currency, post-privacy world?"

"Describe how weather is controlled in a floating city above a hurricane planet."

Some of the best prompts are comparative. You contrast one thing against another to create creative friction:

"How does a pacifist society defend itself against hostile AI?"

"How does a medieval society function aboard a highly advanced alien spacecraft they don't understand?"

"How does a luxury space station orbiting a dying Earth justify its existence?"

Don't forget to world-build inward—within minds and bodies altered by the sci-fi landscape:

"Describe a society where people have internal AI co-pilots who can override their emotions."

"Imagine a culture where everyone hears music instead of voices and has to interpret language through harmony."

"Design the psychological norms of a species that can only reproduce through shared dreams."

The best worldbuilding prompts provoke questions, not just answers. They get you thinking about culture, consequences, contradiction, and conflict. With the help of ChatGPT, you can build societies that feel as real as anything we've ever known—and even stranger than anything we've yet imagined.

Worldbuilding in sci-fi isn't just scenery—it's story, it's character, it's philosophy. And with the right prompt, your world begins to write itself.

Examples of Prompts for Serialized Sci-Fi Story Ideas

Serialized science fiction stories offer the perfect canvas for sweeping arcs, layered mysteries, emotional evolution, and world-shattering consequences. Unlike standalone or monster-of-the-week episodes, serialized stories demand continuity, change, and long-form narrative control. Whether you're crafting a ten-episode limited series or a multi-season saga, serialized storytelling lets you build deep characters, escalating themes, and universes that unravel like cosmic puzzles. The key to unlocking this kind of writing with ChatGPT lies in the prompts you use—how you ask for story arcs, character journeys, and thematic evolution over time.

Great serialized sci-fi begins with a foundational concept that contains both scope and movement. Start by asking ChatGPT to generate overarching series ideas that include built-in momentum:

"Give me five serialized sci-fi story ideas that follow one protagonist through a collapsing multiverse."

"Create a serialized sci-fi show about an alien artifact that activates one piece per episode until it reveals a terrible truth."

"Design a serialized narrative where every episode takes place in a different timeline, and only the main character remembers the last one."

These prompts don't just generate one-off concepts—they seed a framework that can grow into an entire series arc.

Once you have a core premise, you can ask for series-long engines of mystery or tension:

"Write a serialized story about colonists on a newly terraformed world who begin receiving transmissions from their future selves."

"Create a season-long arc where a synthetic human must investigate who programmed them—and why their creators are now missing."

"Design a sci-fi series where reality starts to glitch, and only a janitor aboard a luxury spaceship seems to notice."

You can also center your prompt around change across time—change in the character, in the world, or in both:

"Outline a serialized sci-fi story where humanity discovers immortality, but memory becomes unstable after 200 years."

"Create a ten-episode arc where a time-traveling agent must undo ten historical changes caused by an enemy who has already died."

"Write a series about a ship AI that slowly becomes self-aware while its human crew is cryogenically frozen."

Another rich source of serialization is building toward a reveal. Use prompts that imply secrets, tension, or reversals:

"Design a series where a colony's leader is revealed to be an alien posing as a human—but only in the final episode."

"Write a serialized arc in which each episode reveals a new truth about a shared dream connecting several strangers on different planets."

"Create a story where a war between humans and machines is shown from both sides, until the line between them disappears."

You can also generate arcs that build emotionally, with deep character evolution:

"Write a serialized sci-fi story about a clone who discovers the real version of herself is still alive—and leading a rebellion."

"Outline a story about an alien child raised on Earth who learns the truth about their origin only after Earth is attacked."

"Create a series about a guilt-ridden doctor on a refugee ship crossing galaxies after a failed planetary evacuation."

Serialized sci-fi is perfect for moral and ethical exploration. Use ChatGPT to structure long arcs built on debate, dilemma, or inner conflict:

"Create a serialized show where uploading consciousness is legal, but one family refuses to join digital immortality."

"Outline a series about soldiers enhanced with empathy implants to stop them from killing—and the consequences of overriding that system."

"Write a season arc where AI-run governments begin quietly removing people deemed 'inefficient,' and a whistle-blower discovers they are next."

Mystery-based serials can keep audiences guessing across many episodes. These prompts help ChatGPT give you complex threads to unravel:

"Design a series where a group of astronauts wake up on a ship they don't remember boarding and must piece together what happened."

"Create a serialized show where every episode takes place after the same apocalyptic event—but through the eyes of different survivors."

"Write a mystery-driven story about a rogue planet with ancient ruins that reveal a countdown to an unknown catastrophe."

The best serialized stories often layer emotional arcs onto epic frameworks. Use prompts to fuse scale and intimacy:

"Create a serialized show where an intergalactic rescue ship saves a new survivor every episode—but one of them is not who they claim to be."

"Outline a series about a scientist trying to reconnect with their child while a new alien language slowly reprograms humanity's thoughts."

"Write a serialized arc where a lonely AI repairs a derelict ship and reawakens a cryosleeping crew member it falls in love with."

If you're looking for unusual formats or storytelling structures, try meta-prompts:

"Design a serialized sci-fi show where every episode appears to be a different genre—until viewers realize they're watching simulations within simulations."

"Create a nonlinear serialized story told in reverse chronological order, from the last battle of a war to its first spark."

"Write a show where an ancient alien artifact grants memories of future events, causing characters to behave irrationally in the present."

Finally, you can guide ChatGPT to brainstorm full episode arcs within a serialized framework:

"List ten episodes for a serialized series about a generation ship where society is ruled by algorithms and art is forbidden."

"Create a season breakdown for a story where Earth is destroyed in episode one and the survivors scatter across space."

"Write a ten-part serialized arc about scientists who discover that reality is deteriorating and must stabilize physics before it's too late."

What makes these prompts effective is that they suggest a slow reveal, ongoing tension, personal transformation, or expanding conflict—all hallmarks of great serialized TV. With the help of ChatGPT, you can shape arcs that unfold with drama, depth, and drive, always pulling your audience toward what's next.

Science fiction loves the big idea. Serialization loves the long journey. Put them together, and you've got a galaxy of storytelling potential—and all you need to begin is a great prompt to light the fuse.

Writing a Science Fiction Pilot on a Low Budget

Writing a science fiction pilot doesn't have to mean million-dollar visual effects, elaborate sets, or fleets of CGI starships. In fact, some of the most iconic science fiction pilots in history started with very little. What they had instead were powerful ideas, compelling characters, and worlds hinted at rather than fully shown. A low budget can be your greatest creative ally—it forces you to focus on what matters most: story, mystery, emotional stakes, and character tension. With a bit of smart planning, strategic choices, and the help of AI tools like ChatGPT, you can create a pilot that feels expansive without draining your resources.

The most important decision when writing on a budget is setting. Science fiction often suggests scale: galaxies, future cities, other worlds. But when you're starting small, think *contained.* Limiting the setting doesn't mean limiting the scope—it means choosing one compelling location that tells us everything we need to know about your universe. Think of a spaceship in disrepair, a hidden research bunker, an underground shelter, or even a single locked room where strange things are happening. Use ChatGPT to help you brainstorm low-cost, high-tension environments:

"Describe a sci-fi story that takes place entirely in a single apartment where a wormhole opens in the closet."

"Write a pilot that begins in a basement lab where a time machine prototype is being secretly tested."

These prompts let you focus your writing on dialogue, mystery, and pacing. One of the most effective low-budget strategies is to suggest the larger world through conversation. Let characters *talk about* the galaxy, the government, or the conflict that rages beyond the walls—but keep us planted in one place. Think about how *The X-Files* started in empty forests and small-town morgues or how *Primer* told a time travel story using garages and storage units. Your writing is the special effect.

Another trick is to use character to sell the scale. Give your protagonist a sense of deep history. Maybe they're the last survivor of a failed expedition. Maybe they used to be a space marine. Maybe they're a janitor in a biotech facility where the AI is acting strange. Let their language, habits, and fears point to a world far bigger than we can see. Use ChatGPT to generate this kind of detail:

"Give me a character description for someone who used to pilot cargo ships through wormhole corridors but now lives in hiding on Earth."

"Write dialogue where a character explains why Earth is no longer on the star maps."

These ideas build scope without visual effects. Emotion, memory, and loss are free—and powerful.

Low-budget science fiction also thrives on *objects with meaning.* A mysterious device. A malfunctioning implant. A blinking control panel. One great prop, described well and used cleverly, can anchor an entire pilot. Let ChatGPT help generate plot from one object:

"Write a pilot setup where a character discovers a small cube that projects memories from the future."

"Describe a short scene where a person finds a hidden transmitter embedded in their spine."

These stories work when you focus on tension. Something is wrong. Something is coming. Something is happening. The more you can suggest with less, the more your audience leans in. Sci-fi pilots shouldn't explain everything—they should raise questions, build unease, and introduce strange rules that characters are only just beginning to understand. Ambiguity becomes your visual effect.

When you're writing scenes, remember: lighting and sound are your hidden weapons. What can be heard but not seen? What's happening just off-screen? Think of how often sci-fi relies on eerie sounds, shadows, blinking red lights, or a power outage to build suspense. You can write tension into silence or use a line like: "What was that sound? It wasn't coming from *outside*—it was coming from *inside* the walls." You don't need money for that. You need rhythm.

Also consider structure. A great pilot doesn't need to resolve everything. In fact, it shouldn't. Focus on creating a *contained* story within the episode that leaves us wanting more. Maybe your character finds a strange object. Maybe they wake up in a place they don't remember. Maybe they discover that time has jumped forward. Ask ChatGPT to help you outline:

"Give me a beat-by-beat outline for a pilot episode that takes place in a cryogenic recovery room where only one sleeper wakes up."

"Write an ending for a pilot episode where a lone technician realizes they're not alone in the space station."

Lastly, be bold with theme. Sci-fi lets you talk about human issues—identity, memory, surveillance, freedom—through metaphor. And the best part? These themes cost *nothing*. They're ideas. And ideas, when embodied by great dialogue and gripping conflict, make even the cheapest set feel cinematic.

So don't let budget scare you. Let it sharpen you. Use ChatGPT to brainstorm contained settings, off-screen events, eerie dialogue, small props, and character-driven tension. Focus on mystery. Build your world in pieces. Hook your viewer with what they *don't* see. And remember, some of the greatest science fiction stories ever told began not in space, but in a hallway, a motel room, or a lab with flickering lights and one person asking, "What did we just do?"

Your low-budget pilot is a launch-pad. And the future doesn't need a green screen to feel real.

You Wrote a Sci-Fi Series—Now Let the Universe Watch It Grow

Writing a serialized science fiction TV series is one of the most ambitious, thrilling, and mind-expanding things a creator can do. You've conjured a universe. You've filled it with starships, timelines, biotech, androids, aliens, mystery, and metaphor. Your characters have lived through epic journeys, your worlds have evolved, and your themes have grown larger with each episode. You didn't just write a sci-fi story—you built a living machine of narrative propulsion, emotion, and philosophical inquiry. Now that it's complete, or at least mapped out, the big question is: what next?

The instinct for most writers is to rest. Finishing a season-long arc or even a fully detailed pilot script takes enormous effort. But sci-fi storytelling doesn't end at the last scene. It echoes. It transforms. And with the tools now available—especially AI tools like ChatGPT—you can keep expanding this universe across platforms, genres, and formats. The hard part is done. Now comes the exciting part: letting your creation grow.

First, let's look at what you've built. If you've followed the earlier parts of this journey, then you're holding more than just an idea. You have a season outline. A full pilot. Character profiles. A series bible. Maybe even teasers or trailer scripts. You've likely developed multiple locations, political systems, a visual and auditory language for the world, even alien philosophies. You are already far beyond the average scribbled concept on a napkin. This is your intellectual property. It has shape, scope, and narrative potential. You are ready to present your world to others—producers, platforms, collaborators, and fans.

But there's another layer before that—refinement and growth. Even after writing your series, ChatGPT can help you go back and polish individual scenes, deepen characters, or reshape episode arcs based on new ideas. A series that starts out with one protagonist can evolve into a multi-perspective narrative. A mystery that felt clear in the outline might benefit from extra twists or more subtle foreshadowing. You can ask ChatGPT to test your story's logic, identify pacing imbalances, or even recommend which character needs more screen time. This isn't rewriting—it's evolving.

Once your scripts and outlines are where you want them, it's time to explore expansion. A serialized series is just the beginning of a much wider potential storytelling landscape. You can adapt your show idea into:

- A graphic novel or webcomic, using ChatGPT to help with dialogue and layout concepts
- A podcast-style audio drama, complete with AI-assisted script formatting and episode narration planning
- A novelization or prose short story series that builds out the lore of your universe
- An interactive story, visual novel, or gamebook where users choose how to explore your world

Every one of these formats adds value to your intellectual property, and they serve different audiences. Some fans like to watch. Others like to read, listen, play, or interact. With your core universe built, you can use AI to shift formats smoothly and stay consistent across them all.

This is also the time to think about pitching your show. Whether you aim to reach production companies, streaming platforms, animation studios, or even independent producers, you now have assets: a logline, a synopsis, a pilot script, a pitch deck (which you can outline with ChatGPT), character profiles, and episode guides. You've created a world that a network can invest in. Don't underestimate the power of your complete vision. Many pitch meetings fall apart because the idea is too vague. You, on the other hand, can speak with authority about the arc of Season One, the themes that run through Season Two, and even the mythos waiting in Season Three.

If you're aiming for indie production, AI can keep helping. Use ChatGPT to write visual guides, mock production budgets, casting breakdowns, or even marketing blurbs. You can create a behind-the-scenes "writer's journey" post to share with fans or potential collaborators. You can even write promotional emails and pitch letters, formatted and personalized for specific agents or execs.

And if you want to build an audience before going to market, consider serializing part of your story online. Share short story excerpts on social media. Publish character monologues or scene teasers. Release concept art paired with story captions. ChatGPT can help generate and edit this supplementary content while you stay in creative control. You might even invite fans to participate—vote on a planet name, suggest ship designs, or theorize about the deeper mystery in your story's plot. This kind of early engagement isn't just good PR; it creates a living fanbase that can fuel your series into production and beyond.

So here's where we are. You started with an idea. You used AI not as a crutch, but as a partner. You wrote something that could become television, literature, art, or an entire franchise. What you have now is not just a story—it's a foundation. A blueprint for something that can grow across mediums, borders, and minds.

Let the universe watch it grow. Let your story echo beyond you. Let the future you imagined become part of someone else's imagination. That's the power of sci-fi. That's the power of storytelling. And thanks to your creative persistence—and a little help from ChatGPT—you've built something that might just outlive the screen it's written on.

I hope you found information and inspiration here for your next Sci-Fi series. If you liked this book, please leave a review where you bought it. Thank you from the author.

About the Author

Andrew Parry is a writer and filmmaker with a profound love for film, particularly the genre of science fiction. His passion for the limitless possibilities of sci-fi drives both his storytelling and his creative vision. For Andrew, science fiction is more than just a genre—it's a way to explore the boundaries of human imagination, the future of technology, and the mysteries of the universe. Through his writing and filmmaking, Andrew seeks to create narratives that transport audiences to worlds filled with awe, wonder, and the thrill of discovery.

Inspired by the visionary filmmakers and writers who have shaped science fiction over the decades, Andrew's work often tackles themes of futuristic societies, artificial intelligence, space exploration, and the nature of reality itself. He sees science fiction as a powerful tool for examining the human condition, allowing him to ask big questions about our place in the universe and the potential paths humanity might take.

Read more at https://lonetrail.blog.

www.ingramcontent.com/pod-product-compliance
Lightning Source LLC
LaVergne TN
LVHW082343200926
848481LV00012B/3428